Labyrinths *of* Prosperity

By the same author:

History—the Human Gamble (1983)

Betting on Ideas (1985)

Rivalry (1987)

Gambling and Speculation (with G. A. Brenner, 1990)

Educating Economists (coedited with David Colander, 1992)

Labyrinths
of
Prosperity

Economic Follies,
Democratic Remedies

Reuven Brenner

Ann Arbor

The University of Michigan Press

Copyright © by the University of Michigan 1994
All rights reserved
Published in the United States of America by
The University of Michigan Press
Manufactured in the United States of America
⊗ Printed on acid-free paper

1997   1996   1995   1994   4   3   2   1

A CIP catalogue record for this book is available from the British Library.

Library of Congress Cataloging-in-Publication Data

Brenner, Reuven.
    Labyrinths of prosperity: economic follies, democratic remedies /
Reuven Brenner.
        p.   cm.
        Includes bibliographical references and indexes.
        ISBN 0-472-09556-0 (alk. paper). — ISBN 0-472-06556-4 (pbk. :
    alk. paper)
        1. Economics.   I. Title.
HB171.B6495   1994
330—dc20   94-177
                                                            CIP

To George Petty, an entrepeneur,
one of those whom Jonathan Hughes called
"The Vital Few."

Contents

Preface

How is it that after decades of almost absolute conviction that Keynesian economics is science and that policymakers can rely on it for guiding an economy toward prosperity, there came the eighties, when economists said that it isn't science and that policies based on it can do more harm than good? And how is it that in the nineties the old Keynesian bag of tricks is being partially revived, and economists, politicians, and the media discuss policies about prosperity in its terms once again? And how is it that after years of saying that inflation may be useful, and then years of declaring that it is harmful, economists are once again questioning the pursuit of "zero inflation"? There is a common thread among these contradictory opinions. Each has been offered at one time or another with utter confidence as scientific truth, and policies were based on it. How can that be? What type of science can lead to such flip-flops?

Or, consider economists' and politicians' changing views of broader issues concerning prosperity and ways to achieve it. As late as 1984, John Kenneth Galbraith wrote in the *New Yorker* that the Soviet economy was making great material progress. Galbraith's evidence was the apparent well-being of the people on the street, the rush hour traffic, the spread of apartment houses.[1] He attributed the success to the fact that, in contrast with Western economies, the Soviet system made full use of its manpower. He was not alone among prominent economists to hold such views. For decades—until the eleventh edition—Paul Samuelson's textbook was telling students that it is a "vulgar mistake to think that most people in Eastern Europe are miserable." The major revision in the eleventh edition was that he deleted the word *vulgar.* The twelfth edition, in 1985, omitted the sentence, substituting for it the question whether the economic gains achieved under communism were worth the political repression (a euphemism for the tens of millions killed and starved to death, which he failed to mention in the textbook) and still claiming that this is among the most "profound dilemmas of human society."

Growing up in Eastern Europe, where I lived until the age of fifteen, I knew that these statements were profoundly wrong. They made me skeptical of everything economists wrote and claimed to be scientific. After becoming acquainted with this and much additional material that economists wrote and passed off as science, I set out to solve a number of puzzles:

- How could such well-known economists (some received Nobel prizes for their work), make such misleading statements in their scientific and journalistic writings about policies and prosperity? On what theories and facts were they relying, if any?
- How could such writings, so patently untrue, nevertheless be made credible to so many people and solemnly taught at most universities?
- How could economists be so wrong about what brings prosperity, and how could their views, nevertheless, have such powerful influence on policies?

This book is the result of trying to answer these questions and also to do something much broader and more ambitious. The book sheds light on the process and policies that led to sustained prosperity in the past and can do so today; it also examines policies that led to declines and do so today as well.

While lifting the linguistic veils of prevailing political and economic myths, the book shows that the keys to prosperity can be found through the practice of trade and finance. Prosperity results when people can daringly court risks and can successfully overcome them by commercializing knowledge. Governments can sustain such pursuits both by adopting policies that help the humble to rise and do not prevent the great from falling, and by establishing institutions that discourage erroneous policies. Societies prosper when all this happens, and they fall behind in relative or even absolute terms when all this does not happen.

It is easier to offer this view of prosperity and to reach conclusions on changes required in policies and institutions by first offering my dissenting opinions. To do so, I find it necessary not only to refute but even to ridicule cherished beliefs; to show that many things people accept for facts aren't; and also to show that the language used to debate economic policies and prosperity today obscure what is happening, rather than clarify it.

That is why the book begins by pointing out that macroeconomics is a myth and that the study of national statistics can produce almost any conclusion. Policies based on macroeconomics and national aggregates lost sight of the first principle of prosperity: sustaining conditions favorable to the commercialization of knowledge. Such commercialization means reliance on trade, finance, and a diversity of institutions necessary to carry them out.

In contrast, macroeconomic analyses use a misleadingly neutral language and uniformly computed aggregate numbers across countries, which pass for facts and become part of a scientific mask. Macroeconomists suggest that the manipulation of these aggregates—be they the Gross National Product (GNP), unemployment rates, or productivity measures, which they view as reliable indicators of an economy's performance—can produce keys to prosperity. This approach is wrong. The keys to prosperity cannot be found either by looking at and reacting to changes in gross national products, or by looking at the creation of jobs. Galbraith was right when he noticed that the once-communist countries did not have high statistical unemployment rates, even if he completely misread what was hiding behind the numbers. Communist governments exercised the option of killing millions and sending millions of others to camps. These governments were also paying salaries to everybody who showed up at a workplace, even if workers had nothing to do there, which was often the case. Governments in the West also have the option of calling unemployment benefits "salaries," sending the unemployed to dig holes in the ground (as Keynes suggested), and defining them as being employed. Statistical employment then increases, and statistical unemployment declines. But will such policy train workers, open opportunities and bring prosperity, or will the government's expenditures reflect an additional burden on those otherwise employed? Or, is a decline in GNP, a result of significant cuts in military expenditures (which also led to a significant increase in unemployment rates in California since the Cold War ended), always harmful to prosperity? The answer to both questions is no.

A wide range of evidence—among them the emergence of the successful trading city–states in the past and the present, whose influence radiated over the world—tells us that keys to prosperity can be found when institutions guarantee a mixture of trust and incentives. To be concrete, the keys consist of letting trade and finance flourish within a political framework where the humble can hope to rise and the mighty must fear failure.

Through trade and the "democratization of capital," people can unlock their entrepreneurial talents and get a stake in what the business society is doing by courting risks and, from time to time, successfully overcoming them. Through the political institutions of referendum and initiative, people can express their opinions on government policies and force it to make the respective decisions. Thus, they also get a direct stake in what governments do and help prevent not the committing of errors—that is unavoidable—but *persistence* in error. Once one takes a closer look at the features of such a political system, with the mechanisms of referenda and initiatives in place, one realizes why the Swiss, who have been relying on them, have been less polluted by many bad ideas, macroeconomic ones being just some of them.

This method of controlling political decisions, about types and level of taxation and expenditures in particular, differs from the alternative ones that economists, political scientists, and observers have been discussing and recommending recently. According to the macroeconomists' opinions, governments can decide wisely on expenditures for infrastructure, for public works, for education and training, for targeting research and development in special areas, for designing investment tax-credits, and others. These decisions can be made without either asking people's approval or allowing a reliable mechanism for reversing decisions when politicians and the bureaucracy are proven wrong, a mechanism that referenda and initiatives provide.

Making political decisions through referendum and initiative differs from other political remedies that have been suggested to control governments' expenditures. In recent years many observers have suggested constitutional amendments and term limits on representatives' tenure as the means to force governments to make better decisions. Yet these two methods can be easily circumvented.

The first may only create the illusion that representatives display fiscal responsibility. In fact, it can lead to little more than innovative accounting gimmicks, as New York has shown year after year. The effects of the second are equally questionable. Aside from the question of whether limiting politicians' tenure is constitutional in the United States, it is not clear that new politicians every twelve years would carry out better policies than those who, not facing such constraint, make their moves to secure long-term political careers. And why would one expect novices every twelve years to be better able to deal with the smooth, well-trained, experienced lobbyists who have no term limits? Only in the movies do saints like Mr. Smith go to Washington and withstand the pressures.

Another difference between the effect of the institutions of referendum and initiative and all the others that economists and political scientists have been proposing to control the governments' actions, is that I am not suggesting that I can forecast the exact effect on governments' expenditures and taxation. But I do suggest that within such a system there is a closer correspondence between what governments do and what people receive from their governments than under alternative political arrangements, and that in this system mistaken policies are less likely to persist.

An example: economists do not agree—and never will—on whether or not governments' increased expenditures on roads or education are "investment" or "waste." A road can be built that leads nowhere. It may just redirect government's revenues from taxation into the pockets of one or another politician's constituents. Also, governments can spend more on schools without producing additional "education."

Of course, the contrary may happen too. The road may be extensively used, and students may get good training. It is a trivial exercise to come up with models that lead to either outcome. It is less trivial but not too difficult to come up with evidence that governments made good investments at times, and at other times bad ones. Thus generalized models and contrasting, abstract philosophies cannot help governments to make better decisions consistently, even if they want to. Moreover, even if one makes a stronger assumption that governments always spend money wisely and know which road, school, or hospital will turn out to be a good investment, macroeconomic theory still cannot answer the question: just how much should governments spend on investments altogether?

The institutions of referendum and initiative answer this question directly and also help solve the problem of allocating funds. Assume that a local or federal government wants to increase expenditures on roads, schools, and health care. In a referendum they ask to raise taxes or cut other expenditures. If the majority votes to raise taxes, money will be spent on roads and universities. If the public is pleased with the results in five, ten, or fifteen years, the arrangement continues. If it is not, they may revoke the expenditures through an "initiative," preventing the persistence of erroneous policies and the establishment of rigid bureaucracies and permanent entitlements. In fact, the mere existence of the institution of initiative would keep bureaucrats on their toes.

The institutions can exist at all levels of government, be they federal, state, or municipal, which allows for a diversity of experiments and so, through trial and error, more rapid learning. For instance, one state may opt for public schools, another for private ones. Five or ten years later, voters will be able to compare the outcomes and, through an initiative, cut their losses and shift to the better alternative.

Readers should keep this fundamental option in mind when encountering repeated criticism of one or another policy. The criticism should not imply that I wish to advise statesmen or that I necessarily know the answer. It only means either that the policy was not based on scientific analyses (even if the analyses used the language and methods of what at that moment passed for science) or that a referendum and initiative could have better revealed the correct answer. *Correct* means what the voters would consider as such, neither me nor any expert.

At this stage the reader might ask: If such political arrangements are so advantageous, why have they not become widespread? One answer seems quite simple: neither politicians nor rulers have an interest to introduce them on a regular, constitutionally guaranteed basis since they weaken the rulers' power (though repeatedly people have indicated that they would favor these arrangements). The fact that the Swiss introduced them was due to particular historical circumstances—and, indeed, who has heard of their politicians ever since? It is not accidental either that Switzerland is a prosperous country, consistently among the richest, whatever measure one considers, though they lack natural resources. The fact that they transformed rocks into opportunities reflects their entrepreneurial spirit rather than the blessing of natural endowments.

Nevertheless, there is reason for optimism concerning the introduction of these institutions in some countries, because, as the evidence presented in the last chapter reveals, radical changes in political institutions have occurred when governments are bankrupt and their countries are falling far behind others.

The additional explanation for these political institutions not becoming widespread, is that the military competition between states, which led unavoidably to centralization, prevented their introduction. From this angle, there is also reason for cautious optimism for political experimentations today, at least in some parts of the world.

Briefly, the book shows that ideas, both good and bad, have consequences. Prosperity is sustained when people daringly take risks and bring good ideas to life. When they bring bad ideas to life and there are no political institutions to prevent persistence in error, the bad ideas become myths that lead societies astray.

Communism was one such myth. Macroeconomics, still alive, is another, giving illusions of precision and science. Politicians use both this myth and numbers computed for national units to formulate policies, claiming that such reliance helps navigate a society to prosperity. The book shows not only that this is not so, but also that such reliance on national models and numbers have harmful consequences. Societies cannot sustain prosperity when their governments, relying on these models, tax and spend.

The examination of a wide range of evidence, among them the rise of the open, multinational trading-cities and -states in the past and present, whose influence radiated around the world, show that the keys to prosperity consist of sustaining conditions favorable to the commercialization of knowledge within a political framework that prevents persistence in error. Trade and the democratization of capital allow people, wherever they come from, to unlock their entrepreneurial talents and get a stake in what the business society is doing. Ideally, the political institutions of referenda and initiatives could prevent the persistence of erroneous government policies, even if they do not prevent occasional mistaken decisions (nothing can prevent the latter). These political institutions would also teach people to weigh, reconsider, take responsibilities, and thus better control what governments do. All these conditions combined guarantee prosperity.

And the contrary: societies decline when repressive, corrupt, and monopolistic governments put sands in the wheels of trade, or even break the wheels—the case of communist countries. By so doing they destroy trust and ambition and bring about the destructive traits of envy, resentment, and passivity. Such regimes also destroy civil society, regardless of what national and international statistics agencies measure. Even when these erroneous ways are abandoned, it takes long to restore trust and rebuild the complex and bewildering variety of institutions necessary to sustain prosperity.

The book looks at the two extremes, and shows how both in the past and the present societies got entangled somewhere between them, at times for justified security reasons, at other times because of invented fears, and at still other times because of sticking to outdated myths. The book shows what myths we must discard today to pave the way to prosperity.

Outline

The first chapters discard economic myths. They closely examine macroeconomic models that pass today for science and define public discourse on prosperity. These models turn out to be little more than habits of thought, successive opinions held by contemporaries. Using obscure, vague terms, they were invented to influence policies rather than being part of a continuous process of scientific discovery. They are based on false though logical ideas and on numbers published with a precision of plus or minus one decimal point, which pass for facts but aren't. It turns out that being either logical or numerical does not mean being right. Science becomes mercurial when written with the goal of influencing policies.

The first two chapters show why the aggregate numbers that macro-economists and policymakers focus on are flawed, and to what extent. These two, as well as the third chapter, show that models that bring attention to these aggregates have no solid foundations either. Still, I try to destroy the "business of macroeconomics" creatively, in the sense that, once I discard some views, I offer an alternative way of both looking at facts and solving problems.

Even without going into many details in the first chapter, I conclude that, since the numbers are so unreliable, the much-heated discussions between Keynesians and Monetarists, or between those who build models to justify fine-tuning to sustain prosperity and those who build others to justify stable rules to sustain it, are beside the point. The quality of aggregate data being what it is, a policy of following rules that help establish credibility is preferable to fine-tuning policies, even if one happens to hold Keynesian beliefs. The latter beliefs rely on the assumption that economists and policymakers understand the meaning of changes in aggregate numbers and know how to respond to them. The chapter shows that they don't.

The conclusion that governments should not pay attention to minute changes in aggregates and react to them does not imply that policymakers should avoid paying attention to and reacting to major disturbances. Yet when this is the case, as the book shows in various contexts, the remedies cannot be discussed anyway in the general terms and obscure language of customary macroeconomic models. Changes in policies must be discussed in simple, specific, and concrete terms.

The second chapter deals with debts, deficits, and the government's expenditures. Once again the arguments and evidence show not only that economists have no idea what they measure when they look at debts, deficits, and the governments' expenditures today, but that the theories that justify looking at them are flawed to start with. For example: in macroeconomic models dealing with deficits, it does not matter if the government spends money on the military, on health and education, on roads and bridges, and on bureaucrats wasting money. They all represent "government expenditures." The expenditures can be paid by increasing the deficits, which in Keynesian analysis is beneficial, at times temporarily, at times permanently, no matter what the government does with the money— even digging holes in the ground, as Keynes put it.

Once one gets into the habit of using such generalized language and talking about "government expenditures," it becomes too easy to slip into a line of reasoning implying that, since governments may, at times, spend the money wisely, they will always do so. The careless, obscure language of Keynesian models, still used today in public debates, opens the way to build "general theories" and make policy recommendations based on them. Since these theories disregard the specific historical-institutional background, they lead to both a misinterpretation of numbers and to bad policies. The chapter also shows that it is possible to talk about debts, deficits, saving rates, and macroeconomic policies in everyday language, without using the macroeconomists' specialized vocabulary. Once this is done much of the reasoning and language of macroeconomics seems irrelevant, wrong, or just plain silly. One cannot find ways to deal with debts and deficits by relying on them.

If this dismissal of macroeconomic models and their language sounds radical, well, it is. But it is not as radical as Keynes's own opinion of his followers. When Friedrich Hayek asked him if he was not upset about the ways in which they were applying his ideas, Keynes answered, "Oh, they are just fools." This conversation has never been quoted in any macroeconomic textbooks for graduates or undergraduates, which continue to cover Keynes's followers' approach over most of their pages and which influence public discourse. So, if macroeconomics does not provide the appropriate tools to examine government policies, and neither does it give any keys to unlock the door to prosperity, what approach does?

Chapter 3 looks at the alternative. It shows that once a political-legal setting provides opportunities for the humble to rise by taking risks, the keys can be found through trade and the "democratization of capital." The access to financial markets allows entrepreneurs to unlock their potential and investors to diversify their portfolios. The chapter makes this point by looking at the links between trade and finance in the past and the present, the rise of trading cities in particular, and the way their influence radiated over large areas. While doing so, it also discards many other ideas about causes of prosperity, common in economics and public discourse today, in particular the role of savings.

Inflation and the role of central banks come into the picture in chapter 4, not only because I discuss the merits of pursuing a policy of "zero inflation," but also because of a more fundamental discussion, linking them to the issues covered in the previous chapters: trade and measurement.

After all, the commercialization of knowledge, based on trade and finance, implies reliance on explicit or implicit contracts to buy, to sell, to lend, to work, to pay, to redeem. When prices are stable, people sign contracts on the basis that there will be no material discrepancy between "real" and "nominal" values during the length of their contracts. If people expect a material discrepancy between the two—that is, if they expect inflation—they will try to rewrite the contracts and make other adjustments. Looking more closely at the consequences of both adjustments, the chapter shows: that the costs of inflation are much higher than economists suggest; that inflation is harmful to prosperity, though aggregate numbers may not capture the harm for a long time; that the role of central banks should be to maintain the public's trust by sticking to the goal of keeping the price level stable, and nothing else; how major deficits complicate the central banks' attempts at maintaining price stability and lead to speculation in currencies; and why changes in price indices do not always reflect monetary pressures. When exploring this last issue, the chapter shows that, in spite of reaching the conclusion about the importance of central banks' commitment to maintain stable price levels, in some situations one can say, in a very limited and specific sense, that a central bank's excessive pursuit of "zero-inflation" can be harmful.

Chapter 5 reinforces the conclusions reached in the previous chapters about trade and finance being the keys to prosperity, and price stability a facilitating factor. It also shows how difficult it is to restore trust among people and in institutions once politicians have systematically destroyed such trust. The chapter reaches this conclusion from an unusual angle, by looking closely into a distorted mirror. The mirror reflects what happens when trade, finance, and the institutions of private property that sustain them have been destroyed and denied—the case of communist countries.

The chapter shows more: that a repressive, corrupt, monopolistic state, combined with the prohibition of trade, destroys trust and ambition, and leads to envy, resentment, and passivity, all destructive traits that impede prosperity. Such a state also destroys civil society, regardless of what its rulers measure. To restore trust is not easy: citizens must believe that the state will no longer arbitrarily and violently deprive them of life and property, and people must get used to a system where the distribution of goods and services is based on currency rather than connections and status within the ruling party. Nobody knows how long it takes to restore trust and shift from one system to another by rebuilding the variety of institutions necessary to carry out trade. Unfortunately, too many irresponsible economists raised false hopes about speedy transitions, apparently unaware of the fact that prosperity depends on the crucial, though not always visible, institutions maintaining trust and allowing people to acquire the wide variety of skills necessary for carrying out trade.

Various chapters in the book show that, whereas trade guarantees prosperity, the state must tax and redistribute so as to create among the poor a stabler, more hopeful constituency, and thus sufficiently diminish and rechannel their resentment and envy. These policies relieve the more fortunate from constant guard against their poorer neighbors. When the state finds the proper balance between offering both protection to the more fortunate and a stake in the future to those who are less fortunate, it gives rise to a bond of common interests. Society becomes just and prospers.

It takes time for people to find the policies and institutions necessary to maintain this balance. But the time may be right now. The last chapter shows that radical departures in political institutions happened when the coffers of states were empty and these countries were falling behind others. Introducing the institutions of referendum and initiative could be such departures and could provide the necessary remedies for both limiting politicians' ambitions and reflecting people's wishes.

Acknowledgments

I thank Arnold Beichman, Dennis Carlton, Ronald Coase, David Colander, Leonard Dudley, David Goldman, Leonard Liggio, Richard Lipsey, Joseph Livni, Ejan Mackaay, William McNeill, Joel Mokyr, Robert Mundell, Frederic Pryor, the late Douglass Purvis, Michael Trebilcock, William Watson, Glenn Yago, and anonymous referees for their comments on various chapters. Appendix 3 was written with my previous colleagues at the Université de Montréal, Marcel Dagenais and Claude Montmarquette. Anne-Marie El Hakim gave dedicated assistance on this appendix.

Special thanks are due to Milton Friedman and Anna Schwartz for their encouragement and detailed comments on the numerous versions, and to Colin Day, the director of the University of Michigan Press. This is the sixth time during the last ten years that we have collaborated. Last, but not least, I thank my wife, Gabrielle, to whom I owe so much, and to the kids, who help me to relax.

The encouragement of the people whom I thank was exceptional—many others discouraged me from this venture. But I realized early that the only way to fight myths and "groupthink" is to be willing to stand alone and to distinguish the facts from the myths and prejudices masquerading as "theories" and "facts."

The project was financed, in part, by grants from Quebec FCAR Fund and from the Social Sciences and Humanities Research Council of Canada. I am grateful to the Canada Council for awarding me the Killam Fellowship Award, which gave me the time to work on this project.

The Centre de recherche et développement en économique (CRDE) provided excellent secretarial and other support. Special thanks are due to Sharon Brewer, Francine Martel and Josée Vignola at CRDE, and Cathy Ewart at McGill's Faculty of Management.

Chapter 1

Illusions of Precision

In theory, you're trying to find out what the future is going to be like.
That's difficult when the past keeps changing.
—Martin Zimmerman, chief economist, Ford Motor Company

In Italy, 1987 was called the year of *il sorpasso,* which, roughly translated, means "I leapfrogged you, Mr. Jones." In that year, ISTAT, the government's statistics office, suddenly added an extra 18 percent to its estimate of Italy's real national income. According to the revised numbers, Italy became the world's fourth biggest capitalist economy after the United States, Japan, and West Germany. In fact, the number 18 was chosen to make this jump.[1]

The adjustment was made to take into account Italy's underground economy, though no other reason than leapfrogging other members of the European Community was given for choosing the specific figure. After all, since 1971, when the first study on Italy's black economy was published, the estimates of its size hovered between 20 percent and 30 percent of the Gross National Product (GNP), in some years thought to be less and in others more.[2] Such adjustments render the official unemployment, inequality, and growth figures unreliable and make economic and statistical analyses and policies based on the official pre- and even post-1987 figures dicey as well.[3] Moreover, Italy's prosperity suggests that a country can, on average, do quite well without having access to even vaguely reliable aggregate figures, be they employment or growth rates.

Italy is not the only successful country where income tax returns have had only a vague resemblance to the actual, underlying income patterns. In Taiwan the underground economy is estimated to vary between 25 and 30 percent of the official GNP figure. As in Italy, the existence of this large underground economy is attributed to a high-rate progressive taxation, regulations, and prohibitions, as well as to the history of the Taiwanese, who have had centuries of experience at evading tax collectors.[4] It has been recently estimated that in Spain, another booming country, one-third of the "unemployed" are working illegally and that there too the black market adds between 20 and 30 percent to the official GNP figure. Estimates of the black economy in other countries vary significantly. In the United States it was estimated to add 10 percent to the official figure in 1948, 5.5 percent in 1968, and, according to some, only 4 to 6 percent in 1977.[5] According to others the figure during the 1970s was above 20 percent.[6] In Britain estimates range from 2 to 15 percent; in Belgium, from 5 percent in 1960 to 21 percent from 1978 to 1980; in Greece, from 30 to 50 percent; in Denmark, from 4 to 12 percent; in West Germany, between 4 and 11 percent; and in Canada, around 15 percent.[7] Argentina's black economy is estimated to be 30 percent of the official one, and Peru's as much as 40, whereas in Mexico it is estimated to have increased from 19 to 38 percent of the size of the official one during the last five years.[8]

The existence of black markets due to varying tax rates suggests that not only aggregates but also growth rates and changes in unemployment rates become unreliable, because an increase in tax rates has two effects. It diminishes incentives to work and to invest, and it also diminishes incentives to declare revenues and employment. When the latter effect is significant, as the previous evidence suggests, the recorded growth rates diminish, and recorded unemployment rates increase. To an extent, both may be statistical artifacts. And the contrary: when tax rates diminish, the recorded increased growth rates and diminished unemployment rates are, in part, statistical artifacts too.[9]

None of these observations on aggregates is novel: by 1963 Morgenstern had written that interpreting French, and probably many other countries', statistics poses similar problems. He also noted that the inequality of personal incomes is being evaluated and policies of redistribution are being carried out on the basis of unreliable tax returns.[10]

The wide divergence of opinions about the numbers already suggests that one should be skeptical about attempts to test various macroeconomic theories and to make policy recommendations of the "fine-tuning" type by using official figures. Yet, as the story unfolds in the following chapters, it becomes clear that the problems black markets pose for both interpreting and using measured aggregate numbers for recommending policies, serious as they are, pale in comparison to others.[11]

Behind Veils of the Legal Economy

> None of us really understands what's going on with all these numbers.
> —David Stockman, President Ronald Reagan's budget director

On April 26, the Commerce Department of the United States announced that the GNP grew at a moderate rate of 2.3 percent in the first quarter of 1988. A month later, government statisticians boosted first-quarter GNP growth to 3.9 percent, a change of nearly 70 percent.[12] On July 24, 1987, the Commerce Department announced that the 1984 through 1986 GNP growth numbers were all revised substantially upward, to 6.8 percent from 6.4 percent in 1984, to 3 percent from 2.7 percent for 1985, and to 2.9 percent from 2.5 percent in 1986.[13] Such corrections are typical. Whereas the Commerce Department first announced that the Gross Domestic Product (GDP) grew at an annual rate of 2.7 percent in the third quarter of 1992, it later revealed that the figure was 3.9 percent.[14] In a speech before U.S. executives, Walter Wriston, former chairman of Citicorp, complained when observing these changes that "the government is incapable even of telling us what the last quarter's GNP growth was with any precision: final figures are not issued until three years later [and by then who cares, but the economic historian?],[15] and vary widely from initial reports."[16]

In a study of U.S. GNP revisions, Mankiw and Shapiro (1986) find that the standard deviation of the revision from preliminary estimates of the real growth rate to the final number is 2.2 percent. This means, for instance, that if preliminary figures indicate no growth, the probability of more than a 2.0 percent growth rate exceeds 18 percent.[17] An honest but politically unattractive announcement by the Bureau of Statistics about such a preliminary figure should thus be approximately the following: "The way we measure and weigh total output in the economy, this total probably neither rose by more than 2 percent, nor fell by more than 2 percent during the last year." Such an announcement would be politically unattractive since it would shatter all confidence in fine-tuning policies and raise questions about the usefulness of the statistical bureaucracy.[18]

What are the reasons for these mistakes? The answer is not that they reflect delayed adjustments for black markets. Such adjustments are made rarely and irregularly, if at all. One major source of the underestimation when calculating the GNP by the output method is the undercounting of personal consumption expenditures, in which the category of retail sales is a major component.[19] Those who watch the national income accounts— most recently Wilcox (1988)—have criticized the estimation of this component for a long time.[20]

Here is a numerical example to illustrate the problem. For nearly three years there has been a great and growing discrepancy between the retail sales trends and the numbers released every month by the eighteen largest general merchandise chains (which account for 80 percent of the sales) and the figures issued by the Census Bureau every month (which are used for computing the GNP). On May 8, 1987, for example, the top eighteen retail chains in the United States reported their best growth months in two years, of 13.8 percent. A week later, the Commerce Department reported a 0.1 percent growth for the same period.[21]

Whereas bureaus of statistics could improve the accuracy of aggregate figures by spending more on surveys and doing them more frequently, these expenditures would not be justified since, as explained both below and in the following chapters, the models that draw attention to and justify the building of national aggregates are wrong to start with. Once policymakers discard these models, there can be no reason to compute most aggregates. I shall mention below a few additional though still relatively simpler measurement and conceptual problems, linked with innovations and deregulation. The following chapters will examine the far more difficult ones, linked with the relationship between GNP measures and both the government's expenditures and the historical background.

Numbers out of a Hat

Douglass Lee[22] notes that, in order to calculate real GNP, the Commerce Department deflates the nominal GNP with a price index reflecting changes in prices since 1982. Yet the composition of the GNP has changed appreciably since 1982, as output has tended to rise more rapidly in those sectors where major innovations have been made, and whose prices have lagged behind the overall measured inflation. Thus, when the current nominal value of these sectors is translated into 1982 prices, their contribution to real GNP (which is expressed in 1982 dollars) is exaggerated. The exaggeration is greater for those products and services whose output has grown rapidly while their prices have fallen—precisely the situation with computers and airline tickets (because of innovations in the first case, deregulation in the second).

For example, the Commerce Department reports that from 1982 to 1987 real purchases of office computing and accounting machinery rose by 296 percent, while prices for such equipment declined by 45 percent. The effect of these numbers on the first quarter GNP growth rate in 1988 (when output of computers and accounting equipment increased at an annual rate of 20 percent) was that, although such expenditures totaled $30 billion in today's dollars, they came to more than $97 billion in 1982 dollars.[23] Thus, whereas computers accounted for 0.8 percent of total GNP expressed in current dollars, they represented 2.5 percent of output when the Commerce Department converted the figures into 1982 dollars in order to estimate the "real" GNP.[24]

The inaccuracies due to innovations show up in other aggregate figures as well, such as productivity statistics. The U.S. Bureau of Labor Statistics admits that it finds it impossible to measure productivity in fields such as insurance, health care, real estate, and stock and bond brokerage.[25] All together, services for which no productivity figures are available employ nearly 70 percent of the people in service jobs. It is important to recall that these sectors have expanded rapidly during the last decades and that they account for two-thirds of measured economic activity in industrial economies, and almost two-fifths of world trade.[26]

Productivity measures for the banking industry are published. Though the industry employs only about 22 percent of workers in the service category, this number serves as a proxy for the entire industry's productivity. In recent years this number in the United States compared unfavorably with German and Japanese figures for their banking industry. But the numbers cannot be compared: German and Japanese banks own industrial companies, whereas banks in the United States do not.

The extrapolation based on such limited information and the comparison between countries, which upon closer examination makes little sense, does not prevent bureaus of statistics from continuing to publish aggregate productivity figures with rarely mentioned reservations, nor does it prevent extensive public discourse on changes in the productivity of the United States. In August 1992, for example, the U.S. Bureau of Statistics announced that productivity in service-type business fell at 2.3 percent annual rate, while manufacturing productivity rose 4.7 percent. The decimal-point precision, without any acknowledgement of *varying* margins for errors due to frequent innovations and changes in quality, sustains the illusion that the calculation has sound scientific foundations.

I found only one article that paid attention to the dubious origins of the productivity numbers. In that article, the previous chief economist of the Commerce Department admitted that at the "current state of knowledge, we don't really know what's happening to service sector productivity. It could well be growing faster than manufacturing productivity instead of much slower." If one may suspect such a statement to be politically motivated in an election year—the declaration was made in 1992—there is no reason to distrust the statement of a Bureau of Labor Statistics official in the same article. He said that productivity figures are unreliable not because there are not enough people to do the job but because "in any event [the job of estimating productivity figures] is just about impossible."[27]

Consider an additional measurement problem at a higher level of aggregation. When two methods of calculating the GNP do not fit, "balancing items" running into billions of dollars or pounds sterling are added to or subtracted from various components. For example, in 1987 the income measure in the United Kingdom showed the GNP growing at a real rate of 4.8 percent (to £356 billion), whereas the expenditure measure showed it growing at 2.9 percent (to £347 billion). By definition, the difference of £9 billion had to be put somewhere. Where?

In theory, the current-account balance should equal the gap between domestic savings and total investment. If the British invest more than they save, the difference must come from abroad, and it is there that the £9 billion balancing item has been included.[28] But where one puts this balancing item is important. Economists at Warburg Securities suggested that all the United Kingdom's aggregate measures may be wrong because of the particular way the discrepancy has been interpreted. According to these economists, the source of the discrepancy was the corporate sector. In 1987 the reported financial surplus of this sector (i.e., the difference between retained profits and investment) was £27 billion higher than its identified net acquisition of financial assets.[29] Thus Warburg's economists suggested that the black hole in the national accounts masks a significant under-recording of business investment.

If their interpretation was accurate, the adjustment was of more than statistical interest. If the reported widening current-account deficit has been matched by greater domestic investment rather than just greater consumption, one should have worried less, if at all, about either deficits or capacity shortages.[30] It is surprising that statistical bureaus in Europe continued to pay so much attention to trade figures since, if the European Community's plans go as projected, on January 1, 1993, customs controls will be reduced and intra-EC trade figures, I assume, will change meaning significantly or even vanish.[31]

The discrepancies among aggregates supposed to be equal are not the only ones that lead either to mismeasuring consumption and savings, or to misinterpreting changes in their trends. Many conceptual difficulties also arise from attempts to estimate these two aggregate figures. In public policy debates in recent years, much has been written about the fact that saving rates are too low, being in the range of 3 to 6 percent in the United States, the United Kingdom, France, and other countries, thus preventing adequate investments. Less was written on the ways in which this figure is calculated in the National Income and Product Accounts (NIPAs) in the United States and in accounts under other names in other countries, or on the basic issue that the measured aggregates do not correspond even vaguely to their theoretical definitions.[32] Holloway (1987) and Boskin (1988) are among the exceptions who looked more closely at the figures. They give detailed accounts about the ways savings are calculated and show the formidable limitations of the methods being used, the following being among the main ones:[33]

- Household savings in national accounts are estimated as residuals after subtracting consumer expenditures, taxes, and interest payments to business from the estimated income. This procedure implies that all the errors concerning income and consumption, whatever their nature, show up in the measurement of saving.
- Whereas incomes between 1960 and 1980 became significantly underestimated (because of, among other things, higher marginal tax rates), consumption levels became significantly overestimated, since expenditures on durables, education, and health were counted as consumption rather than savings or investments. According to some estimates, correcting for such overestimation would add five percentage points to the conventional saving figures.[34] (Why is buying a personal computer considered consumption whereas building a classroom is an investment?)
- Examinations of national savings do not come to grips with the well-known conceptual problems of aggregation when drastic demographic changes are taking place and when "households are heterogeneous," as Boskin (1988, 24) puts it. Such an assumption, buried in the midst of a technical text, just shows how common sense can sometimes fail in the face of an apparently precise, logical model and be kept out of sight when using the aggregate language of macroeconomics. After all, when have households *not* been demographically different? Moreover, there have been drastic demographic changes during the last twenty years, and the series of aggregate saving numbers may not be comparable.[35] The number of single parents, unmarried couples, and people living alone has risen significantly, and in many Western countries the average age

of the population has increased. Later chapters will say more about the impact of these changes and provide a far broader context for discussion on "national" saving rates, both private and public.

What Is Real?

One is interested in measuring the GNP, savings, or other variables in "real" rather than "nominal" terms. But how do price indices capture this "reality"?

There is a significant difference between the ways in which the Consumer Price Index (CPI) is computed in the United States and in Canada. The *Evaluation of Issues Relating to the Price Index,* prepared for Statistics Canada in March 1988, emphasized—and criticized—the difference. The Canadian sample is not selected at random, but is referred to as a "judgmental sample."[36] This means that decisions about the number of price quotations and selection of outlets and items priced is based on that of the CPI staff with little, if any, record left about the decisions and their rationale.[37] The reliability of the choices made has never been examined. Thus, if the staff had common sense, the results might be good. If they lacked it, the results might be bad: we just do not know what is happening today in Canada, and no figure of the type that Mankiw and Shapiro calculated for the mismeasured United States GNP is available with respect to price indices (in Canada or anywhere else).

Initially, Herb Segal recommended the method for selecting the outlets in 1977. The selection was supposed to be based on the results of the 1974 Retail Commodity Survey.[38] For various reasons his recommendations about the number of price quotes and types and the number of outlets were adopted, but others concerning the frequency with which they should be sampled were not. Nobody ever calculated the error resulting from this compromise. Also, since no Retail Commodity Survey has appeared since 1974, there has been no systematic update of his work.[39]

The lack of readjustment leads to an overestimation of the inflation rate, as noted in the *Report of the Seminar on the CPI* held in Geneva in 1986, organized jointly by the Economic Commission of Europe and the International Labour Organisation. Improvements in the quality of service that would have lowered prices (since it became less time-consuming to buy goods) are not being taken into account. This particular problem is part of a larger, conceptual one, linked with taking into account innovations of any kind in the price index.

This is an ancient, much-discussed, unsolved problem. Price indices give a distorted view of changes in price levels when many new products come on the market, or when there are yearly, drastic changes in the performance of computers, VCRs, and other communication and home entertainment equipment, as well as in people's expenditures on them. The previous numerical example concerning the computer industry demonstrates the magnitude of the problem concerning just one item.[40]

The Geneva report also raised other issues, like measuring the impact of regulations and of the introduction of antipollution devices in general. Though the consumer pays more, does the change reflect better quality, an improvement in the production of "clean air," and increased welfare? Or do the higher prices indicate diminished wealth and welfare? The participants agreed that there are no general solutions to such problems, and that one has to deal with them on a case-by-case basis.[41] The *Evaluation Report* of the Canadian CPI notes that Statistics Canada, for example, recognizes the importance of taking into account changes in quality, but that "an exact process by which a given quality change is estimated and the relative importance of these changes are not well documented."[42]

This should not provoke one to throw up his hand in despair. But it does imply that paying attention to a figure whose reliability is unknown, dividing already dubious aggregate figures by it, and then arguing that policymakers should react to the recorded changes, will inevitably lead to bad policies, cause embarrassment, and eventually undermine the public's trust.

Grave as these problems are, comparing price indices, both over time and across countries, is difficult mainly because of the totally different and at times arbitrary ways in which their computation takes into account changes in regulated prices and changes concerning homeownership (discussed in chap. 4). I emphasize the latter component because it has about a 40 percent weight in the Canadian CPI (within it a 40 percent weight is given to mortgage interest)[43] and is a major component of most price indices in other parts of the world as well. The problem with homeownership is that owners are consumers, investors, and speculators, which raises numerous conceptual difficulties. For instance, during inflationary periods more and more consumers may turn into "investors" and "speculators" in real estate, yet the CPI, which is supposed to measure things consumed every year rather than investments, will not capture the shift, which leads to a substantial overestimation of inflation. Attempts to correct such distortions have never been made.

Peter deVries and Andrew Baldwin (1985) have examined only what would have happened to the Canadian CPI if the U.S. methodology to calculate homeownership were adopted.[44] They found that, according to the Canadian method, during the twelve months of 1981 the inflation rate as measured by the official CPI was stable, being 12 to 13 percent relative to the year before. However, had the U.S. methodology been used, the inflation rate would have been much higher. They also found that during the twelve months of 1982 the official Canadian CPI varied between 9.3 and 11.4 percent relative to the respective months a year before. However, had the U.S. methodology been adopted, the CPI would have varied between 5.2 and 11.3 percent. While the official CPI would have dropped from 11.4 to 9.3 percent between certain dates, the alternative one would have dropped from 11.3 to 5.2 percent.[45] Which index should have guided monetary policy? And what was the "real" rate of interest?

This large discrepancy in price indices, depending on the method used to take into account homeownership, is not unusual.[46] Alan Blinder (1980) found similar magnitudes when he contrasted alternative ways of calculating price indices in the United States. According to one calculation, the inflation rates in 1977 and 1978 were, respectively, 9.2 percent and 12.4 percent, whereas according to another they were 2.5 percent and 5.7 percent, respectively. Blinder expressed concern that policy was guided by unreliable figures and that governments' entitlements were linked to inappropriate price indices. "The bogus 18 percent inflation rates then being reported by the CPI," writes Blinder, led to credit controls and budget-cutting exercises. Blinder concludes that "this is one inflationary distortion we could all live better without."[47] The same could be said about the situation in Canada, where since 1987 the Central Bank's policy was guided by an almost exclusive focus on minute fluctuations in the CPI; policymakers worried about the possible impact of introducing new indirect taxes. Chapter 4 will say more about price indices and their link to fiscal and monetary policies.

The policy implications of all these measurement problems combined is one of the questions addressed next.

Discretionary Policy

If the aggregate numbers are as unreliable as suggested above—and they are even more unreliable, as the following chapters will show—one can easily conclude that policymakers cannot depend on them to carry out effective fine-tuning policy.[48] Attempts to carry out policies in response to changes in the official figures cause additional uncertainty. Uncertainty would decrease if it were known that policymakers will not try to fine-tune in response to changes in macroeconomic aggregates.[49]

To say that governments and central banks should not fine-tune in response to changes in aggregates does not imply that they should maintain their policies in the face of major disturbances and specific events. Consider the following examples.

During the late 1980s, many observers attributed the decline in the relative value of the U.S. dollar to the fact that central banks around the world decided to no longer hold a large fraction of their reserves in this currency because of its inflationary history and because they expected such history to be repeated. If the Federal Reserve wants to reestablish credibility, it will have to do so through a series of steps. During such times demand for the U.S. dollar will fluctuate (and therefore velocity will not stay constant), so the Federal Reserve will have to look at signals like changes in price indices—the CPI, commodity price indices, and others[50]—however imprecise, to learn about the success of its policies and to react in response to them. Chapter 4 will comment further on the Central Banks' policies.

Consider another example: suppose that the domestic marginal tax rates are significantly changed. If they are lowered, one can expect that part of the income previously earned illegally will now be declared. Measured GNP will rise because of both this effect and the effect of diminished tax rates on incentives to work. At the same time the velocity of currency in circulation will change (since the number of transactions carried out in black and the demand for cash have diminished). In this case too, monetary authorities may decide to react and examine, once again, changes in price indices (but not in other aggregates) for signals of their policies' effectiveness.

Finally, consider the recent events in Germany's monetary history. When the one-to-one exchange rate was chosen after unification, it was estimated that 80 billion DM would be issued during the first year of the unification. This number equaled 19 percent of M1 and 6.5 percent of M3 of West Germany. East Germany's output was expected to add roughly 15 percent to that of West Germany. Growth rates of unified Germany were expected to be around 4 percent, implying a stable price level (using the growth in M1 as a guide to make this prediction). As it turned out, these expectations were way off the mark, and though 100 billion DM was spent in the Eastern part, not much was produced.[51] This unexpected event led the German government to stray from its traditional monetary and fiscal discipline, which it tried to restore in 1992 through a number of abrupt monetary and fiscal steps.

Though one may use the term *discretionary* to describe such policies, he/she should realize that they have nothing in common with the Keynesian meaning of the word. The changes in policy are not automatic, mechanical responses to changes recorded in aggregates figures. They are each specific responses to specific problems and events. It is important to make this point clear since, of the many questions raised in macroeconomics, perhaps the most important was whether or not public policy should be conducted by rule or by discretion, the latter being defined as the policy of reacting mechanically to changes in measured, aggregate variables.

Consider Mankiw's (1990) discussion on this point. He argues—mistakenly—that sticking to rules is always advantageous:

> The argument against discretion is illustrated most simply in an example involving not economics but politics—specifically, public policy about negotiating with terrorists over the release of hostages. The announced policy of the United States and many other nations is that we will not negotiate over hostages. Such an announcement is intended to deter terrorists: if there is nothing to be gained from kidnapping, rational terrorists won't take hostages. But, in fact, terrorists are rational enough to know that once hostages are taken, the announced policy may have little force, and that the temptation to make some concession to obtain the hostages' release may become overwhelming. The only way to deter truly rational terrorists is somehow to take away the discretion of policy-makers and commit them to a rule of never negotiating.[52]

This sounds like a plausible argument in favor of rules. It is a very superficial argument.

Mankiw's conclusion is inaccurate for the simple reason that the term *terrorist* is not defined in a void but depends on specific, historical circumstances. One man's terrorist is another man's freedom fighter, and people do not want to apply the same policies toward freedom fighters as toward terrorists. What at times is called idiotic recklessness, can later be called stout-hearted loyalty to friends, and what is at times praised as prudent foresight, can be condemned at other times as cowardice.[53] In Mankiw's example, sticking to a rule could lead to punishing "heroes, loyalty, prudent foresight"; if enforced, it could lead to diminished resistance to aggression or oppression.

In other words, since a "terrorist act" cannot be unequivocally defined, no rule written to punish it could ever be enforced at all times.[54] Our language is too imprecise to give unequivocal meaning to rules. This is one of the reasons why discretion is not being taken away from politicians. Consistency can be admirable, but not when circumstances change significantly and, as a result, the meaning of words changes.

Let us return to the topic of macroeconomic policy: whereas the existence of measurement problems leads one to favor rules, a rigid rule could impose heavy costs, and people would not expect it to be enforced at all times. Though the previous examples make this point clear, let us examine an additional one to illustrate the conclusion more sharply. Consider the dilemma monetary authorities may be facing. In response to the central bank's perception that there was a significant change in velocity, the bank considers a move in high-powered money. This step involves a calculated risk. Such a move might lead to greater confusion and to expectations of greater fluctuations in price levels if the public viewed the change as a signal that the central bank had abandoned the long-term policy of maintaining stable price levels.[55]

But the public might view the central bank's response as appropriate to the changed circumstances and still expect stable price levels.[56] Obviously, monetary authorities may sometimes succeed and sometimes fail, just like judges, who sometimes make good and sometimes bad decisions. In contrast to what Mankiw is suggesting, nobody is arguing for taking away the judges' discretionary power, though they are expected to rule based on precedents. Yet the existence of precedents themselves suggests that discretionary power has been and is being used, guided by a broader vision.[57] The same thing holds true for monetary and fiscal policies too. Discretion in reference to specific circumstances, but not "in general," is beneficial and should be practiced—subject to a broader vision. What should be the guiding, broader vision for fiscal policy is discussed in the next chapter, whereas the meaning of this broader vision for monetary policy is discussed in chapter 4.

Creating a Myth

At this point a serious question arises. Is the measurement of aggregate variables, besides that of price indices and monetary aggregates, needed at all, and should it be subsidized? The reason for making an exception to monetary aggregates and price indices is simple: governments can control the money supply, and changes in price indices depend on monetary pressures. Information on these numbers may thus forestall abuse of monopoly power (that is, imposing the inflationary tax).

The question about the usefulness of measuring other aggregates arises since aggregate numbers are useless for policy purposes both when rules are followed and when, on occasion, discretion must be used. In the latter case, policymakers must rely on concrete, specific data and common sense, since the meaning of changes in aggregate numbers becomes of even more dubious quality than usual.

There are additional reasons for raising the question about the usefulness of publishing aggregate figures. Recall that Italy, Taiwan, Hong Kong, Singapore, and Spain have prospered without having access to reliable aggregate figures at all, and the communist countries fell further and further behind despite attempts to base policies on what superficially seemed to be meticulously gathered data (as shown in chap. 5).

Indeed, notice that all the problems dealt with until now have been artificial. If governments did not have large statistical bureaucracies measuring macroeconomic aggregates with great solemnity and did not then shape policies in response to them, none of the negative effects of discretionary policy would have happened. Thus the questions are: Why were they gathered to start with? Should we still continue to gather them?

Sir William Petty already made primitive calculations estimating national incomes in the seventeenth century, and many debates followed about what should and what should not be included in their calculation. However, neither economists nor governments paid much attention to what we call today macroeconomic aggregates until the Great Depression in the United States, and until Keynesian ideas during and after the Second World War got hold of some people's imagination. (Before that, the "theory of business cycles" dominated economists' imagination, and great importance was attached to the production of pig iron in an economy.)

In 1932 the U.S. Senate decided that information about national income should be prepared for the years 1929–31, and nominated Simon Kuznets for the task. In 1941 he published the *National Income and its*

Composition, 1919–1938. However, by 1947 and in his later writings he became critical of the thoughtless repetition of his calculations. Meanwhile, Milton Gilbert, head of the National Income Division of the Department of Commerce in the U.S. government, a man influenced by Keynes' ideas, advocated the use of national income measures for examining relationships between defense expenditures and total output.[58] These views gained currency and the expansion of the statistical bureaucracy was on its way. Neither Kuznets's criticism during the 1950s nor that of Oscar Morgenstern during the 1960s had any impact. By then, as Morgenstern wrote, it required "a great deal of strength *not* to use ready-made and commonly available statistics, dealing with important events when there are no substitutes. But great as the temptation may be to continue as if everything were in tolerable shape, a greater service is rendered to economics by insisting that a good theory cannot be built on shaky data."[59]

The use of aggregate statistics gained much legitimacy with the publication of *A System of National Accounts and Supporting Tables* in 1953 by the Statistical Office of the United Nations. In spite of the fact that Kuznets warned explicitly against both the use of uniform methods of calculation for all countries and the difficulties of interpreting such aggregate data in developing countries, the United Nations report, on its first page, described their "outstanding use . . . in connection with public policy."[60]

The illusion of macroeconomics as a science was enforced: wasn't there "hard," numerical evidence to support it? And wasn't macroeconomics taught at every university? The students became teachers, and macroeconomics and the illusion of comprehensible aggregates, a myth.[61]

Of course, the ignorance of what is being measured may not necessarily imply that most aggregate measures are useless. The fact that people lie when filling out their tax returns does not necessarily mean that the data may be inappropriate for formulating policies. If there is a stable relationship between what people say and what they do, one can still use the numbers in order to make predictions. In general, if the relationship between what we measure and what we do not remains stable—because of black markets, corruption, pollution, military or other threats, or innovations and changes in quality—good analyses of data about rates of change would be feasible. But these relationships do not remain stable. Taxes and perceptions of domestic or international threats change significantly, production in modern economies moves away from outputs that gave the illusion that they could be easily counted toward "services," and parents' expectations about the roles of their children and their extended family change significantly too.[62] Thus, the relationship between what is measured as consumption, saving, and investment, and what people view as such, is unstable too—and I did not even raise problems linked with pollution and the environment. When all these things happen, inferring the true state of the economy from national accounts is like consulting a crystal ball or studying the positions of stars.

But for the moment, let us make the heroic assumption that the errors are stable, which would imply that perceptions of how much governments invest and consume (and waste) do not change significantly, that military threats do not change significantly, that new products are introduced only gradually, that no significant changes in relative prices occur, and that there are no major demographic changes. Then one can make good predictions by correcting for the stable errors.[63]

The question is: Who needs the numbers in such circumstances anyway? If everything works well, if everything goes smoothly according to expectations, would anybody want to *change* any policy? Briefly: when the aggregate numbers are "good," i.e., they make good predictions, they are not needed. And when drastic changes in society require a change in policy, the mismeasured aggregate figures provide no useful information. In his presidential address to the Econometric Society, Michael Bruno (1988), also Governor of the Bank of Israel at the time, noted that, although much work following Jan Tinbergen's (1956) suggestions took the form of larger and larger macro-econometric models, pioneered by Klein and Goldberger (1955), he found these models of only limited use, because of, among other things, the rapid regime changes in the countries that interested him.[64]

All this should not discourage consumers and businesses from seeking access to aggregate data today. As long as governments use them to shape policies, businesses and financial markets will need them too. The point made here and in the next chapters is that their use by governments is mistaken to start with, not only because changes in aggregate numbers mislead, but because macroeconomic theory, which calls attention to them, has no foundations. By relying on it, one is sidetracked from the road to prosperity.

Chapter 2

Government Policies:
Illusions of Science

In the school of political projectors I was but ill entertained, the professors appearing in my judgement wholly out of their senses, which is a scene that never fails to make me melancholy. These unhappy people were proposing schemes for persuading monarchs to choose favourites upon the score of their wisdom, capacity and virtue; of teaching ministers to consult the public good; of rewarding merit, great abilities, eminent services; of instructing princes to know their true interest by placing it on the same foundation with that of their people; of choosing for employments persons qualified to exercise them; with many other wild impossible chimaeras, that never entered before into the heart of man to conceive, and confirmed in me the old observation, that there is nothing so extravagant and irrational which some philosophers have not maintained for truth.

—Jonathan Swift, *Gulliver's Stories*

Imagine an economy in which the private sector's annual income is $10 million. In Year One, it consumes $8 million and saves $2 million, which is then invested in a computer factory that produces a future income of $2 million a year. Assume that in all subsequent years the private sector consumes all its income. If the government neither spends nor taxes, both income and consumption in future years will be $12 million.

Suppose instead that the government borrows to spend the $2 million in Year One on civil servants and that the private sector uses all its savings to buy government bonds rather than invest in a factory. Then, total consumption in the first year, public and private, will be $10 million instead of $8 million, and it will stay at $10 million in all future years. Although consumers receive an income from interest on the treasury bonds, that income is financed by annual taxes. The higher consumption in Year One was bought at the price of lower consumption in the future. This example summarizes the so-called neoclassical view of deficits, which serves as the rationale for economists' opposition toward them.[1]

In the previous example the national debt is a burden on future generations insofar as the government uses it to pay the civil servant (the expenditure on whom is viewed as consumption), rather than to pay for an investment.[2] However, if the government uses its funds to finance investments, be they in health, education, or roads, then the effect and the numerical calculation may not differ from the one made regarding the investment in the private computer factory.[3] Or, if the work of the civil servant is an investment (he may work in education or health), then again the same calculation as for the private factory may be the accurate one. Or let us complicate things a bit more by assuming that the government is spending money on houses, roads, schools, and expected immigration (think about Israel). Then the government's current deficits or debts can be compared to those incurred in a leveraged buyout. The investments are financed by the immigrants' expected future incomes, and the government borrows because it anticipates revenues.

If the work of the civil servant is viewed as neither investment nor consumption but as an appointment due to a minority's political power (and thus considered a waste by the majority even if politicians and the statistics bureau call it investment), then the calculation is different since the government's increased present and future expenditures lead to a redistribution of *diminished* wealth. These arguments show that, in order to evaluate the impact of increased government expenditures, which might have resulted in increased deficits, one must look at what the public gets for its money and what political institutions control the government's expenditures. Looking only at the level of the government's expenditures, the level of deficits, or the names that the government gives to its expenditures does not lead one very far.

The calculation is different if one takes into account arguments and evidence about the relationship between governments' expenditures and the use of violence, domestic or foreign.[4] In such instances the government's borrowing of the $2 million might not reflect some arbitrary, capricious decision, or one that served merely narrow political interests, but would be linked with historical events. In order to evaluate the effect of such an expenditure, one must examine not the measured, monetary impact of borrowing the $2 million but the people's expectations. What was the foregone opportunity? What did people expect this policy to *prevent* from happening at that particular point in time?[5]

Suppose that, because of either an increased crime rate or fear of social unrest linked with a new ideology, the government spends the additional \$2 million on the police, the military, or law enforcement. Not only may this additional \$2 million expenditure not crowd out any private investment, but it may even induce people to invest more or at least prevent investments from diminishing further.[6] In this case, the increased government expenditures lead to expectations of unaltered or even diminished taxation in the future.[7] This argument suggests that, in order to evaluate the impact of deficits, the alternatives—the perceived opportunity costs to such spending at a particular time—must be taken into account. Such alternatives are far broader than the customarily considered ones and must be examined within their historical context.[8]

These arguments already show that there cannot be such a thing as a "general theory" about *any* of the following questions:[9]

- How does the general level of a government's expenditures, in particular its debts and deficits, affect either the total production of goods and services, or the national income earned from production?
- How do the debt and deficits affect employment?
- How do the debt and deficits affect the allocation of resources between current consumption and investment?

The reason that no general answers can be given to any of these questions is simple. An increase in either government expenditures, debts, or deficits can have a positive, negative, or neutral effect on national income, employment, or interest rates, and increased deficits may or may not increase current consumption and diminish investments. It all depends on what the government does with the money and on the timing of its expenditures. This is also the reason that neither time-series nor cross-section analyses can be illuminating. By looking at the level of government expenditures over time or across countries, all government expenditures are put in the same basket, which leads to statistical results but no understanding.[10] The statistical examinations done today consist of little more than mining a few numbers with some statistical criteria in mind, without relevance to their source, meaning, or significance.

Not surprisingly, such analyses did not lead to any consistent results. Deficits were *not* found to be necessarily inflationary, to raise interest rates (either nominal or real), or to crowd out investments.[11] These results could have been expected from the previous, straightforward arguments.[12]

These arguments also show why one should not put all government expenditures in the same basket. One cannot add them up and discuss the impact of the resulting sum on the economy. Of course, doing so will produce a number, but it will have no meaning. Instead, one must evaluate case by case the impacts of various government expenditures in their historical context, finding situations that are comparable. The next example, simple and concrete, shows why.

In the 1980 fiscal year in the United States, the budget deficit rose from the original estimate of $36.5 billion to $59.6 billion. Unexpected events caused the difference. An unpredicted decline in the economy led both to diminished tax revenues and to increases in unemployment benefits. There were unexpected increases in expenditures related to the Mount St. Helens volcanic eruption, to the large influx of Cuban refugees to Florida, and to the military operations in the Persian Gulf linked with the Iranian hostage crisis. I cannot see any theory of human behavior that could predict a well-defined impact on the economy from the sum of the expenditures linked with these four events. Some expenditures might have been viewed as investments, others as transfer payments. To evaluate the effectiveness of such expenditures, one should look in the past and determine the effects of government spending on new immigrants, on insuring people against disasters, or on fighting, and then compare the impact of each expenditure over time. But what does it mean to add up the different expenditures and put them in one category? In what context is such a sum relevant?

We shall look next at the context in which people considered such added sums relevant and invented general theories about their predictable effects. Some looked at the problem from a political angle, whereas others—Keynes and his close circle—tried to find specific solutions to particularly pressing situations. Followers—starting with John Hicks and Paul Samuelson—adopted part of Keynes' ideas uncritically, transformed them into caricatures by putting them within narrow, abstract terms, and suggested the discovery of universally valid regularities.[13] In addition to these flaws, frequently little attention was paid to the meaning of numbers used in the statistical analysis on which subsequent policies were based. Nevertheless, government bureaucracies were created to bring bad policies based on bad ideas and numbers to life. The ideas and institutions combined helped create and sustain a myth, which this chapter will try to destroy.

Debts, Deficits, and Balanced Budgets

In its origin the idea of "balanced budgets" in the American tradition had nothing to do with and was not discussed in the mainly economic terms in which it is today.[14] As Savage (1988) puts it: "Prior to the Civil War the debate over deficit spending . . . was discussed principally in terms of states' rights and popular control over a potentially 'corrupt' federal government, . . . [whereas after the Civil War] deficits at the federal level were considered, particularly by the Jeffersonians and the Jacksonians, a reflection of the national government's unwarranted attempt to gain power in a fashion harmful to the fragile balance of powers established in the Constitution."[15]

Jefferson feared that an expanding central government, unconstrained by strong limits on its deficits and debts, would undermine its republican and constitutional foundations, and promote widespread social and economic inequality.[16] He believed that the growing revenues of the federal government, resulting in either surpluses or debts and deficits, would be used to justify a growing bureaucracy, obedient to the moneyed aristocracy. The term *corruption* was used to describe all these negative consequences.

In contrast, debts and deficits run by the states were not perceived in a negative light. In short, the original negative attitudes in the United States were *not* toward debts and deficits, but toward *federal* debts and deficits. Discussions about debts and deficits were thus linked with a general discussion on the advantages and disadvantages of centralized versus decentralized government, and ways to control their size.

This is the reason that discussions referred to the federal government's debts, deficits, and expenditures in general terms. The attention focused on the *level* of expenditures, rather than their composition or the way they were supposed to be financed. The latter two issues—on what exactly the federal government spent the money, and by what methods it raised it—seemed secondary. In contrast, at the states' level, the discussion centered on the composition of the local government's expenditures, whether they represented investment or consumption. The latter discussion did not necessarily view deficits or debts in a negative light.

This political debate about debts, deficits, and balanced budgets, which was specific to the American experience, should thus not be confused with debates about their economic impacts. It is one thing to argue, as did President Ronald Reagan, reminding one of the early ideas about "corruption," that federal deficits resulted from a growing bureaucracy's fraud, waste, and abuse.[17] It is another thing to argue that deficits may be bad because they raise interest rates, cause inflation, or crowd out private investment. President Reagan paid less attention to these latter predictions (he and his economic advisers considered them not only relatively unimportant but wrong).[18] He emphasized instead that his goal was to renew "constitutional government," and to turn "back to states and local communities programs which the federal government has usurped."[19] Yet one should recall that, in the circumstances to which Reagan advocated a return, the states' debts and deficits were not necessarily viewed in a negative light, and neither were the states expected to balance their budgets every year. On the contrary, people viewed in a positive light deficits and debts for financing bridges, canals, roads, and so forth depending on the timing.

The negative views of the general level of federal debt recall but are not the same as Adam Smith's well-known views on government expenditures (and Smith, of course, does not make a distinction between the possible impacts of a federal government's expenditures and those made at the states' level). His negative views of government expenditures, as the following quotations remind us, are linked with the distinction between "productive" and "unproductive" labor. Where power is centralized, Smith views most of the rulers' or their governments' expenditures—including those on the military and the arts (yes, he viewed spending on writers and opera singers a waste)—as unproductive:

> In mercantile and manufacturing towns, where the inferior ranks of people are chiefly maintained by the employment of capital, they are in general industrious, sober and thriving; as in many English and Dutch towns. In those towns which are principally supported by the constant or occasional residence of a court, and in which the inferior ranks of people are chiefly maintained by the spending of revenue, they are in general idle, dissolute and poor; as at Rome, Versailles, Compiegne, and Fontainebleau. (356–57)
>
> Great nations are never impoverished by private, though they sometimes are by public prodigality and misconduct. The whole, or almost the whole public revenue, is in most countries employed in maintaining unproductive hands. Such are the people who compose a numerous and splendid court, a great ecclesiastical establishment, great fleets and armies, who in time of peace produce nothing, and in time of war acquire nothing which can compensate the expense of maintaining them, even while the war

lasts. Such people, as they themselves produce nothing, are all maintained by the produce of other men's labour. When multiplied, therefore, to an unnecessary number, they may in a particular year consume so great a share of this produce, as not to leave a sufficiency for maintaining the productive labourers. . . . Those unproductive hands, who should be maintained by a part only of the spare revenue of the people, may consume so great a share of their whole revenue, and thereby oblige so great a number to encroach upon their capitals, upon the funds destined for the maintenance of productive labour, that all the frugality and good conduct of individuals may not be able to compensate the waste and degradation of produce occasioned by this violent and forced encroachment. (363–64)

Like the American opinions, these statements must also be put in their historical perspective. The national debt had its origins in 1696 in the £1,200,000 raised by the Bank of England after its foundation in 1694, and which was lent to the government at 8 percent in the course of the War of the League of Augsburg (1689–97).[20] The Bank of England was thus founded during this great war, the first of seven that England fought with France as its principal enemy within little more than a century. The others were the Wars of the Spanish Succession (1701–13), and of the Austrian Succession (1740–48); the Seven Years War (1756–63); the War of American Independence (1775–83)—and it was in 1776 that *The Wealth of Nations* appeared—the French Revolutionary War (1793–1802); and the Napoleonic War (1803–15). The national debt grew apace: by 1713 the total debt stood at £56 million; it was £75 million in 1748, £132 million in 1763, and £241 million in 1783 (and £834 million in 1815 after Napoleon had been defeated at Waterloo).[21] The numbers and the events that took place during his lifetime influenced Smith, who thought that constraining governments' ability to spend would shorten wars.

In spite of his previously quoted views, which would suggest looking at the level of the government's expenditures, Smith was not against the role of government in building roads, bridges, canals, and postal services. He only differed with the traditional practice of paying for such investments and their maintenance from the general revenues.[22] Thus the general picture that emerges from Smith's views is that, in striving to evaluate the impact of deficits, debts, and government's expenditures, one should look at both their level and their composition; was it indeed spent on "unproductive workers,"[23] or was it well spent, on investments?[24] His views also imply that statistical job creation is hardly an indicator of prosperity: the nature of the institutions controlling their creation matter. The question is: what type of jobs are being created?[25]

In addition to the aforementioned viewpoints, debates about debts and deficits are shaped today by the views and, maybe even more, by the vocabulary of Keynes's *General Theory,* in which for the first time an economist suggested that one look at the *level* of government's expenditures and deficits for economic rather than for political reasons (instead of at their composition or the way they are financed). Keynes also suggested that increased deficits, increased public debts, and increased government expenditures are good for prosperity. As we shall see in the next section, this argument about the model's universal validity was wrong, even if its policy implication happened to be right for its time; both the model and the vocabulary invented by Keynes, in whose terms discussions about deficits and fiscal policies are still framed today, should be discarded completely.[26]

Keynes's General Theory: Obscure Language, No Theory, Yet Accurate Policy for the 1930s

Within four years, between 1929 and 1933, the price level in the United States dropped by about 30 percent, the unemployment rate increased to about 30 percent, and a large number of bankruptcies occurred. (Yet in spite of the fact that bankruptcies rendered many bonds worthless, the real value of outstanding debt did not diminish, since the large drop in the price level increased it by more than 30 percent).[27] The causes of these events are still open to debate. But the issue during the 1930s was not so much identifying the causes but how to get back on the road to prosperity. On the policies that could achieve this goal there was less disagreement.

For ten years, between 1920 and 1930, the U.S. government had surpluses in its budget,[28] and with a contracting money supply economists did not need a new theory to predict that these changes were deflationary.[29] Nor did they need Keynes to suggest public works and a fiscal stimulus as remedies. Economists Simeon Leland at the University of Chicago and Summer Slichter at Harvard, as well as a large number of others,[30] wrote early in the Depression that major federal expenses were necessary to improve the situation.

What was new in Keynes's analysis was not the recommended policy but the theories he put forward to help him reach his conclusions, the new vocabulary he invented, and his elitist suggestion that depressions could occur regularly in decentralized economies unless politicians' wisdom prevented them. This last feature was the most controversial, since it went against the traditional beliefs that a decentralized economy is self-regulating. It was also this particular feature that seemed most attractive to politicians and bureaucrats, since it gave intellectual, scientific respectability to their increased roles in the economy at all times, not just during recessions.

How did Keynes reach his conclusions? The *General Theory* is a complex, obscure book, in which one can discover many scattered, vague, confused ideas with occasional sparks of common sense, and not one general theory. The next section briefly summarizes and comments on some of his main definitions and arguments.[31]

The discussion is useful for two reasons. Since some people still interpret the changes during the 1980s as fitting predictions of a Keynesian model (see Eisner 1986), and recommend "fiscal stimulus" and spending on "infrastructure" for the 1990s (policies based on Keynesian models, recommended by both James Tobin and Robert Solow), we must approach this model from new angles and put additional nails into its coffin. This is the destructive side of what follows. On the constructive side, we must understand the mechanism through which various forms of government expenditures and policies have an impact on people's wealth and on employment—but which have nothing to do with "aggregate demands." The constructive side clarifies the terms to be used when discussing debts, deficits, and government expenditures on "public works."

Keynes's Language and Ideas

If economists paid more attention to the fact noticed already by a few of Keynes's contemporaries, that he was giving new meanings to well-established words apart from their common usage, the much-heated discussion on the *General Theory* and the policy implications of the Hicksian oversimplification might have been avoided.[32]

One such word was *inflation*. For Keynes this term defined not an increase in prices but something else:

> The view that *any* increase in the quantity of money is inflationary (unless we mean by *inflationary* merely that prices are rising) is bound up with the underlying assumption of the classical

> theory that we are *always* in a condition where a reduction in the
> real rewards of the factors of production will lead to a curtail-
> ment in their supply.[33]

This is a most unusual definition, never used by anybody before or after
Keynes; what else was ever meant by inflation but that all prices are
rising?[34] By making the definition of inflation conditional on whether or
not employment is rising simultaneously with changes in prices, Keynes
misled his followers. When simplifying his ideas, they assumed that the
price level stays unchanged up to the point of full employment, whatever
has happened to the money supply. This assumption was contrary to
Keynes's point; in fact, he recommended policies that would raise the price
level. He just did not *call* the impact inflationary if the increased price
level came together with increased employment, as the quotation shows.

This was not the only term that Keynes used in a very unusual way:
involuntary unemployment was another.[35] Once again, contrary to his
followers, Keynes emphasized that such unemployment had nothing to do
with either the existence of unions or mere wage rigidity. Instead, according to Keynes, the behavior had to do with the fact[36] that "whilst workers
will usually resist a reduction of money wages, it is not their practice to
withdraw their labour whenever there is a rise in the price of wage-
goods."[37] While this view was unorthodox too, at least it was consistent
with Keynes's previously mentioned definition of what is and is not
inflationary, and it also leads to an understanding of a policy he
recommended.

Keynes describes the following scenario in his book. Unexpectedly,
and for no good reason, investors become pessimistic and invest less in the
economy. The output and the price level fall, but the money-wages do not,
and unemployment increases. In these circumstances, increased government expenditures and deficits through a one shot monetary expansion—
even for digging holes in the ground (as Keynes put it)—increase employment since, by raising the price level (which Keynes, however, does not
call inflationary), it restores the value of real wages and debts to their
contracted level.

Maybe it is easy now to understand why, within such a view of the
world, attention was paid to aggregates, to the government's overall
expenditures and to deficits rather than to what the government should do
with the money or how money is raised. We can also understand why,
within such a view of the world, the policy might have been beneficial

during the 1930s even if the theory on which it was based makes, in general, no sense.

Recall that during this period the price level dropped unexpectedly and significantly, and financial obligations and interest rates were contracted in nominal terms. Thus the value of debts in real terms increased significantly. When the price level dropped unexpectedly by 10 percent, instead of paying interest rates of 5 percent, debtors had to pay rates of more than 15 percent. Even if one disregards Keynes's theory, one can suppose that a *reflation* during the 1930s could have improved the situation by restoring the value of the still outstanding debts to their expected level and preventing further bankruptcies. Such a policy could have been effective then, but not today, because it would not have altered long-term expectations of price stability or weakened confidence in the government's monetary and fiscal responsibilities. Also, as Keynes noted, "when we have unemployed men and unemployed plant and more savings than we are using at home, it is utterly imbecile to say that we cannot afford these things [a program of national development]."[38] This statement is examined in detail in the next chapter.

In other words, Keynes recommended the same policies as Irving Fisher and other monetarists, who did not use Keynes's novel definitions or arguments.[39] The policies were useful, not because they were based on a "general" theory applicable at all times, but because at that particular point in time they helped correct previous, erroneous policies.

Elsewhere in the *General Theory* Keynes presents a scenario about why increased government expenditures on public works and through deficit financing in some circumstances may be beneficial for society, but it has little to do with notions of aggregate demand and features of the so-called Keynesian models, or with the previous arguments, but with a far more complex and this time a better and broader view of society. This examination also shows that, by grasping the larger picture, one can put things in context and clarify them rather than make them unmanageable.

Public Works: Irrelevant Theories and Relevant Facts

> Politicians are the same all over. They promise to build bridges, even where there are no rivers.
> —Nikita Khrushchev, in a 1960 press conference

Economists agree that, in spite of the bombastic title, what Keynes intended to present in his book was not a theory but a view of the economy in which disequilibrium persists and risk, uncertainty, and expectations play central roles.[40] Since in Keynes's time these notions were not explicitly introduced in theories dealing with what we call macroeconomics, he felt obligated to adapt the economists' vocabulary to his views first.

That was a mistake: it led to obscurity and even today leads to confusion and controversy. This should have been expected, for Keynes was wrong even to make the attempt. Words that can be defined in models where uncertainty is formally introduced have no meaning in models of certainty. Confidence and "animal spirits," important terms and variables in Keynes's views, have no roles in the latter. And the vocabulary invented by economists at that time to define variables within models where uncertainty was absent, loses its meaning once uncertainty is taken into account.

In the chapters, sections, and paragraphs where Keynes abandons these attempts and uses ordinary language, his arguments become quite clear: at least one knows with what to agree and to disagree. Yet it is exactly these lucid parts of the *General Theory,* where Keynes explains the rationale for the policies he recommended, that most economists have never discussed. The reason for that is clear. Keynes's statements in these lucid parts rely on a view of the world that differs from the one economists assume, and neither this view nor its policy implications are compatible with the mainstream economists' framework.

According to Keynes, then, what causes a crisis of increased unemployment and lowered economic activity, and why must governments intervene?

Although people's weakened propensity to consume and a rise in interest rates can lead to such outcomes, "a more typical, and often predominant, explanation for the crisis is, not primarily a rise in the rate of interest, but a sudden collapse in the marginal efficiency of capital."[41] The collapse, however, has nothing to do with the government's actions—according to Keynes. Once it occurs:

> . . . it is not easy to revive the marginal efficiency of capital, determined as it is, by the uncontrollable and disobedient psychology of the business world. It is the return of confidence to speak in ordinary language, which is so insusceptible to control in an economy of individualistic capitalism. This is the aspect of the slump which bankers and businessmen have been right in

emphasizing, and which the economists who have put their faith in a "purely monetary" remedy have underestimated. (317)

This is the view that led Keynes to his conclusion that public works, even of doubtful utility, may pay for themselves over and over again at a time of severe unemployment. To support this conclusion, Keynes reminds the readers that such policies have been pursued since ancient times:

> Pyramid buildings, . . . even wars may serve to increase wealth, if the education of our statesmen on the principles of the classical economics stands in the way of anything better. . . . Just as wars have been the only form of large-scale loan expenditure which statesmen have thought justifiable, so gold-mining is the only pretext for digging holes in the ground which has recommended itself to bankers as sound finance. . . . Ancient Egypt was doubly fortunate, and doubtless owed to this its fabled wealth, in that it possessed *two* activities . . . pyramid building as well as the search for precious metals. . . . The Middle Ages built cathedrals and sang dirges . . . [42]

Judging by these comments, Keynes did not know much history. The reason for these policies in those ancient times, and the reason for their occasional success, was not a matter of politicians' ability to compensate for "sudden drops in the marginal efficiency of capital" due to private investors' caprices, but something entirely different.

"Public Works"—How Do They Work?

> Let those who have abundance remember that they are surrounded with thorns, and let them take great care not to be pricked by them.
>   —John Calvin, *Commentary on Genesis*

How to deal with the poor and with those falling behind—the term *unemployment* has relatively recent origins—is a question that many rulers and leaders of governments since antiquity have asked themselves, and many writers since ancient times have tried to answer.

These writers made the following point: the poor and those falling behind have less interest in maintaining the status quo and thus are also the greatest menace to its maintenance. Having less to lose, they are more prone to violence, more likely to commit crimes against other people's property, and more likely to bet on revolutionary ideas to rationalize their plunder.[43] Without property or expectations of getting it and climbing from the bottom of the ladder, the poor are less likely to make commitments and to identify their interests with those of the state, or the community. Rulers, politicians, and frequently those in the middle and above, recognized that spending on protecting property and punishing violators was not always sufficient, that, to buy goodwill, transferring wealth to the poor and opening opportunities for them was at times necessary and beneficial.

In fact Keynes's statement on the pyramids echoes that of Sir William Petty, the same gentleman who, as mentioned in the previous chapter, also dabbled with aggregate statistics during the seventeenth century. Sir William Petty proposed using tax money for the construction of useless pyramids on the Salisbury Plain and for "entertainments, magnificent shews, triumphal arches."[44] But his view, no more and no less absurd than Keynes's idea of digging holes and building pyramids, had less to do with employment and manipulating aggregate demands in the short run, than with helping deal with the poor in the long run. The observers of the seventeenth century were preoccupied with *persistent* unemployment of the *same* people, leading to poverty and crime. They thought about lasting remedies for the poor, rather than remedies for occasional, temporary unemployment. Sir William thought that, since the poor must be fed, it is better for them and for society that they be employed and paid rather than given charity. Even if the work consisted of bringing "the Stones at Stonehenge to Tower Hill," it could "keep their minds to discipline and obedience, and their body to a patience of more profitable labours when need shall require it," lest they lose the faculty of laboring.

Sir William's view was not unusual. During the second half of the seventeenth century, all economic tracts discussed employment in similar fashion. The context was not "job creation," but the role of "employment and competencies to civilize all men, and make them tractable & obedient to Superiors' commands."[45] The preoccupation with the poor resulted from their increased numbers and tenuous position. During the seventeenth century, "they had been expelled from a traditional order and as yet were only conditionally and occasionally needed in the new economic structure growing up outside the old."[46] Thus the general view was that "between the dislocation of the past and the expectation for the future," governments must throw a bridge for the dependent poor by employing or retraining them. The nature of their employment seemed secondary to some observers then, as it seemed later to Keynes, and as it seems to observers today.

Such views were held elsewhere too. Giovanni Botero, in his 1589 classic *The Reason of State,* noted that already in Ancient Greece:[47]

> . . . when rumors arrived of a war between King Persius and the Romans, the poor, hoping to see the world turned upside down, sided with Persius, while the "good" people, who had a stake in things remaining as they were, sided with the Romans. When Catiline wanted to set off disturbances in the republic, he made use of those of low life or fortune, because . . . to anyone who aspires to power, the poorest man is the most helpful, since he has no regard for his property, having none, and considers anything honorable for which he receives pay. And Caesar, aspiring to the rule of his country, lent a hand to all who had fallen into dire need, either through debts, bad management, or other accidents. Since they had no reason to be happy, he thought them ripe for use in his project of overturning the republic.

Botero also described how rulers tried to deal with such risks. They redistributed wealth through a wide variety of methods, rationalized this redistribution by a wide variety of ideas, gave the restless some stake in the system, and also spent more on enforcement:

> . . . since not everyone can own land or practice a trade—for [the maintenance of] human life requires that there also be others [who do not]—the prince must provide, either himself or through others, a means by which the poor can earn a living. Dionysius of Halicarnassus says that nothing is more dangerous for princes than the idleness of plebeians. To this end Augustus Caesar built extensively and exhorted the principal citizens to do the same, and in this way he kept the plebeian poor quiet. (243–44)

Offering circuses and building pyramids, cathedrals, or Paris's famous great boulevards are other examples of such public works.[48] The great Elizabethan poor laws, as Jordan (1959) notes, also sprang from the preoccupation with the maintenance of order and the management of the poor.[49] Though the poor laws were criticized, observers were critical of the way they were administered, rather than with the objective—not unlike attitudes toward welfare today. Observers were also critical of the ways the poor were trained—again, not unlike today. However, none of the arguments for or against such interventions had to do with short-run policies and aggregate demands.

Instead, observers held two extreme viewpoints when discussing these policies. Some viewed expenditures on the poor, through public works or otherwise, as beneficial, since they maintained stability by sustaining hopes and in the long run helped form an educated population. Rulers wanted to prevent the predatory behavior of those falling behind, contain the spread of new ideas under which they might be carried out, and diminish political uncertainty.

According to the second viewpoint, such policies eventually encouraged idleness, were harmful to prosperity, and could not provide a long-term solution when the number of poor was increasing. On the contrary, they had the undesirable effects of strengthening existing bureaucracies and creating new ones, of spoiling people into laziness, of diminishing the incentives to invest (because, if taken too far, they led to higher tax rates), and of delaying adjustment to change.[50] But what was the intermediate point at which short-term stabilizing policies turned to unfavorable ones, and when should previous policies be reexamined and canceled? These were two questions to which nobody had yet found precise answers: how the institutions of referendum and initiative could provide a solution, will be discussed below and in the concluding chapter.[51]

Frederic Lane (1966, 414), a historian, illustrated the dilemma in the following words: "Theoretically one might say that violence is productive when it is used to control violence, and is not productive when it is used to transfer wealth from one person to another. . . . The question is: What does the taxpayer receive in return?" He showed that expenditures on controlling violence were productive in some circumstances but not in others. Another historian, William McNeill, captured features of the circumstances in which transfer payments in Venice turned from being productive to taxpayers to being unproductive. Here is his description of the decline of this once-great trading city to a dormant, bureaucratic one:

Active management of industry and commerce passed into the hands of domiciled foreigners, who were tolerated cheerfully enough by Venetian authorities, but whose interests and opinions were not sensitively registered in the deliberations of official boards and governing bodies. As a result, the kind of commercial calculations that had governed Venetian state policy for centuries tended to lose persuasiveness. Simultaneously, considerations of social welfare and poor relief acquired greater scope, for the noble clique ruling the city recognized that its power could only remain secure if the mass of the populace continued to be more or less content. . . . Insofar as such measures were successful in reducing human suffering, it seems obvious that they must also have cushioned the impact of changing economic conditions. This in turn . . . slowed adjustments in the allocation of resources . . .

Another way of describing the matter is to say that political and humanitarian considerations overrode economic and financial calculations. In view of the fact that the men who ruled Venice were no longer active in business, but devoted a large part of their official attention to regulating business behavior, this result is not surprising. In the short run, the measures taken by the Venetian government undoubtedly helped the city to survive acute crisis and gave the poor a definite stake in the maintenance of established administrative and political patterns. In the long run, official efforts at poor relief and public health regulation added to the overall costs of doing business in Venice, and made price competition with northern producers all the more impossible. (147)

What is new? The next chapter will say much more about the rise and decline of trading-cities such as Venice, and extract some lessons about prosperity from their rise and decline.

Thus, Keynes's ideas about the stabilizing effects of increased expenditures on infrastructure, on digging holes in the ground, and on building pyramids, indeed have ancient roots. Yet the temporarily stabilizing effects have less to do with manipulations of aggregate demands, than with politics, political institutions, and specific historical circumstances, totally absent from Keynes's and other macroeconomists' "general" theories and analyses.

The older views shed a different but far better light than Keynes's examples about the *occasional* stabilizing effects of public works, of increased government expenditures, and of fiscal policy. When insuring themselves against domestic instability or international threats, which might already have diminished domestic investments and made interest rates rise, rulers redistribute wealth either directly or indirectly, through increased expenditures on the military, public ceremonies (for which Venice became famous), and other policies. When such policies were successfully combined with the ability to attract *foreign merchants* (today one would call them immigrant entrepreneurs or foreign investors)—as Venice succeeded in doing for a while—prosperity continued.[52]

However, it would be misleading to conclude that increased government expenditures brought prosperity. When the foreign traders left Venice's shores, prosperity vanished. Those who remained were the *cittadini,* the professional bureaucrats who studied law and public administration at the University of Padua. McNeill (1974, 229) concludes that they were "so skilled in maintaining things as they were that the kinds of new growth which a more disorderly society might have allowed were regularly nipped in the bud. It required the ruthlessness of a Corsican upstart, supported by the military as well as by the intellectual forces of the revolution, to shatter forever what so many generations of Venetian rulers had sustained. . . . "

In contrast to this explanation for the occasional stabilizing effects of increased government expenditures and the occasional correlation between increased government expenditures and prosperity, the one within the Keynesian framework makes no sense.

Building pyramids and cathedrals, or spending on arms, are not just "public works," "increased government spending," or "increased investments." People must *believe* that such expenditures contribute to their wealth and thus be ready to trade their time and money to buy whatever the rulers' expenditures produce. Will the building of cathedrals make the country richer? Only if the people are religious. For in this case people are ready to work and trade part of their incomes for whatever service the priests provide, on this earth or the next world. Did the thousands of Lenin statues and paintings make Russians richer? Not necessarily. Were the slaves in Egypt "double fortunate" to build the pyramids?[53] Do public works necessarily help people to learn skills, to forge their own opportunities in the future, and to climb from the bottom of the ladder? Or does the work give them limited skills and force them to stay forever in dead-end jobs while others pay higher taxes?[54]

If people think not in terms of Keynes's framework but in terms of those from whom he borrowed his views, they may occasionally admit that the increased public expenditures for retraining, employing, or otherwise giving greater opportunities to the poor is a good investment in both the short and the long term. Subsidizing people to work and gain marketable skills, is better than giving them incentives to stay permanently idle or to become involved in illegal activities.[55]

With these additional arguments and evidence in mind, let us now return to the question raised at the beginning of this chapter: What could one expect, a priori, from statistical examinations about the relationship between aggregate measures of national incomes, employment, and government expenditures, disregarding the inaccuracies of measurement? These are the answers:

- Increased government expenditures, deficits, or debts may or may not increase employment;
- Increased government expenditures, deficits, or debts may or may not crowd out private investment;
- Increased government expenditures, deficits, or debts may or may not increase interest rates;
- Increased deficits may or may not be harmful for prosperity.

These answers imply that there was no reason to carry out any of the mechanical analyses to start with, since they could not disprove any possibility. Not surprisingly, no consistent results have been obtained.

Unless one examines the numbers in their particular, historical context and looks at them in detail rather than as aggregates, not much can be said a priori on the impact of any particular change in a government's expenditures, in deficits, or in the national debt. Deficit spending may be stimulating in some circumstances, but, as noted, not for what macroeconomists call Keynesian reasons. It may be bad in others, not because deficits necessarily represent dissaving but because the government makes bad decisions, because money is spent on unnecessary bureaucracy and regulation, and because there are no political institutions to prevent the persistence in error. It may have no discernible impact in still other situations, as far as the impact of the method of financing is considered (the Ricardian-Barro view, when, let us say, people view the government's increased expenditures on education, financed by deficits, as a substitute for their own expenditures, but realize that they will pay increased taxes in the future). What, then, is a social scientist or a policymaker left to do today? The next and the final chapter give the broader, more complex answers to this question, taking into account alternative political institutions.

For the moment, here is the simpler, partial answer. Social scientists should use judgment to identify which situations are comparable, rather than use either any "general theory," or rely mechanically on any of the mismeasured, mechanically gathered aggregate numbers, which might not be comparable to start with. This answer also implies that one must examine the numbers in their particular, historical context and look at them in detail rather than as aggregates. So let us look at just a few figures concerning the government's expenditures to make this point clear, in particular the one concerning the choice of "comparable" situations.

Expenditures on Education and National Security

Public education expenditures in Canada, the United States, and the United Kingdom fluctuated between approximately 5.5 and 8.9 percent of the GNP between the 1960s and 1980s. However, before 1958 this percentage was much lower. The big jump in the United States took place following the passage of the National *Defense* Education Act in 1958. The act was passed because of fears that the United States was falling far behind the Russians in their military technology and that its security was threatened by the Sputnik.[56] It was believed that improvement in the teaching of science, mathematics, and foreign languages would close the gap and even help the United States leapfrog its rival. Yet the resulting increased expenditures on education were not classified as military expenditures. Had they been, it would have been easier to discuss cuts in education budgets once the threats diminished or disappeared.

This was not the first time that education and national defense had been linked. When England was falling behind Germany, Prime Minister Forster introduced the Education Bill (later extended by Winston Churchill when the Soviets were perceived as leapfrogging England) on February 17, 1870, with these words:

> "We must not delay. Upon the speedy provision of elementary education depends our industrial prosperity . . . if we have our work folk any longer unskilled, notwithstanding their strong sinews and determined energy, they will become overmatched in the competition of the world. . . . If we are to hold our position among men of our own race [!] or among the nations of the world, we must make up the smallness of our numbers by increasing the intellectual force of the individual." Nearly a

century later, Forster was echoed by . . . Sir Winston Churchill [who said that] "The *Soviet* higher technical education for mechanical engineering has been developed both in numbers and quality to an extent which far exceeds anything we have achieved. This is a matter which needs the immediate attention of Her Majesty's Government . . . if we are—not to keep abreast—but even to maintain our proportionate place in the world."[57]

By custom, governments today continue to allocate significant amounts of money to education. But the question is: if some people believe that expenditures on the military are a waste, what fraction of the education budget should be cut? If external threats diminish, what fraction of the government's expenditures on education should still be considered a good investment? And since government subsidies with military goals in mind helped to build the schools, how much, in Boskin's and his collaborators' estimates of U.S. nonmilitary capital, still belongs to the "military" category, regardless of how accountants classified the subsidies?

Governments' expenditures on education defy categorization. To put it more precisely, their categorization and perceived value depends on historical circumstances, foreign security threats being just one of them. In Russia under the Tsars, for example, policy toward education was constantly shaped by the idea that too much education may bring revolutions, whereas popular ignorance loses wars.[58] This should be kept in mind by all those who carry out thoughtless time-series and cross-country analyses putting education in the neutral-sounding category of "investment."

Governments' expenditures on education are not the only ones that defy categorization. Occasionally the U. S. government uses agriculture as a military weapon too. An embargo was imposed on the Soviet Union in the not-so-distant past, and agricultural aid was given to some countries not on humanitarian grounds but in hopes of shutting out the Soviets.

Brooks (1989) reports that, since 1977, the United States has given Egypt about as much food aid as to all of famine-wracked sub-Saharan Africa. "This isn't aimed just at alleviating the hardships of impoverished Egyptians . . . or ensuring the stability of a friendly regime. It is the price America pays for Egypt's 10-year-old peace treaty with Israel, which was sealed with the promise of lavish aid for both countries. 'Cutting back [the aid] would have the effect of wrecking the Middle East Peace process,' says Marshall Brown, director of the U.S. Agency for International Development in Egypt, the largest American aid mission in the world."

Anticipating such strategic uses (not to mention the domestic advantage of gaining votes), the government may subsidize the agricultural sector either by direct monetary aid or by tariffs, import quotas, or other forms of protection.

But if such agricultural aid is helpful in the military sense and cheaper than direct expenditures on the military for achieving the same goals, how much in subsidies given to agriculture can be viewed as a good investment (saving on military expenditures)? Should the subsidies be classified as military expenditures and not necessarily be viewed as waste? And when should one reexamine whether or not such a strategy continues to be a useful weapon rather than just implying expectations of higher taxes in the future?

Consider more recent events. Germany launched the largest relief program in its postwar history when it began shipping large reserves of food to the Soviets in November 1990. This was no altruism. The Germans made no secret of the fact that the food was sent to prevent a flood of refugees fleeing food shortages during the harsh Russian winter, in particular since the Russians announced that, starting January 1, 1991, they might allow unrestricted travel abroad. Ironically, part of the food being sent to the Soviet Union came from the depletion of the $1.68 billion stock that was stockpiled in Berlin as insurance in case the Soviets repeated their blockade of the city. Whether paying and maintaining this stock was entered in the government's books under the category of "agricultural subsidies" or "military expenditures" no longer matters. It is clear, however, that the expenditures for sending the food to the Soviets should be entered under a category linked with the prevention of migration to the new Germany, which is perceived now as a far more costly alternative to sending food supplies.[59]

This, in addition to the previous example on education, shows that *in order to evaluate the impact of government expenditures and recommend changes, one must have institutions in place that can make regular evaluations of policies, look at the numbers in their particular historical context, and evaluate the "real" composition of expenditures rather than the accounting one.*

International Threats

As shown above, the costs and benefits of subsidies for either agriculture or education depend on whether or not the voters relate them to security threats.[60] This means that by looking at aggregate data on government expenditures, and even at their composition as classified by accounting categories, one cannot get an idea about the present value of these expenditures.[61] This also means that, as some have suggested, distinguishing between the "current account" and the "capital account" when looking at budgets and deficits—something not done in the United States now—cannot lead very far. Let us take a closer look at this problem and examine the more complex relationship between military expenditures and measurement, expenditures which, according to standard calculations, represented 27 percent of the U.S. federal government budget in 1987. The link between military expenditures and prosperity will be examined in the following chapters.

A pure current-account expenditure covers a service of perfectly perishable goods that gives rise to no government-owned assets (and thus produces no future benefits). A pure capital-account expenditure purchases a durable asset that gives the government (i.e., the taxpayers) a future stream of returns, the value of which, one hopes, is greater or equal to the present cost of acquiring the asset. Government debt issued to finance a pure capital-account deficit may not lead to expectations of future increases in taxation, whereas debt issued for financing current-account expenditures does, because current-account deficits do not generate future benefits. These are the deficits condemned by economists. However, as far as capital-account deficits are concerned, the government may act like a firm, borrowing to finance projects that over time are expected to be profitable.[62]

The problem with this vocabulary and these arguments is that they fail to provide a practical, comprehensive framework for discussing either deficits, crowding out, or interpreting the numbers. Even if the U.S. government adopted the distinction between capital and current accounts, the new numbers might not become more enlightening and cannot help voters make decisions. We shall see later how referenda and initiatives provide a solution for making such decisions.

Consider the fact that, even without taking into account the indirect expenditures linked with defense, which we discussed in the previous section, the U.S. government spends about a third of its budget on the military, and that studies by the U.S. Science Council, NASA, and the Pentagon concluded that the main reward of the space program in the not-so-distant past was the "psychic reward" of knowing the country was ahead of the Soviets.[63] If so, how should one classify military expenditures? How much should go toward the current account, and how much toward the capital account? How can one quantify the value of "peace of mind" that citizens receive from the government?[64] To be more precise: how can one evaluate the stream of benefits to one or another generation in terms of the current and future "psychic returns" of expecting to be ahead of the Soviets, when, quite suddenly, they find themselves at the end of the Cold War? Nobody can provide even vague numerical answers to these questions (indirectly, a sequence of referenda and initiatives could).[65]

Indeed, this has been noted in the past and more recently. A February 2, 1984, editorial in the *Wall Street Journal* gave the following interpretation of the 1984 budget:

> The emphasis in this budget, as in others in this administration, is on national security. As the president said in his State of the Union address, national security is the most important federal responsibility and he is giving it his highest priority. Indeed, the entire budget is noteworthy for its emphasis on what can be broadly described as investment. Scientific research (which gets a generous 15% boost), including even that manned space station, is an investment in the future. So is education and training, if properly managed. (One can also add medical care, that expenditures on it will reach $100 billion). So are efforts to save friendly countries from communist takeovers. And so is the defense budget, again, if properly managed. One reason for the strong dollar has been the flow of foreign investment in the U.S. and one reason for this investment is the fact that this country promises to remain relatively secure for the long-term. Its willingness to spend heavily on defense isn't the only reason, but it is one reason.

Although the editorial is outdated, its implications must be kept in mind as far as the interpretation of aggregate numbers goes. When security threats are on the rise, increased government expenditure on defense may promote rather than crowd out private investments. Some investments could have been crowded out by the changed perception of threat *before* the government intervened.[66] Such a view prevents one from evaluating even vaguely the present value of "receipts from the government."

This conclusion is not novel. Robbins (1952), when commenting on the noncomparability of material statistics of war and peace (when the military are included in the measurement of the GNP), wrote that:

A very vivid example of what this means is to be found in Mr. Winston Churchill's account of the situation confronting the Ministry of Munitions at 11 A.M. on November 11th, 1918—the moment of the signing of the Armistice. After years of effort, the nation had acquired a machine for turning out the materials of war in unprecedented quantities. Enormous programs of production were in every stage of completion. Suddenly, the whole position is changed. The "demand" collapses. The needs of war are at the end. What was to be done? Mr. Churchill relates how, in the interests of a smooth change-over, instructions were issued that material more than 60% advanced was to be finished. "Thus, for many weeks after the war was over we continued to disgorge upon the gaping world masses of artillery and military materials of every kind." "It was waste," he adds, "but perhaps it was prudent waste."(47–48)

Prudent or not (and whose perception is one talking about?), if military expenditures are included in the GNP measure, they will be reflected by the same number. That is, whether military expenditures are viewed as insurance or waste, the numbers will not tell the difference. A referendum would.[67]

The rail, aircraft, nuclear, oil, and computer industries, as well as some expenditures on research and development (R&D) in various industries, have all been linked at one time or another to defense and turbulent international politics.[68] Perceptions of such relationships have shaped constraints on trade for a long time, and not only on agriculture. Adam Smith approved of government interventions in the eighteenth-century English shipping industry. He justified the discriminatory and protectionist policies by the requirements of defense (recall that the Navigation Act did not permit shipment to and from England in third-country vessels). Although many substitutes to the nationalized postal systems (and they are nationalized almost all over the world) exist today, postal services in the past fell under intense scrutiny.[69] The argument was the protection of "national interests."[70] Until very recently, governments commonly restricted sale of all sorts of hardware and software to the Soviets, those produced not only in the United States but also in Europe, in order to prevent the Russians from beefing up their military.[71] Freeman (1983) presents evidence that in the United States, the USSR, France, and Britain the public policies toward innovations were largely determined by the

Cold War, which explains the governments' massive support for aircraft, nuclear, and electronics R&D.[72] Even with the sudden end of the Cold War, the mechanical categorization of numbers should still be avoided. Germany gave much help to the new Commonwealth and to Poland, hoping that this would move the Russian army out faster and also prevent immigration. Ex-Soviet nuclear scientists were offered $100 million to stay home rather than sell their services to the highest bidder abroad. Such expenditures are insurance, payments to prevent security threats from happening, no matter how they are counted in the budget.[73]

Domestic Threats

When one takes into account domestic rather than international instability, the interpretation of numbers is equally problematic. Consider Bismarck's introduction of various social security benefits and welfare payments in Prussia at the end of the nineteenth century. The laws introduced in Prussia during the 1880s (imitated later by other countries) established a national insurance system to cover sick payments and accidents, and also a contribution scheme to provide for invalid and old-age pensions.

In justifying the first measure of social legislation introduced in the Reichstag in 1881, Bismarck sounds much like Botero. He declared that the state must "cultivate the view also among the propertyless classes of the population, those who are the most numerous and the least educated, that the state is not only an institution of necessity but also one of welfare."[74] The pressure behind the social legislation came from fear of the socialist movement.[75] Bismarck admitted in 1878 that "if the worker has no more cause for complaint then the roots of socialism would be chained off," and, indeed, he simultaneously introduced social benefits and severely enforced anti-socialist laws.[76]

What do these historical contexts imply about the interpretation of aggregate numbers?

A nonhistorical approach would suggest that economists can evaluate the impact of social security and other insurance payments governments provide, in terms of the citizens' payments and receipts during their lifetime.[77] Not so. What we view today as a matter of private costs and private benefits was perceived in a completely different light in the past. That is, what passes now as an insurance problem, might have been viewed in the past as a far more complex problem linked simultaneously with the issues of creation and redistribution of wealth.[78] Whereas one may count how much was spent, one can only vaguely evaluate what such spending insured against and prevented from happening when domestic and international threats vary.

There are even more reasons that distinguishing between "current" and "capital" accounts in governments' budgets fails to provide a practical framework for discussing and verifying general theories about deficits and crowding out, for interpreting numbers, and for evaluating present values.

Governments have prevented unemployment from rising by spending on "public" works, by subsidizing and nationalizing firms, by imposing tariff and nontariff barriers to imports, and by selectively intervening in declining industries.[79] From an accounting point of view, part of these subsidies—if captured at all in the government's budgets—would be reflected in nonmilitary "capital" accounts. But such a viewpoint has nothing to do with the way people may perceive these expenditures. They may view them either as waste (in part), as a good investment in maintaining social stability (substituting for welfare payments and expenditures on protection against violence), or, who knows, as maybe just a good investment.

Without examining the historical conditions governing the decision to subsidize or nationalize, one cannot categorize the government's expenditures or measure the value of even the nonmilitary capital, and make predictions on their possible consequences—as Boskin et al. do. Expenditures that might be perceived ex post as wasteful, which have imposed additional burdens on taxpayers, might have been initially perceived as beneficial, expected to encourage private investment rather than crowd it out (even if financed by increased deficits and spent on the military).[80] Again then, an examination of aggregate numbers concerning governments but detached from the particular, historical context provides no insights on their possible impact.[81]

It should be emphasized that all these evaluations are needed to start with because the political institutions of referendum and initiative are absent. If they were in place, such calculations would be unnecessary. These political institutions would not prevent waste and mistakes. That is unavoidable: people learn by making mistakes. This political remedy prevents the *persistence* of mistaken decisions.

Preventing Persistence in Error

Whether investments are truly investments depends not on how economists and governments count them but on whether or not the tax-paying citizens expect to earn back, directly or indirectly, over a certain horizon more than their cost. Economists can count government expenditures on infrastructure and education as investment if they please. But a road that is rarely used, an airport that lacks traffic (the case of Mirabel, near Montreal), schools that graduate illiterate students, and government-sponsored films, books, "scientific" publications, and music that are never watched, read, or heard, can all be—and are—counted as investments, though people do not buy the resulting products or would not buy them if given the choice.[82] Of course, private firms' bad investment decisions are also counted as such—*for a while.* The difference is exactly that: how long. Whereas private firms go bankrupt if they persist in their erroneous ways, governments do so more slowly, and waste continues to be counted as investment.

Also, share values on the stock market show that investors look beyond historical accounting standards. For example, five companies can have a combined equity market value of $15 billion in 1989, although taken together they had no reported net income (the five are: McCaw Cellular, Medco, Turner Broadcasting, Viacom, and Circus Circus). There is no similar evaluation of government projects. Polls conducted in Canada revealed that in 1992 the citizens thought the federal government wasted 47 cents of every tax dollar.[83] But because the institutions of referendum and initiative have not been introduced, people cannot force governments to respond to such perceptions. The lack of appropriate political institutions allows the persistence in error.

The two political institutions could also provide answers to an additional question. Assume that each item the government calls investment, taken in separation, would indeed turn out to be an investment rather than waste. This is a strong assumption; for example, it implies that when a decision is made to build a new road, experts calculate how much time it would save, how much it slows down the vehicles' depreciation, how many accidents it prevents (if new roads have this effect to start with), how many lives it saves (another if), and how the latter savings compare with alternative expenditures for saving lives.[84] Assume that the government did such formidable calculations for roads, schooling, and hospitals, and all, taken *separately,* showed that they would be good investments. That does not mean that *all* should be carried out. People also want to enjoy life today.

Which project, then, should be carried out? Choosing the one with the highest expected return is not a practical guide, since, as we can infer from the above, governments cannot make such calculations. Once again, the institutions of referendum and initiative provide a solution. Even if voters make a mistake, later initiatives can correct them. Chapter 6 will discuss in detail how these two institutions operate.

Are There Incentives to Publish Accurate Figures?

In making sense of the aggregate numbers concerning the effects of governments' actions, all these formidable difficulties arise even if one assumes that governments want to publish accurate figures. But do they?

Morgenstern (1963, 20) noted a long time ago that "foreign data are considered secret in some eastern European countries with capital punishment threatened for disclosure! Even in the United States incomplete figures are released in the field of atomic energy. . . . The budget for the Central Intelligence Agency . . . is hidden in a multitude of other accounts in the Federal Budget, invalidating also those accounts. The Russian defense budget is only incompletely known. An example of government falsification of statistics is Nazi Germany's stating its gold reserves far below those actually available. . . . [T]he venerable Bank of England . . . for decades published deliberately misleading statistics . . . suppressing for a considerable period all statistics about its gold holdings." Morgenstern also notes that the national income of Japan "was *negotiated* between the Japanese Government and the American Occupation Forces shortly after the last war. . . . The reason was, of course, that the amount agreed upon influenced the size of economic assistance by the United States."[85]

If patient, one can discover more recent gems—as the Friedmans (1987) did—in the 2,089 pages of information about details in the U.S. government's budget. They found, among other things, that the 1984 budget included a proposed appropriation of $50 million to help finance the Summer Olympics; however, this was included in the Department of Defense budget under Operation and Maintenance, which also budgeted more than $1,500 million for "Wildlife Conservation, Military Reservations."[86] Maybe today, with the end of the Cold War, these problems have diminished. But if so, it makes even less sense to carry out statistical analyses over long terms and try to find long-term cycles, based on numbers that are put in the same accounting category by the statistical bureaucracy though they mean radically different things.

Back to the past and another country. When Alexis de Tocqueville came to America, one of his compatriots, the Marquis de Custine, visited

Russia, about which he wrote a devastating book upon his return to France. Among the many, far more troubling features of life there, he also noted the lack of reliability of much that passed for "facts" in that part of the world and the reason for the unreliability:

> When I tell the Russians that their woods are badly managed, and that their country will in time be without fuel, they laugh me in the face. It has been calculated how many thousands of years it will require to consume the wood which covers the soil of an immense portion of the empire; and this calculation satisfies every body. It is *written* in the estimates sent in by each provincial governor, that each province contains so many acres of forests. Upon these data the statistical department goes to work; but before performing their purely arithmetical labour of adding sums to make a total, the calculators do not think of visiting those forests upon paper. If they did, they would in most cases find only a few thickets of brushwood, amid plains of fern and rushes. But with their written satisfactory reports, the Russians trouble themselves very little. . . . Their woods are immense in the bureau of the minister, and this is sufficient for them. The day may be foreseen when, as a consequence of this administrative supineness and security, the people will warm themselves by the fires made of the old dusty papers accumulated in the public offices: these riches increase daily. (554–55; italics in original)

Far more will be said about those who inherited these statistical practices in communist countries in chapter 5. But the next brief paragraph gives a flavor of their unreliability.

The fact that statistics in the Soviet Union and Eastern bloc countries under the communist regime were not worth the paper they were written on is now officially acknowledged. The fact that the output of all the institutions "producing" torture has been included in the calculation of the GNP (in spite of the fact that this number was supposed to be linked with the measurement of the neutral-sounding term *net product*), and that security forces have employed quite a number of people, has been noted.[87] There have been other reasons for the aggregate numbers' lack of relevance.

Mr. Agabengyan, Mikhail Gorbachev's economic adviser, wrote at one point about the success of maintaining very high employment figures in Russia.[88] Yet he later acknowledged that the figures do not mean very much since, under the current system of management and accounting,[89] Russian factories "inevitably employ 300 or even 400 people when in the West they need only 200."[90] Winiecki (1988) remarks that, in general, the quantities reported by enterprises in communist countries were fictitious: everybody at the enterprise level, from manager to worker, showed doctored performance figures. He quotes A. Shitov, first deputy chairman of the USSR Committee for National Control, who revealed that additions to the actual figures and other distortions were discovered in every third enterprise.[91] Thus, Winiecki concludes, whereas the numbers showed growth, there was no prosperity: enterprises produced, but nobody was buying the shoddy products. Yet because of "soft-budgeting" (which meant justified expectations for continuous subsidies), enterprises did not go bankrupt. Thus growth had no relationship with the welfare of the population. Recently, Alfred Siennicki, head of the office for questions concerning economic relations for the Council of Ministers in Hungary, announced that they must abandon their customary statistics and technical standards because they made no sense. Romania's new leader, Ion Iliescu, accused Ceausescu's government of massive falsification of data on economic statistics, saying that figures for some crops, such as corn, sunflowers, and winter potatoes, had been inflated as much as sixfold by the official press.[92]

During my recent visit to Mexico, the previous director of Mexico's Bureau of Statistics, Mr. Josue Saenz Trevino, told me that for quite a while his bureau estimated that about 10 percent of Mexico's population (about 8 million people) was missing from their sample for a number of different reasons. One reason was that people involved in black market activities refused to answer questions and be counted. Another reason was political, linked with the way in which funds were allocated among cities. Since, apparently, there has been a significant movement to cities other than Mexico City in recent years, there have been pressures not to measure these people (one consequence is that now the other cities want to have their own Census Bureau). Also, since a growing proportion of the population was against the ruling parties, there were pressures not to count them.[93]

Incentives to publish inaccurate data exist not only in national accounts, but in international ones too. By 1982, adding up all countries' inflows and outflows showed around $100 billion more flowing out than in. Investigators from the International Monetary Fund found most of the leakage in services and other money accounts, especially dividend and interest payments, and in official funds like foreign aid, which showed bigger donations than recipients acknowledge. This latter finding led to speculations that part of the money lines the pockets of rulers in countries getting the foreign aid.[94]

When figures about government expenditures enter into the measurement of savings and investment and are used to make international comparisons, the problems multiply if one takes them on face value. Eberstadt (1989) notices that, according to recent World Bank measures of industry's share of gross output, sub-Saharan Africa is today more industrialized than Denmark. Zimbabwe, Bostwana, Congo, Trinidad, and Tobago are, on paper, more industrialized than Japan. Togo, Egypt, Costa Rica, and others have a higher relative level of investment than West Germany.

At the same time, the level of private consumption in all these starving, poor countries is lower than in the Western ones. Yet it is hard to believe, Eberstadt emphasizes, that the poor populations of these countries would, of their own will, risk starvation for the benefit of investing in heavy, nonconsumer goods (or in replicas of St. Peter in the midst of the desert). It is true that in some developing countries—Singapore, Korea, and Indonesia—high rates of investment were followed by high growth rates, but in other countries, where channeled funds led to expansions of the government sector, the outcomes were different, no matter how governments categorized their expenditures. This additional evidence underscores the fact that deficits or government expenditures are not in themselves good or bad; one must consider what governments do with the money.[95]

These observations strengthen the conclusions reached earlier: knowledge of the *aggregate* numbers today does not provide us with reliable information either for recommending any particular short-run fiscal policy, or for interpreting with any confidence statistical results using aggregate numbers. They cannot be used for verifying the traditional theories about the impact of fiscal policies. Maybe their only use is to compare countries with widely divergent incomes—like Russia with the United States, or Portugal with Germany. But with such a goal, comparing numbers of cars or phones, life expectancy, or infant mortality could provide better information. As for other comparisons and uses, one must constantly keep in mind that scientific measurements become mercurial when done with the goal of influencing policies.

Conclusions

The arguments and evidence presented in this chapter show that we must change the ways we think and talk about macroeconomic issues, about the roles of governments and the way these roles are carried out. Words play tricks on us today. We employ the same abstract words when we move from the 1930s to our times, and when we move from country to country.

In spite of worrying about deficits, some economists are still trapped in Keynesian semantics and talk about the stimulus of deficits, of spending on public works (now called "infrastructure"). The *New York Times's* ("Unbalanced," May 10, 1992) main argument against the desirability of constitutional amendments to balance the budget is that it would prevent investments. In this chapter I have tried to show that these are not the issues: not all roads and schools are investments. The issue is responsible governance and political institutions to enforce them, rather than reliance on one or another economic theory, or one way or another of counting numbers. The theories are just frequently repeated opinions without foundation, and frequently the numbers bear no relationship to facts. The roads may lead nowhere, and the schools may produce illiterates with diplomas.

At this point readers might raise the following question: if indeed the aggregate data about governments' expenditures are as incomprehensible as I suggest they are, and they cannot be interpreted in the light of macroeconomic models, is there a problem with the United States and other governments' budgets at all, in particular with their deficits? How can we know if there is a problem? If there is, what should be done? And if there is no problem, why does one get the impression from political discussions and from the media that there is one?

Some people answer the second question by suggesting that too many groups profit from saying that there is a crisis even when there is none. Politicians want to use the idea of crisis to raise taxes; they and the media thrive on nothing but crises and fears and will invent some if there are none; some economists' lifetime work is threatened with oblivion if they can't show that there is a crisis; the army of consultants may have not much to do if everything is going well; and interest groups want specific taxes lowered for them and raised for others.

Add to this list the bureaucracy employed in publishing and using the numbers, and interest groups for whom these numbers help shift the debate from what people are getting for their money to a vague comparison between what the government spends on a program and what the whole society is producing, and one can see why this argument is so tempting. When so many groups have an incentive to make things appear complex and problematic, even if they are not, simplicity has few chances. When so many groups point to a crisis when there is none, bad policies may be adopted that may indeed make the situation worse.

This is not the whole argument, tempting as it is. The intensive debates about debts, deficits, and governments' expenditures, as well as fears about the decline of the United States and other countries, reflect concerns about government institutions, about their ability to govern and guarantee lasting prosperity. They do not reflect concerns about mismeasured, misinterpreted numbers and abstract arguments about their general effects. How to approach and deal with such long-term concerns is a question raised in the next and the final chapters.

Chapter 3

Keys to Prosperity:
Trade and Finance

In the kingdom in which we are now sitting there dwells a princess—a
very clever princess. All the newspapers in the world she has read, and
forgotten them again, so clever is she.
                              —Hans Christian Andersen, *The Snow Queen*

Throughout history, the sudden rags-to-riches story of a poor society
leapfrogging another has provoked envy, admiration, and discussion about
why the richer society tumbled, and the humbler rose.

During the last decades, Japan, Germany, Taiwan, Hong Kong, and
Singapore leapfrogged, or are expected to leapfrog, other societies that
were way ahead of them. As in the past, this provokes emulation, wonder,
and debate. People wonder especially how these societies succeeded when
some had no natural resources at all.

Today's debates never refer to the prosperity of oil-producing Middle
East countries, though they have achieved standards of living similar to
those of the aforementioned countries. Their success is easy to explain; it
conforms to the "finding treasure" image, which poses no puzzles. But
how did societies without natural treasures do it?

This is not the first time in history that economists, historians, and
public discourse have focused on this question, leading to endless discussions about the policy changes needed to catch up. It happened in England
in the seventeenth century. The puzzle was not Spain's and Portugal's
success, which fit into the "finding treasure" pattern. The puzzle was
Amsterdam and Holland—the economic miracles of that century—whose
success did not.

Mainstream macroeconomic opinions today—be they about savings,
trade deficits, jobs, competitiveness, financial markets' power on governments' finances, Keynes's views—can be traced back to this period, when
English economists tried to explain and find remedies to the crisis of
England falling behind the Dutch.[1] To trace them back is useful, since the

larger perspective helps us to discard myths and errors that continue to prevail today. The choice of the period is not accidental: the seventeenth century also happened to be characterized by both a revolution in communication technology—the spread of literacy through extensive use of printing, in the Netherlands in particular[2]—and "global" competition through the commercialization of knowledge.

More important: after we eliminate the errors, the larger perspective helps us to identify the keys to prosperity today. The larger perspective starts with an examination of the abrupt emergence of Amsterdam between 1585 and 1610 and through its persistent glory until the first half of the eighteenth century. Its keys to glory turn out to be the keys to glory today too, whereas many too-often repeated opinions, based on what passes for science today, are not.[3] The keys were political and legal changes that allowed the Dutch and the well-educated immigrants they attracted to unlock their entrepreneurial talents. Their willingness and ability to take risks, because of innovations in financial arrangements that were applied for the first time, resulted in the commercialization of knowledge. These changes and adjustments paved the way to prosperity then, and they can do so today.

The historical pattern of the rise of trading-cities and -states reveals more. It reinforces the view that technological innovations and policies based on macroeconomics do *not* bring prosperity; policies that encourage risk taking do. The policies must be such that entrepreneurs and merchants are willing to take risks and find the financing to bring those risks to life. When entrepreneurship is discouraged, the opportunities technical know-how provides stay unexploited. The state can offer the stability necessary for entrepreneurship to flourish, smoothing the way for opportunities to be discovered.

The decline of the trading-states reveals additional regularities about the relationship between the role of states and prosperity. The trading-states' prosperity was threatened when societies with large populations used technological and financial innovations to increase their military powers significantly. The resulting rivalry between the larger nation-states came to characterize much of what historians now call "the modern era."[4]

During this era economists focused their attention on "nations" as units, study of which, so they thought, would help them understand the keys to prosperity. Most economists were wrong in their focus. They failed to emphasize that risk taking, be it in trade or finance, is the essence of prosperity. Had they been more careful in suggesting their theories, had they admitted that these were not "general theories" of prosperity but political theories fitting circumstances when national rivalries—a political issue—were the characteristic feature of the period, we might have discarded them more easily once such rivalries diminished or ceased. But most economists suggested—and still do suggest—that changes in policies concerning national units, based on information derived from changes in national statistics, could help us find the way to prosperity in general. This chapter will try to further undermine this point of view.

The Dutch Miracle: Facts and Interpretations

People tend first to extrapolate from their own limited experience when confronting new evidence. Some English economists attributed the Dutch success to their natural resources: the tons of herring they fished. Others soon discarded this explanation, noticing that England had grain, timber, and wool, that the French were rich in vineyards and extracted salt from the ocean, yet the Dutch, lacking any of these resources, became the exporters of fine clothing, the biggest traders in grain, the builders of better and cheaper ships than England, and exporters of high-quality salt and wine. This is not unlike some countries today. Switzerland has no cocoa, yet it produces and exports the best chocolate. Japan has no iron, yet Japan produces more and better steel than Peru, which has iron. Theories about natural resources failed to explain prosperity and differences in levels of development in the seventeenth century, and they fail equally today.

English economists, who emphasized the role of natural resources, paid little attention to the fact that Amsterdam had obvious natural disadvantages, for which the Dutch had to pay. (Bernard de Mandeville, of Dutch origin and education, about whose view more will be said later, was among the few exceptions). The city had to be built "on piles to prevent it from sinking into the marshy soil. The port lay far back from the sea, and was difficult to egress when the wind was easterly. Shallow waters made necessary the use of lighters for loading and unloading ships."[5] Nor did the English economists pay much attention to Amsterdam's advantages, unrivaled in that age and far more important than herrings, but not so obvious to those writing from a distance. Because of the access through rivers and canals to other towns in the Netherlands and to regions of Germany and France, transportation and communication were cheaper in Amsterdam than elsewhere.[6] In general, participants in the discussion paid little attention to differences in climate and geography, and the costs and benefits these differences produced, whether in trade or defense.

Even if they were wrong then to overlook these factors, we need not discuss them today. Whereas such differences can explain why particular industries flourished in one place rather than another, they cannot explain either sustained prosperity or differences among societies where climate and geography are similar. After all, the Dutch thrived although they had to pay high overheads for the dikes. The Japanese thrive today although they had to triumph over obstacles and pay overheads for insurance against earthquakes, which other people did not. And within the United States, West Virginia stays poor and inner cities decline, whereas areas nearby, with similar geography and climate thrive.

Once observers discarded the factor of natural resources, they sought other ways to explain the success of Amsterdam and the Dutch. The idea that increased savings for society as a whole—abstracting from historical circumstances—is good, dates from this time.[7] The English economists contrasted the Dutch people's unusual frugality and "legendary work habits" with that of the disorderly, lazy Englishmen. (Sound familiar?) The debate in England led to a large number of protective and discriminatory measures against the Dutch, some justified.[8]

Before discussing false arguments about the origins of the Dutch success and required remedies, which are still repeated today, let us briefly explore what happened and what lessons are still relevant today. What, if not an unusually high saving rate, could make the Dutch the economic wonder of the world during the seventeenth century? How could Holland have both high wages and an increasing population? How could it carry out so much investment, significantly expand credit, have no inflation, and keep interest rates at the lowest level in Europe? All these phenomena greatly puzzled English observers.

After the revolt against the Spanish in the sixteenth century,[9] the birth of the new Dutch republic and its policy of religious toleration far in advance of the times attracted considerable immigration of merchants, moneymen, and those better educated in particular, from both Antwerp and the neighboring countries.[10] The result was a population leap from 1.2 million in 1550 to 1.9 million in 1650.[11] Amsterdam's population went from about 30,000 in the 1570s to 215,000 in 1630.[12] Such demographic expansion, when combined with the expectation of social mobility and political stability, the entrepreneurs and traders attracted by such features, and the subsequent innovations and discoveries of new markets allowed by unprecedented innovations in financial arrangements, created the opportunities that became the keys to the Dutch miracle. The city became a center of growth whose influence radiated not only through Holland, but through Europe and beyond.[13]

But there is no evidence whatsoever that the unusually high Dutch saving rate was the *cause* of these spectacular times (if it was high at all), or that the Dutch avoided buying luxuries—another argument found in the English observers' discussion. (Nor is there evidence that these two patterns later helped either England or the United States to become world powers.) Savings and investments were a *consequence* of credit becoming available to more people than ever before due to innovations in Amsterdam's financial markets and the option of social mobility.

The facts were that political consolidation and well defined property rights opened opportunities for relatively unhindered trade and financial innovations. Together they fostered expectations for Dutch and foreigners of becoming richer, unlocking their potential. More people than before had the incentives to work harder and plough back profits into enterprises.[14] Also, because of Amsterdam's openness, the Dutch collected unanticipated rents because of the inflow of well-connected and educated immigrants, many of them merchants and moneymen (Jews and Huguenots prominent among them), bringing with them information, literacy, and also contacts and money from all over the world. French, Venetians, Florentines, and Genoese, as well as Germans, Poles, Hungarians, Spaniards, Russians, Turks, Armenians, Hindus, and others bargained at the Bourse (the Commodity Exchange), and much of the capital active in Amsterdam was foreign-owned, or owned by Amsterdammers of foreign birth.[15]

Their immigrant status was the feature that Amsterdam's merchants and moneymen had in common—not their "Protestant" ethic, as Max Weber speculated. Although Weber's notion has been quoted frequently enough to pass for fact, it wasn't true in Amsterdam or in other prosperous trading-cities and -states elsewhere in the world. Hamburg's, Hong Kong's, Singapore's, and Taiwan's histories have much in common with Amsterdam's, but shared religion is not a factor. In all these places the state provided an umbrella of law and order that gave people a stake in what the business society was doing, a strategy that attracted immigrants, as in the Netherlands. Hamburg prospered when the displaced Huguenots moved there at the beginning of the eighteenth century and when refugees from the French Revolution arrived at the end of that century. Sir Stamford Raffles designed Singapore as a port at the beginning of the nineteenth century and backed it by a strong administrative, legal, and education system, the latter being offered to its multiracial population.[16] From a small settlement, Singapore rose, attracting Chinese, Malays, and Europeans. Trade and security brought prosperity to the penniless emigrants from Indonesia and, in particular, China. Taiwan (after the seventeenth century), Singapore, and Hong Kong offered the emigrants opportunities denied them by the Chinese hinterland, which was dominated at first by warlords and status-conscious bureaucracy and later by communist bureaucracy. Hong Kong benefited from waves of emigration from China, in particular from the inflow of Shanghai merchants and financiers when Mao Zedong "liberated" China in 1949—much as Amsterdam benefited when Antwerp's merchants and financiers fled the Spanish in earlier centuries, when the Huguenots fled France, and when the Jews fled many parts of Europe. Hong Kong's textile and shipping industries were initiated by emigrants from Shanghai.[17] These Chinese emigrants also established the network of merchants, traders, moneymen, and manufacturers—as Jewish, Italian, Armenian, Parsee, and other migrant groups did throughout history in various parts of the world.[18] However, it should also be stressed that all these entrepreneurial ventures were carried out under the umbrella given by the British Empire's laws and institutions.[19] It should also be stressed that, in addition to commitment to these institutions, without which trade could not have thrived, municipalities of the trading states paid for and supervised the schools. Most children in seventeenth-century Netherlands, ages seven to twelve, attended schools, which were privately run but were supervised by municipalities and Calvinist Churches.[20]

These are the broad regularities. What were the Englishmen's interpretations of the Dutch miracle?

Interpretations

A few English observers, among them Sir Walter Raleigh, attributed the Dutch success to low customs, freedom of foreigners to trade, and superior technique in shipping and fisheries. Sir William Petty emphasized the role of secure property rights, financial innovations, and division of labor in shipbuilding to explain the unprecedented success. In a 1668 treatise, Sir Josiah Child attributed the Dutch prosperity to "toleration of different opinions in matters of religion," by which they attracted industrious and rich dissenters from other countries.[21] These writers were in the minority, and none emphasized the crucial role of financial markets that allowed access to capital and helped unlock people's entrepreneurial talents.

The majority discussed the situation and prescribed remedies in terms of what we would today call macroeconomic perspective. They observed that the Dutch saved more, had lower interest rates, and made more investments in infrastructure. (The latter was Roger Coke's observation after looking at Holland's canals and interconnected cities.)[22] These English writers concluded that Amsterdam's success could be *replicated* if Englishmen saved more, if interest rates were lowered, and if governments invested in infrastructure. This inference was wrong.

The English observers paid less attention to the changes needed in the political-legal-regulatory setting, those concerning financial innovations and institutions in particular. They ignored the fact that the Dutch drew power from their federalism and openness when absolutist centralization was the norm.[23] They confused consequences with causes, a confusion those in power had the incentives to promote. The rulers publicized those views that fit their political interests and bestowed upon them an aura of respectability and science.[24] (What is new?)

The Dutch success was built on trust and the expansion of trade, the latter based on an unprecedented expansion of the art of finance. It was not based on the manipulation of saving rates or interest rates, or on investments in infrastructure. Nor was it based on reactions to international trade figures, much discussed in England and France, but not in Holland, nor in today's flourishing Asian city-states.

Trade and Finance

Amsterdam, like Venice and the other Italian city-states before, thrived by becoming a trusted center for trade. Access to new financial instruments allowed its people to unlock their entrepreneurial talents, to invest and expand trade. Cheques and double-entry bookkeeping had already been invented in Florence. According to historians, these innovations, along with the number and effectiveness of ad hoc corporations and holding companies, explain the Italian city-states' prosperity. They allowed people to coordinate "important aspects of the routine activities of indefinite numbers of men across barriers of both time and space."[25] Amsterdam's entrepreneurs and moneymen used these and made other innovations in finance, smoothing the flow of credit, which helped commercialize knowledge.

Marine insurance expanded, and courts were set up to handle commercial, maritime, and other insurance cases.[26] The Chamber of assurance was set up in 1598, the Bourse in 1608, and a special one for grain in 1616; the Exchange Bank was set up in 1609, and a lending bank in 1614.[27] Price lists on everything traded in Amsterdam served as indices all over Europe.

They were found in archives of trading establishments in Copenhagen, Vienna, and Florence.[28]

Amsterdam's prosperity was based on the management of the flow of information—ours is not the first information age. The seventeenth century saw the spread of literacy, a process in which the Dutch played a prominent role. The city gathered and sold knowledge of market conditions around the world; it developed its skills in appraisal and classification of merchandise and credit, and in wholesale service (and practicing the idea of "on-time delivery," in grain trade in particular). All these innovations were supported, and none could exist without financial credit, insurance, informed brokerage and exchange facilities, or the spread of literacy and printing technology.

Access to financial markets and financial innovations explain a number of things. The saving and investment patterns of the Dutch were indeed different from those of people in other countries. Whereas elsewhere people could, at best, buy or lease farms and other small properties, the Dutch, even of small and moderate means, could—and did—put their savings into shares in ships and mills, into fishing and trading voyages, and into the much-trusted loans to the city of Amsterdam, the province of Holland, or the United Provinces.[29] The Dutch had the incentive to plough back profits and savings in commercial enterprises, an incentive people in other countries lacked.

Those who subscribed to particular merchant ventures—building, buying, or chartering a ship, or a mill, or a fishing and trading voyage—could do so in shares as little as one sixty-fourth, and others could bet even smaller amounts on futures, be they for speculating on the actual outcome of the voyage and its profit, or on price fluctuations, which, just as today, were influenced by news and rumors.[30] Already then brokers put up shows as bears (*contremines*) or bulls (*liefhebbers*), and moved "small batches of shares, or packets of split shares at low prices. And they lived off their wits rather than means, since it became common practice to offer shares which either were not yet in their possession or for which they had not yet paid, on the assumption that they could be off-loaded for a profit by the time their initial obligation fell due."[31]

Grain futures were traded in Amsterdam in the mid-sixteenth century, and in the seventeenth there were optional and conditional contracts in herring, spices, and whale oil. By the second half of the seventeenth century, brokers recorded the various types of sales, "the arts of time bargains, optional sales, buying on margin, 'ducat-actions' by which *small* speculators followed the market, winning or losing a ducat for every point of rise or fall in the price of actions."[32] It was in Amsterdam that "shares"—in our meaning of the term—were invented.[33] Again the English observers were puzzled and showed no understanding of the reasons for such markets:

> They invent new ways of Trade, great quantities of Brandy being disposed of every year, which are never intended to be delivered, only the Buyer and Seller get or lose according to the Rates it bears at the time agreed on to make good bargains; such a Commerce in England would be of little advantage.[34]

Yet these financial arrangements allowed people to take out insurances and diversify their portfolios, and enabled entrepreneurs—born in Amsterdam or not—unprecedented access to capital.[35] Such access opened careers in Amsterdam, as it had in the Italian trading-cities to anyone shrewd or lucky enough to do well in trade, be he young or poor,[36] and gave rise to a bond based on common commercial interests.

There was freedom to export monetary metals too, rare elsewhere in the seventeenth century. This brought the business of bills of exchange as negotiable instruments of credit to Amsterdam too. Barbour notes, "In the trade of no other country in this period . . . was the bill of exchange used so freely and flexibly, and no other city in this century had a business in them equal to Amsterdam's. Neither French, Spanish, Scottish, nor Italian cities could provide direct and current exchange with northern and north-eastern Europe, and London was in little better case; hence exchange to and from these countries flowed through Amsterdam."[37] Familiarity with the bill of exchange both for settling balances and as a means of anticipating credits led to the acceptance of other forms of paper credit: merchants' notes, receipts for bullion deposited at banks, merchandise stored in warehouses, debentures, and municipal bonds.

Manufacturing flourished, relying on the traders' knowledge of foreign industry and markets. The Dutch established their reputation and exported ships, glass, typecasting, printing, scientific instruments, and cutting and polishing lenses for spectacles and diamonds. Sugar refining became a big industry (financed by Portuguese residents). Foreign visitors were surprised by the numerous innovations in mills (protected by patent laws), which the Dutch adapted to industries as diverse as breweries, foundries, and the production of gunpowder.[38]

Amsterdam's influence radiated due to not only its innovations in finance but also those in industry and the organization of industries, spreading information about them around the world:

> Where Dutch capital went, there swamps were drained, mines opened, forests exploited, canals constructed, ships built, new industries established, mills turned, and trading companies were organized. . . . "It may be said," observed Huet about the year 1694, "that the Dutch are in some respects masters of the commerce of the Swedish kingdom since they are masters of the copper trade. The farmers of these mines, being always in need of money, and not finding any in Sweden, pledge this commodity to merchants of Amsterdam who advance them the necessary funds." . . . [The Dutch] were capitalist entrepreneurs who raised the commercial and industrial potential of the countries whose resources they developed. An authority on the economic history of Sweden in the seventeenth century has said: "Dutch immigrants dominated almost everything that was new in the economic life of Sweden at that time."[39]

The same was true about Norway, Denmark, Russia, and many other parts of Europe and beyond, where the Dutch both brought information about trading opportunities and helped finance them. This is what the "unlocking" of people's potential means. It paved the way to Amsterdam's prosperity, as it can pave the way to prosperity elsewhere. Amsterdam's entrepreneurs, like those of the Italian cities before, thought "globally," even if nobody bothered to use the term then.

Briefly: knowledge of distant markets and anticipatory ability are trading skills. These skills—discovering the location of supplies and demands, anticipating fluctuations in them, pioneering trade and finance, helping and improving the flow of commercial information[40]—are not as visible as technical skills, which lead to mechanical innovations, or artistic skills, which bring pleasure to the eyes and ears.[41] Yet allowing these skills to be practiced and reflected in financial innovations brings prosperity. Technical knowledge without commercialization doesn't. There is no better proof for this assertion than the long list of wide-ranging technological innovations and discoveries in China that stayed unexploited until they were either rediscovered in Europe or transferred to the rest of the world by traders. The list covers porcelain and paper, magnetism and gunpowder, the wheelbarrow and the seed drill plow (with hopper), blowing engines for furnaces, and many others.[42] At times, more than 1,500 years elapsed before these technological advances were transmitted from China to the West. Trade and finance eventually allowed people to commercialize this knowledge, accumulating experience in the process. Formal, statistically-measured "education" or "human capital," of which we may have plenty today, like the Chinese Mandarins', was no substitute for experience in the past, nor is it today.[43]

The Meaning of Economic Development

The freedom to trade leads to the commercialization of novelty—of innovations, in a very broad sense of the word—and to what one may call economic development. Novelties continue to appear when people encounter *diversity*. This means coming in contact with strangers—traders and immigrants—who bring information, money, and contacts, or with adversity, which in some circumstances forces people to deviate from routines and bet on new ideas.[44] Such events prevent societies from settling into routine behavior. People do things in new ways, hoping to restore their wealth or to catch up with and leapfrog their fellows.[45]

Initially, societies developed in places where geography encouraged more frequent encounters among strangers. Over long periods of time, ports or places where international trade routes passed became the centers where novelty emerged. Foreigners brought information, which opened people's eyes to new opportunities. The encounters led to an endogenous process of growth over the area where traders could move. Today, technology and institutions of industrially advanced societies give their members the option both of being in touch with strangers—without moving—and of leapfrogging their fellows by entrepreneurship and innovation. This process results in specialization, renewal of diverse skills, and continuous division of labor.

It is no accident that China now grows quickly, and that Hungary and Poland are expected to grow more rapidly than Russia, Romania, and other parts of Eastern Europe. There is a large Chinese diaspora in the West (estimated at 55 million), as there is a large Hungarian and Polish one (in 1956, after the failed uprising against the Soviet army, about 10 percent of Hungary's population left for the West). It is estimated that 75 percent of mainland China's 28,000 enterprises with significant foreign equity are financed by ethnic Chinese living outside China.[46] Hungarian and Polish rulers, strapped for cash, have tried to lure back their entrepreneurial diaspora since the 1970s. Armenia's president was born in Syria, its foreign and energy ministers in California. In contrast, Mikhail Gorbachev had no Russian diaspora who wanted to come back. He and his followers were unwilling to bet on private foreign entrepreneurship and its financial resources, even though these were at the root of Russia's brief, fourteen-year growth spurt between 1885 and 1899.[47]

However, the fact that people innovate and outdo their fellows also means that skills become obsolete and some people fall behind. The reactions of the latter group, which could be violent, explain why there are obstacles inherent in the previous process, which we call growth.

Bringing novelties to life means that traditional trades fall into oblivion and new ones must be learned. Traditions must be abandoned and new habits acquired. There are new centers of skill and traditional groups break up. These consequences set in motion a process that slows down the trend toward specialization, toward increased diversity, and thus toward prosperity. The danger exists that in some societies the transfer of wealth will lead to the persistence of traditions, to maintaining rigid routines, and to limited interaction with strangers. Thus prosperity is not inevitable.[48] Societies can—and did—close themselves through a wide variety of regulations and policies, sustained by various beliefs, some supposedly based on science. The difficult task is to discard such myths and maintain a society poised between tradition and change. This is the condition necessary for creativity, for the emergence of novelty, for prosperity.

Unfortunately, it is not a sufficient condition. Even if a society succeeds in keeping itself vulnerable, poised between routines and change, its future also depends on what other societies do.

The relative decline of Amsterdam and other trading-cities, and the rise of England and France, as well as the relative, temporary rise of communist societies that tried to suppress both trade and the financial arts—features whose consequences are discussed in chapter 5—are explained by the latter's ability to bet on the military option. Let us see how this option confers advantages and disadvantages. It has probably led to the most fundamental confusion about the meaning and measurement of growth and prosperity, a confusion deeply embedded today in the notion of macroeconomics and the measurement of national aggregates.

Economic Development and the Military

It is no accident that the Dutch were uninhibited by abstractions of nationalism and by economic theories that, explicitly or implicitly, carried a nationalist message. A country poor in natural resources—land in particular—can only prosper by unlocking the potential of people living within its borders, and by relying on trade and activities depending on trade. Holland's dense but (in absolute terms) small population then, like that of the Far East Asian city-states today, could not indulge in nationalism and forego trade.[49]

However, more populous countries (and the military option this characteristic allows) with access to natural resources, can, did, and will pursue such an option. Its availability has a number of effects. One is that it imposes costs on cities and states that opted for trade, leading to their relative decline. The relative decline will be faster when the governments of the more populous countries adopt the techniques of financial management and trade first invented in cities. England did so after the 1688 Revolution and improved on both the Italian banking techniques and the Dutch principles of funded debt.[50] At the same time its military expenditures, though having the obvious effect of imposing a tax on Englishmen, also raised the protection costs of competing enterprises of other nations— the Dutch in particular—which benefited Englishmen by redirecting trade.[51] The relative decline of the Dutch after the 1730s is due not only to the three wars fought against the British and the two against France, which led to one of the heaviest tax burdens of that time, but also to the fact that, as a result, the merchants and the skilled—those that Jonathan Hugues called "the vital few"—left its shores.[52]

Expenditures on the military confer what the historian Frederic Lane has called "protection rents," which economists will then measure as increases in national income in the country receiving them. When many governments of populous nations emulate one another and have access to trade, finance, and military options, we see the origins of the maze of interactions confronting us today: both the centralized, modern nation-states and the theories, economic ones in particular, whose departure point is the political and military unit called "the nation." [53]

The resulting abstract theories and statistics (national accounts and trade balances) obscure the historical context. The meaning of changes in aggregate numbers are all blurred by the availability of the military options, by the competition between the political-military units to achieve or maintain the "protection rents," and by the varying degrees of military threat to which such competition leads.

The national statistics of societies that successfully obtain the protection rents will record high measured growth and productivity rates, as well as job creation. The country will have a high standard of living and a large government sector strongly involved with industry. The interpretation of the aggregate measures gets even more complex when the military sector also exports its products, as happened in France, the United States, and the former USSR during the last decades.[54] If, during such periods of time, economists look at aggregate data and try to prove that the size of government (including military industries) is negatively related to "productivity," "growth," or "standards of living," or that governments cannot create employment, they will all be proven wrong.[55]

Once again, from a much broader angle than in previous chapters, we can see why macroeconomics misleads. Its neutral language and uniformly computed aggregates across countries suggest independence of political, legal, military, and social setting, and offer—not surprisingly—possibilities for *national* economic development *without* profound political, legal, military, and social change. Macroeconomics is a tautology and a myth, a dangerous one at that, sustaining the illusion that prosperity is necessarily linked with territory, national units, and government spending in general.

In conclusion, the relative decline of the trading-cities and the rise of the modern, centralized nation-states that competed with their military technologies should not have confused economists examining the keys to prosperity—regardless of what they measured. But it did. Economists examined growth in terms of political units that created the statistics, which obscured the fact that these units are not crucial for understanding prosperity. The diversity of people's skill, based on the practice of commerce and finance, is. Denmark and Sweden grew during the seventeenth century, and Southern China grows today. But the prosperity of these areas cannot be understood without taking into account the role of Amsterdam's, Hong Kong's, and China's diaspora; they brought the trading skills, the business experience, the contacts, and the finances and the information that come with them. Vancouver is also booming while the rest of Canada languishes. Neither can these changes be understood without taking into account the powerful influence of Hong Kong and some other Far East immigrants and their trade with Asian countries.[56] Looking just at China's or Canada's average growth rate, at Ottawa's policies, or at any national statistics will not help us understand the keys to prosperity.[57]

This and much additional evidence notwithstanding, economists continue to examine growth in terms of national, geographic units and aggregate statistics.[58] The following sections show how in detail, by looking at influential trends in macro-economists' writings today. There are two reasons for such discussion. First we need to see how ideas can mislead and turn an already not straight road to prosperity into a labyrinth. Second, we need to prevent these new ideas, covered by scientific masks, from being established, leading to bad policies and becoming another myth.

National Saving Rates: Consequence, not Cause

Before examining the origins of today's opinions on national savings and the policies recommended to manipulate them, let us straighten out the definition of saving and show where the macro-economists have misled us again.

Here is Paul Krugman (1990) repeating the standard definition:

> Saving means setting aside some portion of your current earnings to provide for the future. There are only two ways that the nation as a whole can save. It can use some of its current income to build more factories, improve its telecommunications, rebuild its streets and bridges, etc. That is, it can add to its stock of productive capital by investing more than enough to replace old capital as it wears out or becomes obsolete. Or it can buy assets from foreigners, either by investing abroad or by paying off debts incurred to foreigners in the past. The national rate is therefore measured as the sum of net domestic investment . . . and net foreign investment. (65–66)

This definition makes no reference to the creation of credit, its flow, and to education. For example, when a large fraction of women plan to enter the labor force, whatever the reason, they will spend more on education.[59] Measured savings will decline when this adjustment takes place, which may take a long time. If this change takes place in one country (the United States) and not in others (Japan or Germany), as was the case during the last fifteen years, its measured *relative* rate of savings declines too. There should be less concern about prosperity in the future when identifying declines in saving rates, either absolute or relative, during such times. People just shift from one traditionally measured investment to others, which is measured as "consumption," if it is measured at all.

There are economists, as well as Republican and Democratic politicians in the United States, who link low national savings with the budget deficits. They argue that by eliminating them, national savings will rise, and thus there will be more investment. Without a frame of reference, this argument is wrong too.

As shown in the previous chapter, the argument may well be correct if governments have not invested but have consumed (or wasted) the money. However, if governments have made additional investments—and if they are indeed investments rather than just counted as such—then the increase in deficits has not diminished national savings, and there is no reason to worry. Following Krugman's definition, if governments have spent money to repair bridges and streets as efficiently as the private sector would have, and have financed the repairs through deficits, or if they have built dams and hydroelectric power stations, there should be no reason to worry about deficits at all. That is the case *if* the repairs have sustained or helped expand trade, and *if* electricity has been bought (at a correctly calculated price).[60] The story is different if governments have wasted the money, even if they have counted the expenditures as investments, and even if the expenditures have created jobs in some areas. But how does one know, unless political institutions were in place to help infer that people got approximately what they voted for?

Those who argue for cutting the deficits because they diminish savings must thus perceive that governments waste money, no matter how they label the expenditures. Or, they must perceive that governments make so many commitments that redistribute wealth toward consumption that, to remain solvent and maintain their credit ranking, they must raise additional revenues. In such instances one can say that governments should cut the deficits. This can be done in a variety of ways.

Governments can solve the problem of commitments (and even of waste and mistakes) if they broaden the tax base, by inducing more privately created employment. Governments can also raise taxes or diminish expenditures. However, no matter what option governments choose, the issue with savings is not what the private sector does, but what governments do. Discussing changes in national saving rates obscures the fact that, as far as prosperity is concerned, the focus should be on incentives to invest in and access capital markets. The issue is not the manipulation of measured, or rather mismeasured, national saving rates.

Krugman criticizes such a conclusion on the following grounds:

> On the left, there were the advocates of "industrial policy": people like Robert Reich and Lester Thurow, who thought that by playing a more active role in the market place, the government could accelerate productivity growth. On the right there were supply-siders: people like Arthur Laffer and Jude Wanniski, who believed that getting the government *out* of the marketplace would unleash a wave of private sector dynamism. Although these groups were at opposite ends of the political spectrum, they had much in common . . . [T]hey offered the political system alternatives to the dreary virtue preached by the economics establishment. They offered free lunches—a chance to invigorate the economy without pain. (15–16; italics in original)

But Krugman is wrong again, whether one agrees with the Left or the Right. If governments pursued a mistaken policy in the past, correcting for it improves the situation. The correction can take the form of either abolishing a previous law, regulation, or tax, or an additional intervention, as shown in the previous chapters. Though both Left and Right will argue correctly that abolishing a mistake, or trying to counteract for the unexpected effects of policies, will improve the overall situation, neither of them argues that the change is a free lunch. They merely argue that governments can learn from their own mistakes and correct them.

The Right and the Left are well aware of the fact that all laws, regulations, taxes, or tariffs—whether they perceive them as good or bad—create groups interested in maintaining them, who will find pliable intellectuals to rationalize their interests. The latter will invent any number of ideas to maintain the tariff or the tax, and advocate national security or protection of culture and public welfare, calling the theories surrounding these terms "social science." This is part of what people in the Right and Left have in common, rather than a belief in free lunch.

They differ in their solutions. The Right to whom Krugman refers—which includes George Gilder, Jude Wanniski, and Arthur Laffer—advocates abolishing arrangements that bestow monopoly powers, by facilitating entry and individual risk taking helped by financial markets.

Krugman's Left also wants additional entry—Reich advocates training and retraining workers, and encouraging new firms. But according to Reich and Thurow, this goal can be achieved through additional government action, that is, collective risk taking rather than individual risk taking through access to financial markets. Thus neither the Left nor the Right advocate free lunch, contrary to Krugman's statements. Both want to abolish monopoly powers and disturb the status quo by *unlocking additional potential.* They differ in the policies they recommend to achieve this goal.

Savings and the Dutch Miracle in Keynes's Frame of Reference

Keynes framed the issue of savings through the following question: Can governments' actions prevent expectations from being lowered, or can they even raise them? He discusses the answer with unusual clarity (relative to the rest of the book) and at great length in the final chapters of his book, linking it with what later became known, misleadingly, as the "paradox of savings." He relies on Mandeville's *Fable of the Bees,* whose verses he quotes extensively, and which once again links this discussion with the English views of the Dutch miracle.

Keynes thought that people will try to save more when they lower expectations and aspirations, and become pessimistic about future incomes. He felt that governments should try to prevent aspirations from diminishing after prolonged periods of rising unemployment. On this point Keynes agreed with Gessell, Hobson, and Malthus. But his arguments have nothing to do with the simplistic mechanics and algebra of the Hicksian IS-LM framework. He wrote:[61]

> Adam Smith has stated that capitals are increased by parsimony, that every frugal man is a public benefactor, and that the increase of wealth depends upon the balance of produce over consumption. That these propositions are true to a great extent is perfectly unquestionable. . . . But it is quite obvious that they are not true to an indefinite extent, and that the principles of saving, pushed to excess, would destroy the motive to production. *If every person were satisfied with the simplest food, the poorest clothing, and the meanest houses, it is certain that no other sort of food, clothing and lodging would be in existence.* . . . The two ex-

tremes are obvious; and it follows that there must be some intermediate point, though the resources of political economy may not be able to ascertain it, where, taking into consideration both the power to produce and the *will to consume,* the encouragement to the increase of wealth is the greatest. (363; italics added)

This is the broader context of Keynes's policies. He thought that governments could restore confidence, encourage consumption, prevent people from lowering their aspirations, and thus "unlock savings." I would prefer to say "unlock innovative and entrepreneurial potential," to avoid confusion. But in contrast to the rest of his obscure book, there can be little doubt here about what Keynes means, since he says it in plain English. His view has nothing to do with the simplistic ways in which savings and investments are discussed today, or with the whole framework of macroeconomics.

Keynes's next question was: How can governments raise expectations and unlock people's potential? He discusses in this context the eighteenth-century, Dutch-born Mandeville's *Fable of the Bees,* which was one of the most widely debated pamphlets in England at the time. Keynes says that his "general theory" is in agreement with Mandeville's views and that Mandeville's fable shows best why public works at particular times of unusually high and persistent unemployment will improve the situation by preventing the trap of lowered expectations and "the paradox of savings."[62] Let us look at Mandeville's text that Keynes quotes and see how it identifies the engine of sustained growth.

Mandeville satirizes the conflict between virtue and prosperity. One day the bees are smitten with virtue and begin leading sober lives, giving up ambition and becoming modest and frugal. The result is the Great [Bee] Crash:

> But, Oh ye Gods! What Consternation,
> How vast and sudden was th'Alteration
> In half an Hour, the Nation round,
> Meat fell a Peny in the Pound.
>
> As Pride and Luxury decrease,
> So by degrees they leave the Seas.
> Not Merchants now, but Companies
> Remove whole Manufactories.

> All Arts and Crafts neglected lie;
> Content, the Bane of Industry,
> Makes'em admire their homely Store,
> And neither seek nor covet more.
>
> For 'twas not only that They went,
> By whom vast Sums were Yearly spent;
> But Multitudes that liv'd on them,
> Were daily forc'd to do the same.
> In vain to other Trades they Fly;
> All were o'er-stock'd accordingly.

However, before the bees lowered their expectations, the situation was quite different:

> The Root of Evil, Avarice
> That damn'd ill-natur'd baneful Vice,
> Was slave to Prodigality,
> That noble Sin; whilst Luxury
> Employ'd a Million of the Poor,
> And odious Pride a Million more;
> Envy itself, and Vanity,
> Were Ministers of Industry;
> Their darling Folly, Fickleness,
> In Diet, Furniture and Dress,
> That strange ridic'lous Vice, was made
> The very wheel that turn'd the Trade.

And the moral of all this is:

> Bare Virtue can't make Nations live
> In Splendour. They that would revive
> A Golden Age, must be as free,
> For Acorns as for Honesty.

This view of human nature implies that prosperity depends on provoking among people "envy and vanity: the ministers of industry," which leads them to trade. This may sound sarcastic, but it is not, or at least not as much as it may sound to modern ears. Although we are now accustomed to give a negative interpretation to the term *envy,* and a positive one to *emulation,* throughout the seventeenth century the two terms were synonyms.

Envy also meant "wish, desire, longing, enthusiasm," without connotation of bad will. It meant the desire to equal others in achievement, and people spoke about "honest, virtuous and innocent" envy.[63] At the same time, the term *emulation* had the negative connotations that today we associate with *envy.* It meant not only "ambitious rivalry for power" but also ill-will between rivals, grudges against the superiority of others, and jealousy. So Mandeville's "Envy Itself and Vanity / Were Ministers of Industry," published in 1705, had a different meaning than it does now. Which policies encourage ambition and emulation (in today's sense of the words), and which ones discourage them and provoke envy (in today's sense of the word) are among the questions raised later in this section and in chapter 5.

Mandeville also noted that the reputation of the Dutch for frugality does not date from the *good* times but from the *bad* ones, when Philip II of Spain "began to rage over them with that unheard-of Tyranny."[64] It was during these times that the Dutch, "rather than to become a Victim to the Spanish Fury, . . . were contended to live upon a third Part of their Income, and lay out far the greatest part of their Income in defending themselves against their merciless Enemies."[65]

But savings spent on the military for fighting the Spanish can hardly explain the Dutch people's eventual prosperity, concludes Mandeville with obvious good sense (otherwise why should one ever cut down on military expenditures, even during peace?). His explanation for the Dutch success lies elsewhere:

> The Dutch may ascribe their present Grandeur to the Virtue of Frugality of their Ancestors as they please; but what made that contemptible Spot of Ground so considerable among the principal Powers of Europe, has been their Political Wisdom in postponing everything to Merchandize and Navigation, the unlimited Liberty of Conscience that is enjoy'd among them, and the unwearied Application with which they have always made use of the most effectual means to encourage and increase Trade in general. (185)

Expectations of "hardships and calamities of war" made the Dutch save more and invest more in the military and resistance to oppression (however measured). But their political institutions and trade made them rich.

There is no evidence that savings and investments in the face of hardships explain the eventual prosperity of the Dutch. As Simon Schama notes in his recent book on the Dutch Golden Age, travelers to Holland described them not as frugal people but as "free-spending prodigals." Public ceremonies reflected their taste for opulence. The Flemish towns developed during the Golden Age a tradition to produce "Renaissance ceremonies of unrivaled splendor in the North."[66] In fact, many observers deplored the prodigal behavior, though Schama adds that:

> This was no more than the latest version of the Roman stoic lament for the sybaritic corruption of republican virtue. That it was much rehearsed by Dutch moralists throughout the seventeenth and eighteenth centuries is not in doubt, but whether the flocks ever heeded their Jeremiahs (except in times of national crisis) is more doubtful. (295)

Mandeville was not the only eighteenth-century writer who was skeptical of a causal relationship between frugality and prosperity. Nicholas Barbon, John Houghton, Dudley North, Hume, and others also thought that the gratification of wants was wholly compatible with national fortune.[67] What else but the expectations of fulfilling such wants by trade motivates people to make greater efforts? These observeps viewed private investments and harder work, whatever form or shape they took, as consequences of expecting better times.

Can government policies induce people to expect such times by manipulating savings or by calling their expenditures "investments"—the view implicit in macroeconomics? The answer is *no,* although, as shown in the previous chapter and sections, there are situations when government expenditures are useful, when funds are spent on education, health, or welfare of the poor, giving them hope and stake in what the business society is doing by helping to unlock their potential. But these expectations have nothing to do with the manipulation of savings and aggregate demands, or any "general" models.

Some macro-economists admit their partial failure when they state, for example, that "good macroeconomic policies . . . are not sufficient for outstanding productivity performance." (De Long and Summers 1992, 5)

The last quotation appears at the beginning of a recent article by De Long and Summers that displays all the flaws of typical macroeconomic research. It uses official aggregate data from a number of countries around the world, ranging from Israel to city-states of Hong Kong and Singapore, as well as countries like Italy, Brazil, Argentina, and others. Without discussing the meaning of the numbers and in spite of the quoted reservation, they conclude their statistical analyses with the recommendation that governments subsidize investments in "equipment," because only such an investment has "externalities." (What investment can be carried out without "equipment"?) They also suggest that "certainly cases can also be made for strategically selected investments in infrastructure and in education," though they admit that they cannot measure their benefits. Finally, they add that "even in the absence of compelling evidence of external benefits, there is a case for increasing public investment in those countries where investment rates have lagged and are low by international standards" (25). They do not specify what, if not political advocacy, explains this case.

Economists' Growth Theories: The Latest Fashions

In order to show how off the mark macro-economists' views of growth continue to be, let us take a detailed look at Robert Barro's recent sequence of influential studies on the subject.

The latest in the sequence starts with this observation: "A key issue in economic development is whether economies that start out behind tend to grow faster in per capita terms and thereby converge toward those that began ahead." This is a startling beginning.

Every economist who is interested in economic development knows—or should know, if she/he examines stretches of a hundred years—about the rise and decline of regions, cities, nations, and empires. The decline was at times relative, at times absolute: the Amsterdam episode is not an exception. Here is an observation made 2,500 years ago by Herodotus in his *Histories* (Book 1):

> For most cities which were great once are small today; and those which used to be small were great in my own time. Knowing, therefore, that human prosperity never abides long in the same place, I shall pay attention to both alike.[68]

There is plenty of evidence that societies, be they cities or larger units, leapfrogged one another not only in Ancient Greece and Rome but in many other parts of the world. Societies that were far behind not only caught up with those who were ahead but even outdid them. Of course, this also means that societies that were ahead fell behind, which implies that poor places grew faster than richer ones. Athens and Sparta, Rome, Byzantium, Spain and Portugal, the Italian city-states, the Arabs, the Ottoman empire, the Dutch, the English, the Chinese, South American countries—they all rose and also declined, not only in relative but also, at times, in absolute terms.[69]

So why does Barro even raise the question "*whether* economies which were behind tend to grow faster"? Everybody knows the answer. Some societies not only caught up but outdid others, whereas other societies fell behind and did not catch up for decades or centuries.

The hotly debated key questions are: Why does leapfrogging occur? How does it occur? How long does a society need to catch up? Can the neoclassical models of growth explain why some societies fall behind not only relatively but in absolute terms? Barro's framework, relying on Robert Solow's "neoclassical growth model," is incapable of handling either these questions or many of the problems to which it claims to give answers. As for Barro's statistical results: as shown below, they are little more than statistical artifacts, though some of his ideas are sound.

The transitional growth process on which Barro relies, draws on Solow-type neoclassical models, within which the important questions cannot be dealt with. In these models there is no uncertainty, no opportunities for trade to be discovered, no financial markets, no poor, no government, no wars, no cities, no diversity of skills, and no commercialization of knowledge. The only human thing in this model is a trivial choice between physical and human capital, depending on relative returns. Thus, although growth rates may vary, the possibility that there will be no growth or that societies can fall behind just does not exist in terms of the model's postulates themselves.[70] The model makes one prediction: a country's per capita growth rate tends to be inversely related to its starting level of per capita income. The convergence between poor and rich countries is brought about under certain conditions through the adjustment of capital-labor ratios. Barro claims that, based on his statistical examination, this model describes growth patterns around the world. Close examination reveals that this is not so.

Statistical Results, and Their Database

As noted above, historians know that many societies and regions have suffered not just short-term, cyclical declines but declines over very long periods of time. Barro's international sample makes additions to this list. Since the model on which he relies excludes such a possibility, isn't such evidence sufficient to invalidate and discard his model? The usual defenses, that generalizations are necessary in science and that the appropriate method for judging the relevance of a theory is to examine whether the statements are valid in a statistical sense, do not apply in this case.

Yes, generalizations are necessary in science, but for only one reason: to discover exceptions to the rule. However, in this case the exceptions have already been discovered. We already have sufficient reason to discard the Solow-type models.[71]

Although Barro presents no model that would show how to link growth, violence, and black markets with Solow's simple-minded, neoclassical growth model, on which he claims to rely, he makes a strong statement. He argues that for the international comparison he obtains the inverse relationship between a country's growth rate and its starting position—as predicted by the neoclassical model and as he obtained for the United States too.[72] Upon closer examination, the result is not a miracle. It just shows that if one is ingenious and patient enough to mine a body of national and regional statistics with a statistical reliability in mind, but without relevance to the source, meaning, or significance of the data, one will be able to get pretty much whatever statistical result one wants.[73]

Where do the aggregate numbers come from?

In the latest international investigation, Barro (1993) uses aggregate data from seventy-three countries, each with only five observations, whereas in the 1991 investigation he used a larger sample, where about a quarter of them referred to African countries notorious for their unreliable statistics, be they about demography or aggregates.

Here are two examples. In 1992 it was widely publicized that Nigeria did not have a population of 100 million, as claimed, but of only 80 million. In Cameroon, nobody knows what happened to life expectancy or fertility: the last census was done in the mid-1970s. The numbers that appear in official statistics about these countries are based on projections from that time—which also produced Nigeria's now-discarded 100 million figure. Looking at aggregate data from countries getting international aid, I am always reminded of the numbers that came from an area in China in two enumerations. In one, the population was 28 million. Five years later, it was 105 million. The reason for the difference: the first census was done for tax and military purposes, the second for famine relief.[74] What if all the sub-Saharan African data—for which Barro uses a dummy—and other data as well suffer from such problems?

One of the explanatory variables in Barro's statistical analyses is the black market premium on foreign currency. But if there was a black market in foreign exchange, one would like to know how many other goods and services were traded in black markets and whether or not they were captured by the national statistics. As discussed in chapter 1, there is an extensive literature about black markets in South American, African, Asian, and even European countries (Greece, Spain, and Italy having the largest estimated shares), none of which (or in Italy's case part of which) is counted in national statistics. Barro does not refer to any of these problems.

There are other difficulties with international comparisons. For a long time, the number of children in rural families has been far greater than in urban ones, one reason being that the opportunity cost of raising kids on a farm is lower than in the city. Thus, a lower per capita income in rural areas exaggerates the poverty of these families: income per capita, correctly calculated, could be similar. When this situation applies, one would like to know how much of the differences in average incomes among and within states and countries in Barro's examinations were no more than statistical artifacts. There is a vast literature on the subject of comparing cost of living between urban and rural settings when life expectancy or other demographic variables differ or change and when small-scale agriculture experiences a relative decline in the course of economic development.[75] Barro does not raise any of these topics either. He uses the official figures, known for their unreliability.[76]

Political Stability

One of Barro's conclusions is that "the message from the policy variables included in the regressions is that more interference with markets and political instability are adverse for economic growth" (1993, 10). One problem with this argument is that frequently societies which were politically stable were among those whose governments interfered with trade.

To be sure, Barro does not want one to conclude that growth has been adversely affected by political instability in Spain following Franco's rule, by political instability in various Latin American or South American countries after throwing out one dictator or another, or by political instability following the fall of communist regimes.[77] And, although the current constitutional debate in Canada will never lead to a revolution and may not be captured by Barro's political instability variable, Canada no doubt suffers from political instability. Even if Canada does not break up, there will be a redistribution of powers from the federal government to the provinces. Does such political instability necessarily have adverse effects? Since, in general, countries do not break up without being politically unstable for a while, one wonders when political instability is favorable to prosperity and when it is not.

A brief summary of historical events will clarify this point and will also come up later in an additional context.[78] The 1688 Glorious Revolution was a critical factor in England's growth. Repeated fiscal crises of the Stuarts led them to engage in forced loans, to sell monopolies, and to render property rights less secure in the early seventeenth century. Parliament and the courts became engaged in the struggle against the monarchy, which led to civil war and a series of failed experiments with political institutions. The Glorious Revolution restored stability, with Parliament controlling financial matters, and an independent judiciary. The long period of instability led to the establishment of those institutions that played a critical role not only in England's but also in Singapore's and Hong Kong's rise centuries later.

Or consider a more general example, far more troubling in its implications, for those who want to study growth through narrow, disciplinary, technical prisms. The religious wars in Europe were terrible, but eventually they led to the separation of Church and State. Societies where the two remain linked—Russia before the Communist Revolution, Islamic countries, China during long periods in its history—have prospered less than others. Some historians and legal scholars view the lack of separation, with its greater monopoly of power and limited diversification of ideas, as one of the greatest obstacles to prosperity. Yet these societies may be considered politically stable for long periods of time.[79]

The breakup of communist regimes requires a separate discussion, though in this case too the eventual failure of the system had to do with the fact that trade and finance were prohibited.[80] Barro's type of statistical analyses would superficially confirm the positive correlation between political stability and growth rates in these countries—when they were communist. Except for recoveries after wars, this would be little more than a statistical artifact. The numbers that passed for national statistics in these regimes were little more than tricks pulled out of a hat. They were meaningless: outputs were exaggerated and goods were recorded at fictitious prices. The resulting aggregate numbers showed growth, but life expectancy was declining, infant mortality was rising, and people had to wait an increasing number of hours for food, and years for phones, cars, refrigerators, furniture, and apartments—all recorded by official statistics as being available at low prices. Thus political stability in those regimes had an adverse effect on growth, whatever was measured—chapter 5 will say more about this.[81]

I mention the case of communist countries because, in one of his articles, Barro predicts that it would take East Germany about 35 years to catch up partially, closing half of the gap between the eastern and western parts of Germany by relying on his statistical results. Based on the arguments about the importance of trading and financial skills in explaining growth, I would have made the same prediction: it would take them more than a generation (about forty years) to catch up. This prediction can be made without reliance on statistical manipulations of numbers whose meaning is far from evident.

The reason for the "one generation" prediction is that it takes about a generation to learn the diverse trading skills and to gain business experience of the type that political frontiers prevented East Germans from learning for a generation. I am not talking here about statistically measured "human capital" but about trading skills. During this time the older generation, who learned useless and even harmful material, will retire. (Remember the biblical story about Moses letting the generation of Jewish people raised as slaves die in the desert and letting the younger generation make a fresh start? I am not sure that we know much more about human behavior now than the biblical writers knew then.) I emphasize that the Germans were only a generation behind, because if they were further behind, it would take much longer to catch up. The shrewdness necessary for trade is passed from one generation to another through a variety of complex channels and institutions about which we know little. Formal education may help in using such skills. But formal education is no substitute for experience that can only be gained in open societies.

"Public" Goods

Barro (1993) concludes that "interference with markets and political in-stability are adverse for economic growth." Following this statement, he makes others showing how education has a positive effect on growth. Yet if there was a sector where governments obviously interfered with markets, by now for decades, it was education. One expects Barro to discuss this obvious inconsistency, but he doesn't.

Some economists have suggested that "education" is a public good and that the sector producing it should therefore be treated differently from others, which justifies government interferences. (Is it just a coincidence that people in the education sector write these studies? I am afraid that once again models and empirical tests come perilously close to confusing promotion of knowledge with the advocacy and rationalization of policy.)[82] Maybe Barro buys the "public good" argument, and that is why he treats education separately, in spite of accumulating evidence all over the world, and in the United States in particular, about the failure of the public system of education on every level.[83]

The argument about externalities to education is troubling on other grounds too (though, as argued in the previous chapter, there are good reasons to allow the poorer yet talented young people access to credit to finance their education). One can build just about any mathematical model—a logical speculation, that is—showing that if a sector has external effects, one government intervention or another can bring about a magical cure. Some make this argument about education, others—Bradford De Long and Lawrence Summers (1992)—just about any machinery and equipment. The latter two claim, as shown before, that because of big spillover effects, the return on such investments to the economy as a whole is far greater than to any individual firm (because of quicker diffusion of technology throughout the economy), which justifies government interference.[84]

What is one to conclude from such advocacy? If all sectors can be shown to have positive externalities and should be subsidized, then who will be taxed? If subsidies are selective, which industries will get them? And how are these conclusions compatible with the negative effect that Barro obtains about the effect of government interference on growth? Ronald Coase gave the best answer to these questions: one should worry as much about solutions that economists propose, as about the problems they claim they have solved. There are no magical cures, contrary to what all these mathematical speculations based on externalities suggest.

These observations should not imply that economists cannot generalize about historical change and examine which portions of general theories are relevant. But for one to use economic and statistical analyses effectively, it is not enough to know their principles. As Frederic Lane once pointed out, the principles of mechanics and electricity are the same for every machine and electric circuit. But knowledge of them will not help the engineer or technician to repair anything unless he knows the type of machine he has to repair. Likewise, an economist should be acquainted with the institutions of the society he/she is investigating before suggesting any repairs.

The United States Results: What Do They Tell Us
About Prosperity?

Barro's research started with the examination of growth patterns in the United States, looking at the fifty states. He considered them as small, isolated, closed economies producing identical goods—as required by the Solow-type growth models. He interprets the catching up of the poorer states as the result of adjustment of capital-labor ratios.

But that is not the story I read when looking at the numbers. What I read were two main stories, one general, the other more state-specific, both linked with what was said about the rise of trading centers.

The general one is that growth results from the diversity of skills that people practice in cities once a certain incentive structure is in place.[85] Amsterdam's typical case illustrated that, as income in the city grows and diversity and specialization increase, income increases, which affects more distant areas. As buying power in these more distant areas increases, markets grow even if population in the city from which growth radiates does not. If the new centers of growth attract people, the process is reinforced.[86] This is what happened in the United States. The urban population grew at an annual rate of roughly 2.79 percent between 1900 and 1930, and 2.00 percent in the next thirty years. Less urbanized areas grew more quickly than those that were already urbanized. The measured convergence between and within states reflects increased specialization and increased division of labor as growth radiates from various centers, and has nothing to do with substitutions between undefined labor and undefined capital.[87]

In his comments on Barro's U.S. investigation, Blanchard (1991) also criticized the findings, though on very different grounds. The next quotation reflects his main point and leads to my next main one, linking growth in some areas with specific innovations:

> In light of [Barro's] model, the reader may conclude that the *main* fact about regional growth in the United States has been the convergence of personal income per capita, presumably caused by the adjustment of capital-labor ratios. This conclusion would be wrong. Surely, an equally important fact is the amazing range of employment growth rates across states . . . over the last 40 years average annual employment growth rates have ranged from close to 0 percent for West Virginia to above 5 percent for Nevada, Arizona, and Florida. The challenge is to reconcile this range of growth rates with the authors' fact of convergence in incomes per capita. (160; italics in original)

Blanchard's observation is the same one that puzzled English observers during the seventeenth century when looking at Holland: how can one have both increasing employment and high wages?

The answer is simple, although aggregates will not reveal it. It is the emergence of state-specific novelties (i.e., unlike Barro, not dealing with the states as if they were producing identical goods)—keeping in mind that we are talking not about people in different countries but about people making decisions under similar institutions and thus similar incentives.

The story of Nevada's novelty is different from those of the rest of the states, and the lesson it gives for growth theory is indirect, although it still shows how an innovation, legal one in this case, brings prosperity to an area. The innovation was that Nevada legalized the gambling industry when other states outlawed it.[88] The southern states' link with an innovation—the air conditioner—is more interesting.

Heat and humidity prevented some industries from spreading, but nice, dry weather attracted others. Initially, two of southern California's biggest industries—entertainment and aerospace—came there for the latter reasons. Textile mills, for example, could not be built in humid places. They demanded solutions for controlling moisture in textiles by adding measured quantities of steam into the atmosphere. (This procedure was initially called "conditioning the air," and was the origin of the word *air conditioner.*) A physicist, Stuart W. Cramer, presented the first scientific paper on the topic before the American Cotton Manufacturers' Association in 1907.

Printers and lithographers were the other major industrial group looking for solutions. Fluctuations in humidity and temperature caused them numerous problems: paper expanded and contracted, ink flowed or dried up, colors varied between printings.[89] Willis Carrier, an engineer graduating from Cornell, came up with the first commercial air-cooling system in 1902, responding to an assignment from a Brooklyn printer. But only in 1919 did the first air-conditioned movie theater open in Chicago. Offices and department stores installed them during the 1930s and 1940s, and claimed that it increased productivity: all employees voluntarily arrived early and left late. Because of the war, not until the 1950s did air conditioning spread over the United States—coinciding exactly with the rapid growth in both employment and per capita income starts in the warmer states or the warmer parts of states (like California). Between 1950 and 1988, employment grew at a rate of more than 5 percent a year in Florida and Arizona, whereas the U.S. average is between 2 and 3 percent.[90]

In brief: innovations (technological as well as statutory) led to the significantly larger growth in employment rates in the southern states, to specializations across states, and to additional division of labor. The commercialization of knowledge was the engine of growth. Adjusting labor-capital ratios—the main feature of the Solow-Barro arguments—reveals nothing about prosperity and the way it spreads.

Conclusions

If one wants to learn something about prosperity and to draw conclusions about policies, one need not look at aggregate national statistics. Instead, one must pay attention to the incentive structure and the costs imposed on trade. To do so one must draw on a detailed examination of taxes, regulations, traditions, and institutions. I suspect that economists avoid such examinations because they rely on models of *national* aggregate units. They hide the fact that commercialization of knowledge, combining trade, finance and innovations, and the resulting diversity of skills enhances a society's ability to sustain prosperity.[91] The focus on national aggregates and policies also prevents us from viewing these changes within the international context. During the last decade many countries became hospitable to foreign investments and more stable politically, which implies that Western governments' ability to tax has diminished significantly. Entrepreneurs, merchants, and financiers—the "vital few"—can leave the Western countries' shores and set up businesses in new, hospitable climates, bringing prosperity to new centers.[92] Attempts to deal with the resulting problems by reacting to changes in macroeconomic national aggregates can only mislead.

Thus, to learn about prosperity, economists should focus their examinations on features of centers of skill that either radiate influences through "innovations" or fall into oblivion, rather than on national aggregates. They should compare Moscow and the port of St. Petersburg; Venice and Milan on one side (one a port, the other on trade routes) and Rome on the other; Barcelona and Madrid; once-cosmopolitan Montreal, now falling behind, and thriving Vancouver; Shanghai and Beijing—the list is long. Economists should stop focusing on nations as units, even if that is in the politicians' interests, or on administrative units that create national statistics; they should concentrate instead on trade, finance, and the institutions required to practice them.[93]

With these reminders let us look next from yet an additional angle at institutions facilitating trade. The commercialization of knowledge relies on a system of *promises* to buy, to sell, to lend, to rent, to deliver, to work, to pay, to redeem. All these exchanges are made in trust that the value of the currency in which they were made does not vary significantly. How to maintain such trust, what the consequences are when it is lost, and how this loss is linked with both government finances and political institutions, are subjects discussed in the following chapters.

Chapter 4

Inflation and Central Banks: Matters of Trust

Anyone who is convinced that he can fine-tune the economy doesn't
know what he is talking about.
  —Arthur Burns, as quoted in *Time,* December 28, 1987

Volatile inflation causes uncertainty because it interferes with trade. Trade
is a system of explicit and implicit contracts to buy, to sell, to lend, to
work, to pay, to redeem. When there is price stability—which, as explained below, is not the same thing as "zero inflation" as measured by one
or another rigidly computed price index—people sign contracts on the
basis that there will be no discrepancy between "real" and "nominal"
values during the length of their contracts. As Alan Greenspan, Chairman
of the Federal Reserve, put it: "For all practical purposes, price stability
means that expected changes in the average price level are small enough
and gradual enough that they do not materially enter business and household financial decisions."[1]

If they do "materially" enter business and household financial decisions, people will rewrite the contractual arrangement, adding a clause
about adjustments in case prtce levels fluctuate. As shown in this chapter,
this is indeed one of the things that people did when facing volatile
inflation. The practice is called indexation. If all contracts had such
clauses, and if measured fluctuations in price levels would perfectly
capture monetary pressures, nobody would care or write about inflation. In
fact, there would probably be no inflation.

However, for reasons briefly mentioned in chapter 1 and examined in
greater detail here, indexation is a distant second best to a policy of price
stability. This is so not only because price indices suffer from many flaws,
but because one type of contracts in the economy—those between businesses and households on one hand, and the government on the other—are
not indexed. They are renegotiated only after a lag, or not at all (capital
gains tax in the United States, for example).

If one looks more closely at the emergence and consequences of both new contractual arrangements and new markets in response to volatile inflation, he/she can answer a number of questions:

- What are the costs of inflation?
- When and in what sense can one say that there is too much pursuit of price stability?
- What are appropriate roles for central banks, and why it is difficult to carry them out? How are these roles linked with the governments' fiscal policies?

Costs of Inflation

Since contracts between governments and the private sector—tax brackets, in particular—are not always renegotiated, households and businesses end up paying more taxes when inflation rates rise, whether the inflation is expected or not. Also, since brackets are not adjusted even if interest rates correctly anticipate inflation, part of people's savings will be transferred to governments.[2] If inflation is not anticipated, an even greater fraction of savings would be transferred (due to the government's outstanding debt and progressive taxation in particular).[3] Of course, this is exactly why inflation existed in the past. It is also the reason why some societies have it today, and others expect it.[4]

Governments tried to neutralize partially the fiscal consequences of their inflationary policy in a number of awkward ways. When they did not index tax brackets, they allowed both government employees and employees in the private sector to get untaxed benefits in kind.[5] (One should not be surprised to see that when people are pushed into higher brackets, because of inflation or just steep progressive taxation, they increase demands for government benefits in kind, be they schooling, health care, food, or transportation.)[6] Governments also offered subsidies to businesses.[7]

The volatility of tax brackets, combined with the capricious ways in which households and businesses were compensated, complicated the ability of businessmen and financial institutions to make calculations and raise funds on the private market, which distorted decisions on investments and led to additional demands for government intervention.[8] Thus one impact of volatile inflation was an increase in faulty decisions.[9] Another was the increased volatility of interest rates and emergence of markets and institutions to deal with it. Let us look at such adjustments in some detail.

Responses to Volatile Inflation

The inflation rate in the United States during the late 1970s hovered between 10 and 14 percent. After 1982 it hovered around 4 percent. During the 1970s short-term interest rates fluctuated between 5 and 10 percent, rising above 20 percent at the beginning of the 1980s and hovering at around 8 percent after 1983 for the rest of the 1980s. Whereas the volatility of interest rates complicated some businesses' calculations, it provided opportunities to others.

Financial markets responded by developing a wide range of financial instruments in response to the change in expectations about future inflation and interest rates. Financial markets offered interest-rate swaps and caps, which provided insurance against sudden interest-rate change. They offered new financial instruments for long-term financing and also the trading of mortgage-backed securities, which reduced the risk in home lending.[10] People invested more in housing and real estate as hedges against inflation.[11] The emergence of some markets, the expansion of others, the additional government intervention in response to fluctuating inflation, and the attempts to insure against it show its costs. However, aggregate data will not reveal them.

I make this last, trivial remark because, in spite of the evidence on the costly adjustments that people make when inflation is volatile, some economists still ask "Why is inflation a bad thing?" "That's a surprisingly hard question to answer," writes Paul Krugman (1990, 52). "In fact, it is one of the dirty little secrets of economic analysis that even though inflation is universally regarded as a terrible scourge, most efforts to measure its costs come up with embarrassingly small numbers."[12] Krugman is not alone in holding this opinion. In another typical cross-country, macroeconomic research project relying on aggregates, Alesina and Summers (1992) find neither a substantively nor a statistically significant relationship between central bank independence and high unemployment or slow growth, nor evidence that the monetary discipline associated with central bank independence, which reduces the level and variability of inflation, induces large benefits "in terms of real macroeconomic performance."[13]

To jump from a statistical examination of aggregates to these conclusions just shows from an additional angle why the whole idea of "macroeconomics" and the measurement of aggregates misleads us. Consider the emergence of innovative financial instruments and the expansion of financial markets in response to the greater inflation and interest-rate volatility. These markets impose additional transaction costs on trade, which could have been avoided.[14] In other words: as far as the national economy is concerned—and here one must talk about the "national" economy since we discuss issues linked with a "national currency"—the costs of carrying out trade have increased. When inflation rates fluctuate, more intermediate goods are needed to produce the same amount of trade. But national aggregates will not reveal the additional transaction costs since they just add up everything: for instance employment will diminish in the manufacturing sector but increase in the real estate and financial sectors.[15]

Let us put this observation differently. Both the innovative response and expansion of financial markets and the option of investing in real estate make people better off when governments pursue inflationary policies. But if an economist wanted to evaluate the costs of fluctuating inflation and decide on their magnitude, she/he should examine which markets, among all those counted in national aggregates, existed or expanded *because* inflation was volatile. Then one could have seen that their output is a tax on trade rather than an intermediary product helping to expand it, as is the case with other financial outputs.

The examination also could have revealed how many investment opportunities were forgone because people invested in real estate, gold, art, stamps, coins, foreign currency, etc., as hedges against inflation only (or, in the United States, also as hedges against paying higher taxes, since mortgages can be deducted).[16] But aggregate accounting does not (and cannot) distinguish between the impact of different financial instruments or identify the expansion of the real estate and other sectors as hedges against inflation.[17] This flaw should not have confused economists on the nature of the problem they claimed to examine. However, as shown above, it did.

When these measurement problems are added to all the additional ones discussed in the previous chapters, one can understand why neither time-series nor cross-section analyses of aggregates computed in countries with different institutions and expectations can reveal much about the costs of volatile inflation. What reveals the costs is exactly a look at the emergence of new arrangements to insure against such outcomes, regardless of how they were counted in national statistics.

These observations should not imply that economies experiencing fluctuating inflation did not grow (as measured by the GNP), or that they grew necessarily less than other economies in which there was no inflation. Frequently we do not know what measured growth measures. And as shown in the previous chapters, the underlying process behind what we think of as growth is a complex process on which government policies, other than the monetary ones, have a powerful effect.

Neither should these observations imply that interpreting changes in price indices becomes problematic only when there are monetary pressures. Price indices, like all aggregates, have inherent flaws, and when inflation is volatile, more flaws develop, as shown in the following sections. One can only inform the public about their existence and explain that they are inevitable even in the absence of monetary pressures. Once central banks establish credibility in maintaining stable price levels, people will cease paying attention to changes in price indices anyway.

Practicing Indexation

Indexation is a method of protecting incomes against volatile inflation by linking them to changes in the general price level in the economy. An alternative method of protection is to guess the future rate of inflation and renegotiate contracts if there are deviations from such guesses.

If this were the case, a $10 payment when there is no inflation would become $11 when 10 percent inflation was anticipated. However, if the guess were incorrect and the realized inflation was higher than the one expected, then one of two things might happen. Either one party would lose, or the parties would renegotiate the contract. The latter option is a costly process, occurring with considerable lags.

In contrast, an indexation clause achieves the inflation protection automatically when inflation rates vary: $11 will be paid since the negotiated contractual agreement states that the payment will increase if there is 10 percent inflation. As a result, indexed contracts, be they in financial or labor markets, can be entered for a longer duration than non-indexed ones. The advantage of indexation for long-term contracts is greater than for short-term ones. Let us say that an individual gives a loan for three months at an annual rate of 10 percent on the assumption that inflation will proceed at a rate of 4 percent. Instead, unexpectedly, he faces inflation that proceeds at an annual rate of 12 percent. The individual will lose 0.5 percent of the real value of his initial principal. In contrast, the value of a loan to be repaid with accumulated interest at the end of five years will, under the same circumstances, lose almost 10 percent of its value.[18]

At first sight—superficially, as it turns out—all parties in private markets should have viewed indexation as beneficial. It was expected to maintain the purchasing power of financial obligations and of incomes. It was also expected to reduce the costly and laborious transactions involved in frequently renegotiating contracts. It didn't work out that way exactly.

As inflation persisted, the practice of indexation spread. But many countries that enthusiastically adopted the practice, decided later to alter, abandon, or even outlaw it.[19] When incomes or bonds were fully tied to the CPI, many problems linked with its measurement surfaced, one of them being that changes in the CPI did not reflect monetary pressures. The problems were hardly trivial, and they led to difficulties in conducting monetary and fiscal policies, to arbitrary redistribution of wealth, and to increasing demands for government intervention as a result of the latter.

Close attention to indexation practices reveals additional costs of volatile inflation. It also shows what a policy aiming at "price stability" means, and why it should not be confused with a policy of pursuing "zero inflation," as measured by one or another index. From an unexpected angle this experience also sheds light on the much-debated question of the relationship between inflation and unemployment.

Wage Indexation in Canada

Wage indexation has been practiced in Canada with varying frequency since the Second World War. The practice became widespread when inflation rates fluctuated considerably from year to year, and was abandoned once there was no inflation. For example, indexation clauses existed in 21 percent of all collective bargaining agreements in the early 1950s, when inflation rates varied between 2 and 10 percent. However, by 1967, after a long period of price stability, this proportion had dropped to 2 percent. Whereas in 1969, after a long period of price stability, only 9 percent of wage contracts contained cost-of-living adjustment clauses (COLAs), 54 percent contained them by 1975, when inflation rates started to vary again between 3 and 11 percent.[20]

Krugman (1990, 53) suggests that "for an economy with inflation of

10 percent or less . . . the demonetizing effect of inflation is trivial." This is a strange comment: even an annual inflation rate of 5 percent doubles the general price level in fourteen years. Can the doubling of the price level every fourteen years have no effect if tax brackets are not adjusted? Since the indexation practices reflect a demonetizing effect, and as the Canadian evidence shows, they happened even when inflation rates varied in this range, Krugman is obviously wrong. People went to great lengths to adapt to the volatile inflation even within this lower range, demonetizing their contracts. Both the adaptations and their consequences were costly, which suggests that the demonetizing effects of even moderate inflation were far from trivial. Let us see why.

The Partial Indexation of Wages

When import prices rose, the index to which wages were linked reflected this increase. Since the importing country became poorer, not everybody could be compensated for the resulting increase in a price index.[21] Either wage contracts had to be renegotiated and wages lowered to reduce costs, or costs rose faster than prices and unemployment increased, or some combination of both.[22] That is what happened.

There was widespread indexation of labor contracts in Brazil during the 1963–73 period, when the inflation rate varied between 16 and 85 percent; in Israel, where since 1948 the inflation rate varied between 5 and more than 100 percent; and in Belgium, Canada, Denmark, Finland, and the Netherlands during their experiences with both moderate and high, variable inflation of the 1950s and 1970s.

Indexation clauses gave only partial protection against inflation. Even when there was full indexation on paper, a partial protection was achieved through a variety of means, in particular the blatant manipulation of the price index (in Brazil, for example).[23] Partial indexation in these countries also resulted from the recognition that changes in indices, to which wages were linked, did not reflect monetary pressures only.

The cost-of-living clause in Danish wage contracts, though automatic, was suspended for one year following the 1967 devaluation, so as not to compensate for something that a country cannot be compensated for when its terms of trade are worsened. In Belgium, whenever the CPI rose 2 percent, an automatic adjustment was paid. The average inflation rate between 1962 and 1972 was about 4 percent. It jumped to 7 percent in 1973 and to 16 percent a year later. As a result, the employees received eight separate automatic increases in 1974, not counting any "real" ones. Thus, nominal wages rose by 20.9 percent in 1974, unemployment doubled to 7 percent, and industrial production was running at about 70 percent of its capacity. After a series of strikes, unrest, and negotiations, the practice of wage indexation was changed. The renegotiated contracts a) reduced the frequency of salary increases to two a year; b) froze that part of workers' salaries above $1,000 a month; c) raised wages by less than the increase in CPI; and d) revised the index used for indexation practices.

After a surge in import prices, indexation was abandoned and banned by law in both France (in 1958) and Finland (in 1968). Following the rise in oil prices, the practice was suspended in the Netherlands in 1974 and 1975. In Norway the government had the right to decide what proportion of the change in import prices would be compensated for. It decided on 70 percent until 1973, before the jump in oil prices, and 45 percent immediately after.

It would be misleading to think that only import prices and devaluations can cause problems when inflation is volatile and people try to adjust by indexing contracts. In June 1974, a steep rise in the price of potatoes in Belgium threatened to trigger a new wage hike and caused a national crisis. The problem was solved by deliberately understating the price of potatoes in the Belgian CPI.[24]

Thus, after strikes and negotiations the contracting parties end up with partially indexed—that is to say, partially demonetized—wage contracts.[25] But the partial indexation clause becomes only one component of the wage contract.[26] Another component is its duration. Contracts with indexation clauses are, in general, of longer duration than those without.[27] In 1970 in Canada, when there was no inflation, the average duration of all contracts was about twenty-six months, whereas in 1977 it was only sixteen, and even those with indexation clauses lasted only twenty months, on average. This suggests that volatile inflation shortens planning horizons, even when people have the option of including an indexation clause in their contract.[28]

Other countries had similar experiences. In Israel wage indexation was never full. The terms of the indexation clause were negotiated between the Histadruth (the labor union),[29] the Manufacturers' Association, and the government. The agreement defined a ceiling wage, up to which the automatic COLA was to be paid (as in the revised Belgian system),[30] and determined the frequency of payment and methods of calculation. At times the automatic compensation was given for only 70 percent of the increase in the CPI, as the remaining 30 percent was assumed to reflect changes in prices caused by variations in the effective exchange rate, in international prices, or in indirect taxes.[31]

This evidence shows a number of things. First, volatile inflation imposes costs even if people adjust their contracts. Second, changes in price indices reflect more than monetary pressures; they reflect both changes in relative prices, which in theory they should not, and political manipulations, about which the theory says nothing.

Indexation in the Public Sector and Financial Markets

During the 1970s increases in family allowances, old-age security payments, tax brackets, and wages in the public sector were also partially demonetized in Canada. They were adjusted to movements in the CPI, although the adjustment was neither complete nor automatic. (Yet recall that inflation during those years fluctuated between 2 and 13 percent only.)

The indexing of tax brackets, family allowances, and public utility rates prevented both faulty decisions and the lengthy renegotiation required in revising legislation or regulations.[32] If this hadn't been done, incomes would automatically have been pushed up into higher tax brackets even if the purchasing power of incomes before taxes had not changed. Brazil and Israel are the two countries whose governments also issued indexed bonds, where the principal and interest were linked, more or less, to the CPI.[33] Let us see why it was sometimes more and sometimes less.[34]

Before introducing the indexed bonds, the capital markets in Brazil collapsed because of high and variable inflation (43 percent in 1959, 32 percent in 1960, 43 percent in 1961, 61 percent in 1962, and 81 percent in 1963). Yet, contrary to what one might expect, the Brazilian-indexed treasury bonds were not a great success during this period (even at the end of 1973 they accounted for only 19 percent of the government's outstanding debt). One reason was that these bonds yielded a lower return than other assets, since there was a five-month delay in the availability of price-index statistics. Another reason was that the government used an underestimated inflation index in calculating the nominal return on these indexed bonds.[35]

Conditions were similar in Israel: between 1950 and 1953, the average inflation rate was 23 percent, with large variability around it.[36] Beginning in 1955 and ending in 1962, for reasons to be explained below, the Israeli government applied the principle of indexation to both its borrowing and lending.[37] The "index bonds," however, were not all linked to the CPI: some were linked to the dollar, some to the CPI, and some to both in equal proportions. The sale of the new issues quintupled between 1955 to 1956, and quintupled again between 1956 and 1962. The practice came to an abrupt end on February 9, 1962.

The reason was a 67 percent devaluation. The debtors in dollars found themselves with an overnight nominal debt increase of 67 percent. Within two weeks, the government abolished or modified—retroactively—the terms of the linkage. The experience also revealed that indexing to foreign currency on a large scale imposed severe constraints on the government's ability to carry out monetary policy. A successful devaluation must be accompanied by a restrictive monetary policy. The existence of large portfolios of dollar-linked bonds, whose nominal value would automatically increase as a result of the devaluation itself, worked in the opposite direction. (Notice, however, that to a lesser extent this same problem arises if contracts are linked to an index that does not exclude the impact of devaluations.)[38] The Israeli government ceased issuing bonds linked to the U.S. dollar. From 1962 on, the government's bonds were linked to the CPI only.[39]

During the 1970s, when inflation rates rose and became more volatile, the nominal market price of the indexed bonds rose to their maturity value—exclusive of indexation—so that their real rate of return became zero.[40] One reason for the indexed bonds' popularity was an anomaly in the income tax law that treated as income the full receipts of interest on the nominal bond while not treating as income that part of the money return on an indexed bond that represented indexation. There is no logic for such a distinction.[41] In 1976 and 1977, the indexed bonds were no longer fully indexed. The rate was lowered first to 90 percent and later to 70 percent of the increase in the CPI, in order to exclude, approximately, the impact of changes in import prices and in indirect taxes, similar to patterns negotiated in wage settlements.[42]

While making these innovations, the government did not tie the loans from its development budget to either the dollar or the CPI, not even partially.[43] This mistaken decision aggravated the problems the government was facing in the more inflationary 1970s.[44]

This discussion of indexation practices around the world reveals additional aspects of the costs of volatile inflation. More important, it draws attention to flaws in another mismeasured aggregate—the inflation rate. Implications of taking these flaws into account when discussing monetary and fiscal policies in general are examined next.

Inflation as Measured by the CPI

During the last few years, the CPI in Canada became one of if not the single most-watched economic indicator, not because of indexation practices but because the Bank of Canada seemed determined to reduce the rate of growth in this particular index to zero. However, while politicians, the public, and the Bank of Canada paid much attention to the monthly figures, several economists and officials in Canada, the United States, and other countries have expressed dissatisfaction both with its computation and with the harm of "too much pursuit of price stability," (as De Long and Summers put it, though they do not discuss any measurement problems).[45]

In the wake of such interest, and of the idea that monetary policy should produce a stable "price level"—which indeed should be its aim—we should take a closer look at the ways price levels are actually computed, while keeping in mind the previously described experiences with indexation. This clarification shows not only the specific circumstances when *too much* pursuit of price stability can be harmful, but helps us better understand the links between monetary and fiscal policies and measured changes in price indices.

The Weighting Issue

Recall briefly the observations made in chapter 1 on the computation of price indices. There is a significant difference between the ways the CPI is calculated in the United States and in Canada. *The Evaluation of Issues Relating to the Price Index,* prepared for Statistics Canada in March 1988, emphasized—and criticized—the difference. The Canadian sample of prices is not selected at random but is referred to as a "judgmental sample."[46] This means that the staff at the statistics bureau decides the number of price quotations and the selection of outlets and items priced, with little if any record left about the decisions or their rationale.[47] The reliability of the choices made has never been examined. If the staff had common sense, the results might be good. If they lacked it, the results might be bad: we do not know what is happening today.

Initially, Herb Segal recommended the method to select outlets in

1977. The recommendation was based on the results of the 1974 Retail Commodity Survey, conducted almost twenty years ago.[48] For various reasons his recommendations about the number of price quotes and types and number of outlets were adopted, but others concerning the frequency with which they should be sampled were not. Also, since no Retail Commodity Survey has appeared since 1974, there has been no systematic update of his work.[49]

Sampling is not the only problem with infrequently adjusted fixed-weight indices. Until the spring of 1982 the weights in Canada were based on a 1974 basket. "The inflation rate" measures the percentage change in the cost of this basket, even though consumers change their consumption patterns to adapt to changes in relative prices. For example, between 1967 and 1974 the inflation-rate calculation was based on a basket of goods in which food represented 24.8 percent, housing 31.4 percent, and recreation 6.9 percent. In 1974, when these weights were reestimated, it was determined that people were spending relatively less on food and more on housing and recreation. As a result the weights were changed to 21.5 percent, 34.1 percent, and 8.3 percent, respectively.[50]

Yet for seven years the changing consumption patterns were not taken into account when changes in the CPI were being solemnly calculated and announced. A simple numerical example, relevant for the period that these numbers cover, shows how. Suppose that the prices of gasoline and heating oil unexpectedly increase by 25 percent. As a result, people reduce their average consumption of these items from 15 to 11 percent of their expenditures. Simultaneously, they increase their demand for warmer clothing in winter and lighter clothing in summer (because offices and homes are less heated in winter and less cooled in summer), for public transportation, fuel-efficient cars, and vacations closer to their homes. The calculation of the CPI does not take these substitutions into account. Instead, for years, it is being calculated as if people continue to spend 15 percent of their incomes on gasoline and heating oil.[51] Thus, although this sudden, unexpected 25-percent increase in the price of gasoline and heating oil leads to a 3.75-percent increase in the CPI (15 percent multiplied by 25 percent), this number is meaningless in economic terms. Similarly, the CPI overestimates the change in the cost of living when either the domestic currency depreciates or the prices of imported versus locally produced goods unexpectedly increase. In such instances as well, substitution from imported to locally produced goods is not being considered. Changes in the price index reflect the increased cost of a basket of goods and services that people can no longer consume, since society has experienced sudden impoverishment.

Consider another numerical example from a later period. Two widely used price indices in the United States—the CPI and the personal consumption expenditures (PCE) deflator—have been close for a long time, but they diverged substantially in 1979 and 1980.[52] In 1979 the CPI increased by 12.7 percent, the PCE by 9.5 percent; in 1980,—they increased by 12.5 and 10.1, respectively. (At the same time, what was then the experimental rental equivalence series for the CPI, about which more will be said later, increased by 10.6 and 10.8, respectively.) One source of discrepancy is their different way of measuring housing costs. Another is that, whereas the CPI is a fixed weight index, the PCE is essentially a variable or current-weight index. (Note that in 1979 the 2.9 percent difference between the CPI and PCE deflator was still attributed to changing weights or differences in weights on gasoline purchases.)[53]

Changes in sales (indirect) taxes, as reflected in the CPI, also overestimate changes in the cost of living. Assume that, instead of increasing revenues by raising indirect taxes, the government raises revenues by increasing income taxes. I am not aware of any argument that could explain how changes in the latter form of taxation can be "inflationary." But then, how can it be that the effect is inflationary if the government raises the same amount of money through indirect taxes?

When governments raise indirect taxes, the measured inflation is a statistical artifact. To see why, consider the following question. What does the government do with the money it raised through the increased indirect taxes? Assume that other taxes were not lowered and there was no monetary expansion. The increased revenues will either be spent to diminish the government's debts or be given back in subsidies, transfer payments, or salaries of government employees. This means that wealth will only be redistributed. But then how could the impact be inflationary? Some prices will go up, and others down. This conclusion is even more obvious if, with the increased indirect taxes, other taxes are diminished. In this case too, it is unclear how the resulting reallocation can cause inflation. Only relative prices change unless, simultaneously, there is a monetary expansion. But that is another story, discussed later.

Several governments have been successful in making this point clear to their citizens when introducing sales taxes (Netherlands, Scandinavian countries, for example). They used an adjusted price index series for a while, which excluded the influence of both increased taxes and diminished subsidies.[54] These revised indices were used for the inflation correction of wages, of income tax brackets, and of other contracts, rather than the customarily used CPI. However, this was not done in Canada, in spite of the fact that Statistics Canada released studies showing that in 1991 regulated prices increased at a much higher rate than non-regulated ones: 10.5 percent for the former, which have a weight of 26 percent in the basket on which the calculation of the CPI is based, compared to 4.4 for the latter.[55] Over a longer period of time, between 1983 and 1989, regulated prices increased by more than non-regulated ones, 6.1 percent for the first group versus 3.9 for the rest.[56] Just two items in the first group— tobacco and alcohol—have the substantial weight of 5.6 percent in the CPI.[57] The taxes on both are viewed as major sources of revenues and have been substantially raised in recent years.[58]

The implications of the resulting mismeasurements are important. Assume that the increase in regulated prices is not only due to the fact that governments wanted to raise taxes but also because the respective industries are becoming less efficient. That means that the country is becoming poorer. Yet, if significant portions of governments' expenditures are linked to the mismeasured CPI, the outcome is either unexpected increases in taxation or increased borrowing. So, before central banks adopt a policy of pursuing a stable price level, they must understand the flaws in the calculation of price indices, in particular those linked with changes in taxation and regulated prices.

If they do not, central banks end up pursuing a far too restrictive policy when reacting to every upward movement in the CPI. Such a policy's impacts are the same as that of linking wages and financial contracts to price indices that reflect other than monetary pressures: diminished production and higher unemployment. Only in this sense can there be such a thing as "too much pursuit of price stability."

New Products and Quality Changes

The Seminar on the CPI, held in Geneva in 1988 and organized jointly by the Economic Commission of Europe and the International Labour Organisation, reported that the fixed-basket concept of calculating the CPI requires the set of outlets to be constant throughout the index period. This does not happen because some close and new ones open. But even if the "physical" product stays the same, the change in the quality of service should be taken into account (meaning, for example, that it takes less time for the buyer to purchase the product), which would lower the price. This problem is linked with a far broader one, that of taking into account innovations of any kind in a price index.

How to figure in new products and quality changes when measuring both price indices and the "real" GNP is an ancient, much-discussed, and still unsolved problem.[59] It may pose particular problems now, when there are drastic annual changes in the performance of computers and VCRs;[60] when the picture quality of color television sets and the sound of stereo equipment and other home entertainment equipment becomes better; when microwaves in most households produce unmeasured savings in time and effort, and so forth.[61] The Geneva report (1988, 7) dealt with quality changes. But the only thing that the participants could agree upon was "the need to take [such] changes into account when measuring price changes." There was no agreement on how: some argued that seasonal products, new fashion lines, etc., should be excluded. Others said that they should be included but that attention must be paid to discounts. There was general agreement only on the fact that, if such items are introduced, it should be done in such a way as to give a "representative picture of the year" and that "the methods used [should] be generally understood and accepted by the public."

The Geneva report also raised more serious issues, like measuring the impact of regulations, the use of catalyzers in cars, and the introduction of antipollution devices in general. Though the consumer pays more, does the change reflect an improvement in quality, and should the "real" price of the final product therefore be lowered? The participants agreed to deal with this issue on a case-by-case basis.[62] The *Evaluation Report* of the Canadian CPI (1988, 28) notes that although Statistics Canada recognizes the importance of taking into account changes in quality, "an exact process by which a given quality change is estimated and the relative importance of these changes is not well documented." This report, in addition to the one written in Geneva, emphasizes that economists did not find ways of solving the problem.

This should be no cause for despair. But it does imply that paying undue attention to a figure whose reliability is unknown, and either basing monetary policies on it or linking financial assets to it, may lead to bad surprises—as such policies did. Next let us turn to a problem in the measurement and interpretation of price indices that makes all those mentioned pale by comparison.

The Measurement of Homeownership Costs

The main problem with measuring the yearly value of homeownership is that owners are consumers, investors, and speculators—although the only distinction between the latter two is that one buys and sells more frequently than the other.[63] Volatile inflation and demographic changes turn more and more consumers into "investors" and "speculators," yet the CPI will not measure the shift. This leads to a substantial overestimation of inflation. This component has about a 40 percent weight in the Canadian CPI, and within the component a 40 percent weight is given to mortgage interest.

Indeed, the Geneva report arrived at only one main conclusion shared by all participants: the major causes of the international non-comparability of consumer price indices were differences in the behavior of housing markets and in the treatment of owner-occupied dwellings, and the problems of taking into account rent controls. The report suggested that, if one wants to make international comparisons, one should calculate an index that excludes housing.[64] (None of the macroeconomic studies mentioned in this or the previous chapters did so.)

Alternatively, one could try to calculate a domestic price index according to methods adopted in other countries. Peter deVries and Andrew Baldwin (1985) did such an exercise and looked at what would happen to the Canadian CPI if the methodology used to calculate homeownership were the same as the one used in the United States.[65] Their recalculation suggests that, at times, the two measures will diverge significantly. For example, during the twelve months of 1981 the inflation rate as measured by the official CPI was stable, being between 12 and 13 percent relative to the year before. Had the U.S. methodology been used, the inflation rate would have been much higher, during four months being above 15 percent relative to the respective months a year before.

However, during the twelve months of 1982, the official Canadian CPI varied between 9.3 and 11.4 percent relative to the respective months a year before. Had the alternative methodology been adopted, the CPI would have varied between 5.2 and 11.3 percent. In fact, while the official CPI would have dropped from 11.4 to a mere 9.3 percent, the alternative one would have dropped from 11.3 to 5.2 percent.[66] Which index, then, should be used for guiding monetary policy (if price indices are chosen as guides)?[67] And what were the real rates of interest?

The Canadian treatment of homeownership costs is arbitrary. Ownership housing is not treated as a capital good (which would result in the "rental equivalence approach" now used in the United States). Nor does it reflect a user-cost approach.[68] According to DeVries and Baldwin, the Canadian approach " . . . is designed to detect the impact of price changes on homeowners' specific costs of shelter, as opposed to tenant's specific cost of shelter." In contrast, the U.S. approach is designed to answer the question: "How much rental income do the owners of housing units forego when they choose to occupy the units themselves instead of renting them out?" The owned accommodation costs by components is calculated here according to these weights: repairs, 9.2 percent; property tax, 20.1 percent; insurance premium, 4.7 percent; mortgage interest, 40.2 percent; replacement costs, 20.6 percent; other, 5.2 percent.[69] Yet apparently only Canada and the United Kingdom include mortgage interest costs in their consumer price indices. Japan does not, and whereas the United States did so for many years, a reform in the early 1980s took these costs out of the index.[70]

This large discrepancy in price indices, depending on the method used to take homeownership into account, is not unusual. Alan Blinder found similar magnitudes when he contrasted alternative ways of calculating the CPI in the United States. According to one calculation, the inflation rates in 1977 and 1978 were, respectively, 9.2 percent and 12.4 percent, whereas, according to another, they were 2.5 percent and 5.7 percent, respectively.[71]

Blinder's major point was similar to the one made here. He warned of what might happen when economic policy is guided by unreliable numbers, and if transfer payments were linked to such numbers. In the United States the credit controls and budget-cutting exercises of early 1980, for example, were apparent responses to what Blinder calls "the bogus 18 percent inflation rates then being reported by the CPI"; he concludes that "this is one inflationary distortion we could all live better without."[72] Also, a major worry in the United States was that many of the government's expenditures (Social Security benefits, for example) were in fact indexed, and that the index was inaccurate for this purpose.

Monetary Policy

Whatever the difficulties with price indices, there should be little doubt that when monetary pressures dominate, all the aforementioned measurement problems become relatively less important. When the price level increases by 950 percent (as it has in the United States since 1933), or by 4,000 percent (as it has in England since 1933), monetary policy is at fault, not the techniques of computing price indices. Neither should we doubt that, when and where central banks commit themselves to maintain a stable price level, they can do it. The examples of the Swiss, the German, and recently the Canadian experiences should leave no doubt on this point. Gavin and Stockman (1993) document another case: Sweden's, between 1930 and 1936. This last case is unusual, as the authors emphasize, because of the following reason:

> To our knowledge, there is only one case in which a central bank based its policy actions on a price-index target. This was a six-year episode in the 1930s when the Swedish central bank, the Riksbank, targeted that nation's CPI at around 100. . . . [T]he actual price level stayed well within 3 percent of this figure throughout all six years, crossing the price target twice. Although this was a rather brief period in history, it illustrates that a measurable objective for price stability can be achieved. (311–12)

The fact that the central bank can do it does not mean that it should. The question is: What is the meaning of the change in the price index? If the change is due to mismeasurements because of any of the non-monetary disturbances discussed before—be they in fiscal policy (the introduction of indirect taxes), import prices, demographic changes effecting housing prices, regulated prices, and so forth—then pursuing the policy of "zero inflation" would be a mistake. It can lead to the same harmful effects as did widespread indexation to rigid indices: diminished output and increased unemployment.

Only in this very limited sense can one say that governments can choose between a bit less unemployment and a bit more inflation. Otherwise this choice—once reflected by widespread belief in the Phillips curve (unfortunately still solemnly included in all the textbooks)—does not exist.[73] When, then, can monetary policy be guided by changes in price indices, if at all?

Recall that in 1968, when Milton Friedman advocated monetary targets rather than price-level targets as guides for policy, his reasoning was based on practical grounds rather than theoretical ones:

Of the three guides listed [exchange rates, price index and money stock], the price level is clearly the most important in its own right. Other things the same, it would be much the best of alternatives. . . . But other things are not the same. . . . [W]e cannot predict at all accurately just what effect a particular monetary action will have on the price level, and, equally important, just when it will have that effect. Attempting to control directly the price level is therefore likely to make monetary policy itself a source of economic disturbance because of false stops and starts. (108)

This argument and the evidence on the relatively constant trend in velocity in one monetary aggregate in the United States (M2, but neither M1 nor M3) led Friedman to recommend that controlling for its stable growth could prevent unnecessary economic disturbances. Relative to the alternatives, this seemed the best option then, since it was the stablest relationship he found.

This does not mean that the relationship stays stable at all times. The 1980s saw significant changes in financial markets: deposit deregulation (due to reduction in reserve requirements),[74] substitutes for deposits (new securities in response to the higher interest-rate volatility in particular), technological innovations in handling cash, and disturbances linked with the significant increases in governments' deficits—about which more will be said below—which led to speculations about how the monetary authorities will offset them. Also, although there was a large increase in the level of currency in circulation in the United States (about 9 percent annual rate in 1992), much of it left its shores to replace domestic currencies in Eastern European and Latin American countries. Roughly two-thirds of the currency is now estimated to circulate outside the United States, a much higher proportion than in the past.[75] Also, in 1992, the sharp drop in short-term interest rates has made bank deposits unattractive compared with bonds and equity mutual funds. People shifted their savings out of bank-time deposits, included in M2, into other assets which are not. All these effects combined have led to a volatile velocity and to the conclusion that since the 1980s the control of short-range targets for monetary aggregates provides less information about inflationary pressures than it did in the past.[76]

When this is the case, monetary authorities who want to maintain a stable price level face difficult choices. They may decide to look at many things, in addition to the standard computation of monetary aggregates. If they choose to look at changes in price indices, they must be aware of their flaws.

Consider the 1991 U.S. data. The producers' price index rose by 0.3 percent, whereas the CPI rose by about 4 percent. Central banks that would emphasize the harm of the 4 percent inflation, and the goal of eliminating it, shape the perception that the index measuring the 4 percent change is the targeted, correct "inflation" rate. If the bank will pay attention to this rate and shape monetary policy accordingly, financial and labor markets will pay attention to this rate too. Interest rates and wage negotiations will reflect this figure. But what if 0.3 percent was the "correct" rate?

The outcome of tight monetary policy would be diminished production, increased unemployment, and increased rates of bankruptcy. Such were the outcomes recently in Canada, where the central bank fought "inflation," although a 15 percent sales tax was introduced during this time. Though the very tight monetary policy (the money supply dropped by more than 5 percent during 1990) no doubt succeeded in lowering measured inflation, it raised interest rates significantly and brought about a severe recession.[77] The effect was worsened when the higher interest rates drove up the value of the Canadian dollar and diminished exports significantly, causing additional hardships. Canadian taxpayers had to pay interest on foreign debt and also cover the expanding gap between imports and exports. These sequence of events did not escape the attention of international financial markets. In 1992, after more than two years of such misguided monetary policy, the Canadian dollar dropped, and taxpayers lost more in the central bank's additional misguided speculation to prevent the drop.

In this sense, there can be such a thing as "too much" pursuit of "zero inflation."[78] The sequence of events in Canada started with the proper objective of restoring price stability, but the policy then turned into an absurd pursuit of "zero inflation."[79] However, the unusually tight monetary policy in Canada and other countries should be seen in additional, broader perspectives.

The Independence of Central Banks

When velocity is volatile, monetary aggregates flawed, and measured changes in price indices have their flaws as well, there are no perfect solutions. One anchor left to monetary policy is its tradition and the views of the individual who happens to be the central banker. When the bank even lacks the tradition of political independence and success in maintaining a stable price level, the anchor is nothing more than the views of the central banker and his attempts to establish credibility.

No economic or other theory explains how a central banker can reestablish credibility or how long it will take, when the confidence was shattered because of the bank's inflationary policies in the past. It is in this context that one must see the Canadian monetary policy described in the previous section, and also interpret the recommendation of Paul Volcker, the chairman of the Federal Reserve Board from 1979 until 1988, to pass a statute defining the purpose of monetary policy as the stability of the currency and nothing else. He wrote:

> I believe the recurring difficulty in acting before inflation builds momentum could be reduced if central banking statutes in the U.S. and other countries stated more explicitly that the main continuing purpose of monetary policy should be the stability of the currency. That would follow a pattern already set in Germany. No doubt the manner and intensity with which that goal is pursued at specific times will and should be influenced by surrounding circumstances. For that reason I don't have much faith in setting specific targets for reducing inflation; the pseudo-precision implied would risk undermining rather than reinforcing credibility. But the vacuous admonitions that a monetary authority be all things to all men—for growth, full employment and stability—risk confusion and misunderstanding about what a central bank can really do.[80]

Can the passing of such statutes today serve as an anchor? Probably so, as the German and Swiss monetary histories suggest (though the first only after bad cases of hyperinflation, and the second showing recently that it still can make mistakes in controlling inflation). It can also help eliminate inflationary expectations more quickly. But as Mark Twain once said, "laws are sands, customs are rocks," and nobody knows how long it will take for laws to become customs.

Volcker notes that such a statute can also achieve something else. Once people believe that central banks pursue the goal of price stability and nothing else, they will pay no attention either to variations in one or another price index, or to the exact technical details by which central banks control targets for monetary aggregates. Also, people will neither request nor expect the pseudo-precision of zero inflation, when they are confident that, whatever central bankers do, "nominal" and "real" values will be substantially the same over longer periods of time.

However, as pointed out above, passing a statute does not necessarily mean that people will expect its enforcement. Statutes are only words on paper. How does one assert independence of the central bank from government? It is possible to see some central bank's tight monetary policy from this perspective. As long as economists and policymakers talk in terms of Keynesian trade-off between inflation and unemployment—the first a technical issue concerning central banks, the other a political one—and no established traditions prevent them from playing with monetary and fiscal policies before elections, then no very clear-cut policies will establish credibility. Passing a statute does not guarantee it, though it could serve as a start.

Insulating central banks from political pressures today is important, because it changes expectations about the likelihood of governments' monetizing their rapidly rising debts. Let us see next how this last feature enters into the picture, complicating central banks' tasks.

Monetary Policy and Deficits

Monetary policy in the United States, Canada, and other Western countries has been complicated during the last few years by the unprecedented deficits, and in Europe also by attempts to limit fluctuations in exchange rates while pursuing widely divergent fiscal policies. How are such policies linked with monetary ones?

Friedman's and the monetarists' views are frequently identified with rigid adherence to a stable monetary rule and opposition to discretionary policy. Yet Friedman's (1969, 107) writings suggest a far more pragmatic approach, as can already be inferred from the previous quotation and also from the next one, which links discretionary monetary policy to deficits. Although he argued that during "normal times" the best thing monetary authorities could do was to provide a stable background for the economy, he also thought that monetary authorities should deviate from rules at times, since they "can contribute to offsetting *major* disturbances in the economic system" (italics added).

One such disturbance, for which Friedman justifies departure from rules, happens when "an explosive federal budget threatens unprecedented deficits . . . [In this case] monetary policy can hold any inflationary dangers in check by a slower rate of monetary growth than would otherwise be desirable. This will temporarily mean higher interest rates than would otherwise prevail—to enable the government to borrow the sums needed to finance the deficits—but by preventing the speeding up of inflation, it may well mean both lower prices and lower nominal interest rates for the long pull" (107).[81] Whether or not the tighter monetary policy succeeds in achieving this stabilizing goal depends on a number of things, in particular what the government does with the borrowed funds.

Here the link with the discussion in the previous chapters should be made clear. If the funds raised by the government, whether on the domestic or the international markets, serve to finance increased investments, repaying them should be no problem, and the monetary policy Friedman recommended may indeed turn out to be beneficial. But if the use of funds is such that deficits do not diminish, government revenues do not increase since domestic production diminishes, and governments do not cut their expenditures, then there is a wide range of possible outcomes. Let me illustrate a few.

A common one occurs when governments misspend the borrowed funds. Krugman (1990) remarks:

> In April 1981, to take a representative example, Harvard economist Jeffrey Sachs wrote that "Much of the growth in LDC debt reflects increased investment and should not pose a problem of repayment. . . . This is particularly true of Brazil and Mexico." Only 16 months later Mexico announced that it was stopping payments on its debts; Sachs himself has become the leading advocate of large-scale cancellation of Third World debt. (185)

(In all, losses on Western loans to the Third World are estimated in the hundreds of billions of dollars.)[82] Borrowing, combined with tight monetary policy, may bolster the currency's value for a while. However, if the borrowed funds are misspent, the policy leads eventually to devaluation, and the cost of the loan becomes a burden.

Another case is Germany's. The optimistic expectations that with West German help the Eastern part would catch up quickly, have been disappointed. The 100 billion DM spent there did not produce much. But it led the German government to stray from its traditional monetary and fiscal discipline, which in 1992 it tried to restore through a much tighter monetary and fiscal policy.[83] For the moment, commitment to stable domestic price level and high interest rates, combined perhaps with expectations that the funds are invested and will eventually bring goods for sale in markets, has bolstered the value of the DM. If the latter expectations are disappointed, the DM will fall relative to other currencies.[84] If not, the tighter monetary policy will prove beneficial in the long run, as Friedman's arguments suggest.

The picture is more complicated for the United States. Recall that although budget deficits grew in seven of President Reagan's eight years, long-term interest rates and inflation fell, and prosperity increased, no matter what measure one looks at.[85] Expenditures on the military grew until the USSR and the Eastern bloc collapsed. As explained in the previous chapters, there were good reasons to look upon the United States's "Star Wars" as a good investment. It hastened the demise of communist regimes by imposing on them rising protection costs, which they could not finance. The more rapid end of the Cold War saved many resources for this and future generations in the West, although just how much will remain a matter of speculation forever. However, such a sudden demise has additional consequences.

In 1992, military expenditures in the United States were in the range of about $300 billion, when the deficits stood in the $350 billion range and the servicing of the federal debt at about $200 billion. The taxes that paid for the military spending showed up in costs and prices in the private sector, just as the costs of dikes showed up in Holland. If the oceans receded permanently, the taxes paying for dikes, which were productive before and helped produce trade, would cease to be so. Though they might be accounted in national statistics in the same manner, the taxes paying for the dikes would become transfer payments and a tax on trade, whereas before they were necessary expenditures that allowed trade to flourish. The same thing is true about military spending when threats disappear.

Consider now two countries similarly affected by the disappearance of security threats. One has more flexible political institutions than the other, and succeeds in adjusting its military expenditures and taxes more quickly. If both governments should borrow on the international financial markets, the one making the faster adjustment would see its ability to borrow enhanced (by lower interest) and its currency appreciate. If the other country tried at such times to tighten its monetary policy and raise interest rates, this would bolster its currency but diminish its exports. Unless fiscal adjustments are made and trade is liberalized, the latter country would fall behind, its currency would eventually fall, and its citizens would find themselves with a greater burden of debt. While all these processes took place, there would be speculation in both currencies, suggesting that exchange rates should certainly not be used as indicators for guiding monetary policy.[86]

Conclusions

Let us go from the simpler to the more complex implications of the facts and discussion presented in this chapter.

At the very least statistical bureaus should regularly publish two price indices: one recording price changes determined in unregulated markets and another in regulated ones. Next, they should simultaneously publish two series of price indices whenever there are significant changes in fiscal policy and import prices or a devaluation, one including and the other excluding their effects. Together with the publication of such series, bureaus of statistics should also acknowledge that they all may be subject to errors.

Such information by itself might help put monetary policy on a sounder footing. Nobody will announce with great solemnity that the CPI rose by 2.1 percent a month, when the error may be such that there is either a 20 percent chance that the rate of change is zero, or a 20 percent chance that the rate exceeds 4 percent. The additional information could also be useful in negotiating contracts in the private or public sector.

All the above may be useful when central banks try to reestablish their credibility and prove that their long-term goal is to maintain price stability. But keep in mind that commitment to this goal is not the same thing as commitment to the pseudo-precision of zero inflation as measured by one or another price index. Central banks should distinguish between the message and the noises that might come with it. Once they do, people will pay attention to the message, forget about the noises, and focus their attention on their everyday business.

The most important lesson of this chapter is the simplest: that the central banks should concentrate on price stability and nothing else. By pursuing any other objective, central banks impose a tax on trade.

Chapter 5

From Great Failures to
Great Transformations

Harm comes from not taking instructions from discussion before the time
has come for action.

—Pericles

Drab, dusty, decaying, devastated, dilapidated—these terms describe
Moscow. In the summer of 1991, it had just two bright lights that brought it
in line with western capitals: performances at the Bolshoi and the small
number of well-kept architectural delights within or just beyond the
Kremlin walls. And yes, during May and June 1991, just weeks before the
coup, it had a third.

Under the auspices of USSR's Ministry of Culture, the Church of Ivan
the Great, within the Kremlin walls, housed in the midst of such despair,
neglect, and lack of anything but the simplest food, one of the most
spectacular modern jewelry exhibitions by the Swiss Gilbert Albert. There
were tiaras, necklaces, bracelets, masks, and clocks in gold, silver, and
diamonds, all lavishly sprinkled with black, Burmese and Chinese pearls
as well as scarabs, emeralds, and black sapphires, gems that Princess
Diana and Nancy Reagan would have had difficulties finding occasions for
wearing, even during their days of glory. At least they could afford them,
something that could not be said about any Soviet woman or man, whose
average salary stood then at about 300 rubles, or $11 using the rate of
exchange being given to tourists, which was also the black market rate.
But it equaled $150, according to one of the official rates. (By 1992, these
fictional rates were abandoned, and the average salary stood at about 900
rubles, which in dollar terms went down to $8).

On the surface, absurd. But no more so than many other aspects of life
there, some of which will be examined here from an insider's/outsider's
perspective.

I was born and spent the first fifteen years of my life under a
communist regime. My first impression during recent visits was that, in the

thirty years that elapsed since I left that part of the world, everything was left to depreciate, from housing to factories, from roads to hospitals to machinery, no matter what the official statistics were showing.

In fact, until the eighties the official statistics of the USSR were showing growth. By now, however, it is acknowledged that even the CIA's much lower estimates by far overestimated the Soviet income per capita and underestimated the fraction spent by the Soviets on the military— something that came as no surprise to anybody who lived there.[1]

The fact that the situation had been deteriorating rather than improving since the 1970s could be inferred from some simple demographic numbers, whose political manipulation is less feasible. Infant mortality was increasing and life expectancy was diminishing.[2] Additional simple figures, like changes in the number of telephones and cars, the waiting time for apartments—even without adjusting for quality—captured the worsening situation far better than the changes in manufactured aggregate numbers. They showed that the USSR was falling further and further behind Western economies. By the mid-eighties, the United States had about 80 telephones per one hundred people, the USSR about 10. The United States had about 550 cars per one thousand people, the USSR about 36 (although, according to the aggregate, official measures, per capita incomes were getting closer).[3] If one adjusted for "quality," the discrepancy became much larger than these numbers suggest. One could spend hours on the phone trying to call distant localities, and if one really wanted to arrive at a destination, he would be well advised to get official transportation, having a chauffeur with good contacts who could get the car fixed each time it broke down.

The fact that the stores are empty, that the quality of available food, clothing, and cosmetics is shoddy, and that people spend hours in line to get even the simplest food at the still-low official prices (even after the January 1992 reforms), is by now well known. How did this happen? What are the immediate and long-term effects of prohibiting trade and finance— a characteristic feature of the once communist countries? This chapter starts by answering these questions. Then it shows something more: that a repressive, corrupt, monopolistic state, combined with the prohibition of trade, have led to envy, resentment, and passivity, and destroyed the tenets of civil society and prosperity—which are its people's ambition and the trust they share.

Our close look into this distorted mirror thus reinforces the conclusions reached in the previous chapters about trade being a key to prosperity. This examination also reveals that trade is not a simple matter of "freeing prices." Trade means reliance on implicit and explicit contracts, based on trust and a complex maze of institutions. In a society where the rulers weakened and even destroyed the trust people shared, and who prohibited the emergence of institutions necessary for carrying out trade, a decree from above to free prices will not bring about quick prosperity. It is a grave mistake to raise people's expectations and suggest that declarations—be they constitutions or decrees about prices—will bring about change. Time will pass before trust is restored and institutions necessary for enforcing the decrees' promises can come to life. It will take a long time to climb the road from serfdom—to paraphrase the title of Friedrich Hayek's book—and longer in some post-communist societies than in others, depending on the extent to which trust among people has been destroyed and the length of time that people were prevented from carrying out the trades of everyday living.

Trade under Communism

There were no "communists" in the communist countries, only opportunists and members of the Communist Party who adopted the label. The continuing resistance to change since 1985, to allowing other parties to emerge and come to power, occurred not because those who had been so long in power came to believe sincerely in communism, but because, after getting accustomed to the privileges of power, the members of the ruling party, the bureaucracy, the military, and all those who came to depend on them, did not want to end their lives with a significantly lower standard of living at best, or in jail at worst.

This opportunistic behavior was evident when, hardly days or weeks after the collapse of the regimes, many high-ranking officials, whose adherence to the regime had never been in doubt, announced that they favored democracy, pluralism, and other ideas that, if expressed just a few days beforehand, would have put them in jail.[4]

This rapid change should have been expected by anybody familiar with life under those regimes. Few people living there ever doubted that the regimes represented more than a minority's use of monopoly power in its own interest, with all the benefits that such power provides. The power was derived from a monopoly on all resources; it was rationalized by the obscure, confusing vocabulary of an ideology enforced by the army and security forces, and by the fact that those in power had nothing to fear during fictional elections.

Yet the officials' declared change of mind should not have misled observers any more than years of declared adherence to other slogans did; no one should have expected that the transition would be smooth or without risks, or take little time. One reason is that institutions necessary for trade, and others limiting political authority, are nonexistent, helping the *nomenklatura* to maintain power—under new names. The consequences are continued monopoly power, lawlessness, arbitrariness, and lack of trust, consequences of the rule of men rather than law.

Fearing such rule and denied access to use their skills, people lowered their aspirations and became less ambitious in the past. It was the fear and lack of opportunities that turned dogma into obedience in the Eastern bloc rather than any adherence to an ideology. Though we may diminish this fear, we do not know how long it takes to cure people of their long history of obedience to repressive regimes when they still expect backlashes and many of those who had power under the communist regimes still possess it.[5]

How long will it take to establish credibly that the institutions favoring political freedom and trade will endure and flourish? The previous chapter showed how difficult it is to reestablish trust in just *one* institution even in the West. Imagine the difficulty of establishing credibility in a society where institutions protecting people's rights to trade and to reasonable doubt did not exist for centuries. People freed from 72 years of communism in Russia may have become less obedient, but they have stayed suspicious, and with good reasons.

Many of the changes that happened until now are matters of semantics, and the *nomenklatura*'s skill of double-talk serves them well. Instead of calling themselves "top officials," the previous apparatchicks call themselves now "managers." This confuses Western observers into thinking that these "managers" are suddenly in favor of an open business climate just because they call themselves managers and their institutions "holding companies" rather than "branch ministries." In truth, although these managers preach competition in theory, they resist it in practice. The new vocabulary, music to Western ears, confuses observers and academics about what is going on. It shouldn't. Fortunately, it does not confuse too many businessmen: of the 60,000 Western businesses that tried to venture inside Russia, only 600 carried out their plans.

What is happening, not only in many parts of the former USSR but also in former Eastern bloc countries, is that the *nomenklatura* takes good care of itself and continues to reward those who obey them. The *nomenklatura* has first access to transfer assets to themselves and food to both themselves and their followers. Though the assets are officially held by "private" syndicates, they are not "private enterprises": at every step they still depend on enterprises owned by the state and need the *nomenklatura*'s backing. Also, as late as 1989, the more fortunate followers received the Zakaz, the special bonus food baskets customarily offered at factories and offices at the end of the year through the Communist Party patronage channel.[6] For the Soviet workers the provision of food *now,* rather than promises of plenty in some distant future, is a major concern. So the persistence of such arrangements maintains the nomenklatura's grip under a new "free market" name, penalizing those who try to deviate from depending on them.

Briefly: connections and getting favors are still the main games in town, and the idea of letting "ordinary" people have access to institutions to unlock their skills remains a foreign idea.[7] Of course, Western businesses willing to venture into Russia need the old *nomenklatura* under the new mask. Both sides can benefit by making a deal. That doesn't mean that the *nomenklatura,* even as a new business partner, will favor an open society. On the contrary, they are quite happy to maintain their monopoly power *and* become richer. The process is not different from what has happened in many Third World countries. And Russia is very much a Third World country, though one with nuclear arms and a still-powerful military.

The *nomenklatura*'s continuing attempts to maintain a system relying on connections rather than currency to allocate goods and services, though covered up by new pro-business vocabulary, slows down the emergence of trade. This is a problem today, rather than lack of entrepreneurial talent and aversion to trade among Russians. The latter is a myth the *nomenklatura* likes and has the incentive to spread. The next sections present the evidence that leads to this conclusion, before turning to more fundamental matters.

The Past

The way to get along and advance within the communist system was either to make a career by adhering to the ideological guidelines or at least to keep good personal contacts with the enormous bureaucracy making the decisions. This bureaucracy decided which factory to favor in the provision of materials and increased budgets, who would be punished and who would be forgiven for not meeting a plan's goals, who would get bonuses, who would get vacations and where, which workers would get the easier jobs or the more convenient shifts in a factory, and who would be conveniently overlooked when engaged in either dubious accounting practices or plain stealing. This arbitrariness, the rule of men rather than laws in every facet of people's lives, also grew from the fact that many of the laws in these countries prohibited activities required for normal life.

In the USSR, article 154 of the criminal code forbade "speculation," which was defined as "the buying and selling with the purpose of making a profit"; articles 153 and 162 forbade commercial "middlemen" and a number of other professions; and article 88 forbade foreign trade transactions and foreign currency "speculation" (Eastern bloc countries had similar prohibitions).[8] The Statute on Crafts and Trades of May 3, 1976, listed a number of forbidden activities, of which the most important were the preparation of food products (except for one's own use, or from self-produced material), the production of chemicals and leather goods, and the transportation of passengers and goods.[9] In Romania the use of cars was restricted, typewriters had to be registered, and access to libraries was denied. Since commodities like quality textiles and clothing, appliances, coffee, tea, and good cigarettes, not to mention "exotic" food like oranges, bananas, and chocolate, were available on black markets only, their purchase turned everyone into a lawbreaker. The local bureaucrats got many of their privileges not only because they had first crack at many commodities, they got items "under the counter," and decisions at the workplace depended on their goodwill, but also because of their power to disregard widespread stealing at the workplace and to enforce prohibitions—selectively.[10]

It was no secret that, while farmers in the USSR could own at most 0.5 hectare of land for their private use, they supplied and sold from these tiny lots 30 percent of the agricultural products, in spite of the aforementioned code on speculation.[11] The illegal private sector produced far more than just food; wine, liquor, spare parts for cars and domestic appliances, clothing, and books and records (illegally brought in after travelling abroad) were all available.[12] The nomenklatura got percentages or part of the goods.

Theft of liquid fuel by professional drivers, who resold it on the black market to car owners, has been a regular practice. When supervised, ten gas stations in Kursk took in 273,000 rubles. But during an equal but unsupervised period the sum turned out to be a mere 88,000 rubles. Numerical indicators of the magnitude of such thefts were the same elsewhere: in Orel the receipts rose by 200 to 1000 percent during supervised periods. The *Izvestia* thus estimated that a third of private cars ran on stolen fuel, although others' estimates ran as high as 80 percent.[13] Trucks were regularly "borrowed" from the workplace, be it the kolkhoz or the factory, and used for transportation. This was just one of the ways by which managers, bureaucrats, and administrators exchanged favors with the "second-class" citizens. Managers and high-ranking officials of enterprises had their houses and dachas built and repaired by enterprise personnel with materials belonging to the enterprise. In turn the managers closed their eyes when the cars and trucks owned by enterprises were used by the employees for their own purposes. There were many other exchanges among the privileged and those who were not: from the buying and selling of illegally imported goods,[14] to the practice of *tolkachi*, when middlemen—who were present even if not called by this name—ensured firms that they could bribe officials and thus guarantee supplies and permits.[15]

Thus bribes were common, and young workers were quickly taught to pay them. If, by chance, they happened to be starry eyed and did not want to pay bribes, or were reluctant to steal (or worse, tried to unmask the crime), they were rewarded with some back-to-back shifts, denial of vacations, being moved to the end of the waiting lists for an apartment (which could happen when one was demoted or dismissed), and the threat of being exiled to faraway places. Among the most pitied occupations was teaching: what could teachers steal to bribe their superiors or to resell to other members of society? Chalk?[16] Lord Acton noticed a long time ago that official corruption, which would ruin a commonwealth, was in Russia a salutary relief from the pressure of absolutism.[17] Without the customary bribes, everyday life would have been impossible under such regimes.[18]

Bribes did not necessarily take the monetary form one would expect in the West. In a society where most commodities, be they food, clothing, housing, electronic appliances, furniture, or cars, took much time to obtain, either getting the products themselves, or being informed about their availability and having a priority claim to them, was a privilege, not unlike a monetary bribe in other societies. Thus party members lived far better than the rest of the population, although how much better was a matter of rumor and speculation until the collapse.[19]

Not so after the collapse: the existing communication channels rapidly diffused the living standards of the East German party leaders, the Ceausescu clan, and the Bulgarian elite. Their lifestyles surpassed all that the second-class citizens imagined. At Wandlitz, in the isolated compound built for the narrow elite of twenty-three families in power, two maids were provided free for each house; the families had access to a department store, a swimming pool, and Western movies, banned for the rest of the East German public, among other privileges. The information about the Ceausescus, with their golden-plated bathrooms, their stocks of shoes, their caviar, their Swiss bank accounts, and their personal use of the national treasures, palaces, jewelry and art, was quickly diffused on television. The revelations about such standards of living, comfortable even by Western customs, suggested that party members had access to far more wealth than the customary bribes could allow them, bribes that common people there more or less learned to live with.

This information led to investigations of major embezzlements and confirmed what people in the Eastern bloc and the Soviet Union had already guessed.[20] It did not take long to find that much of the earnings of Communist Party–owned businesses in East Germany, in the range of $4.4 to $7.6 billion per year, were unaccounted for, which led to arrests, and that leaders of Bulgaria's Communist Party had Swiss bank accounts, which led to their arrests too.[21] Where these numbers appeared in official statistics, if at all, is anybody's guess.

Even the lower-level bureaucrats, who lacked all the privileges of their higher-ranking counterparts, such as higher pay, country houses, vacations, and preferential access to education for their children and to medical treatment, and who did not get any "tangible" bribes either, fear that, under a decentralized system, they stand to lose. These powerful groups will not give up money and power for the sake of their country's welfare, and they do not care about the fact that people's skills go untapped. The obstacles to trade have hardly been lowered in Russia, the exceptions being types of trade that benefit the renamed nomenklatura.

The Present: Entrepreneurs and What Is Stopping Them

It is frequently argued in the press and in academic circles that the Russians and the Eastern bloc need entrepreneurial help, since seventy years of communism have destroyed this trait of human nature there. As shown above, this is not the case.

There were plenty of entrepreneurs behind the facade of order in communist regimes, and not only were they taking "business risks," but they were even risking their freedom and lives when making such deals, something their Western counterparts never had to worry about.

Exchanges in black markets in both the Soviet Union and the Eastern bloc, contributed an estimated 30 percent to official production as far as food, transportation, building, repairs, and supply of clothing and smaller appliances was concerned—anything that could be produced on a small, less visible, scales. Thus we are talking here not about a small number of entrepreneurs but a rather large one.

Nor should one make the mistake of thinking that all black marketeers under the communist regimes can be compared to the Mafia in the United States, a comparison that Russian bureaucrats and intellectuals like—and have the incentive—to make. (After all, if entrepreneurs can manage the economy, who needs the bureaucrats and intellectuals advising and supplying them with theories and numbers?) "The black marketeers" were mainly involved in the supply and distribution of goods necessary for everyday living, rather than drugs, prostitution, or weapons.[22] One should remember Edward Shevardnadze's experiment in 1979, when he was the Georgian Party leader. After initially trying to eradicate black markets, he became convinced that it would be far better to legalize the activities that were previously outlawed. He thus legalized black-market industries so as "to tap their entrepreneurship," allowed "self-managed" firms, and abolished controls over the press and the arts.[23] The result of his policies? Georgia flourished far more than other republics.

What is missing in the new commonwealth today is not the ability of people to take risks, to spot demands, and to carry out a vision with discipline. The diversity of skills necessary to carry out trade is much smaller—never mind how many scientists and engineers they have (about 1.5 million), or how literate the population is.[24] Only a society open to trade produces diversity of occupations and adjusts its institutions. Trading in black markets in an essentially static society requires far fewer skills than trading in an open, changing society. Moreover, communism was also based on the idea of achieving economies of large-scale production, which further limited the range of skills and prevented diversity. (The idea also further centralized power by locating specialized gigantic enterprises in different republics, so as to make all depend on Moscow.)

Still, the entrepreneurial skills are there, as is the willingness to try things and incur hardships. Institutional obstacles prevent people from learning and using such skills and, through the experience of trial and error, diversifying them. What are these institutional obstacles today?

Entrepreneurs, Competition, and the Law

One role of governments is to maintain law and order. Under the communist regimes their other role was to make all decisions about production and allocation of resources. The government decided how much one factory should produce and to whom it should supply its production. This meant, however, that the whole idea of contract and the legal institutions interpreting it were redundant. In fact, there was and still is no independent judiciary system in Russia.

By departing from centralization in words, but without canceling regulations and abolishing institutions, the Russian leaders created a void that causes much uncertainty today. On one side the nomenklatura ventured into the void, transferring assets to themselves. On the other, this void also increased the Russian Mafia's power—opportunities are discovered and exploited under every system of government. If some institutions are absent, the entrepreneurial talent will be diverted into costly acts, trying to enforce property rights by other means. When the institutions appear, the talent will often go in more beneficial directions.

Declarations on "freeing prices" and reforms on paper did not mean what they implied in the West (after wars), since no one expected them to be enforced. On the contrary, passing laws and regulations that continue to be casually disobeyed (at times because nobody has even heard of them) brings into disrepute the new enterprise, the legal one in particular. And what is true about laws holds true for taxes as well. The government introduces a new tax or raises an old one, but they are not collected.

I happened to be in Moscow when the government announced that apartments would be privatized and that dwellers could buy them for symbolic sums. A very small percentage of Russians showed interest at the time. The same thing happened in November 1992, when privatization vouchers were issued. Again, only a small percentage of the population picked them up. A number of articles were written in the Western press about the Russians' lack of interest in private property. That's just not the case. When I asked Russians about their lack of interest in owning apartments, their answer was simple and pragmatic, though I confess, I don't have a scientific sample. Rents are low, and people do not expect the government to raise them. But they did expect private property to be taxed and ownership of apartments to bring costly responsibilities. So why bother buying up anything now? As to the vouchers: people don't believe that any of the state-owned enterprises issuing vouchers have any value. They know that only a small portion of government property is to be privatized by this method, and they also know that whatever value they might have had, the old nomenklatura–new managers have succeeded in putting their hands on it already. So why pick up valueless paper?

What else happens in such an uncertain environment, where nobody knows what the laws are, and nobody quite knows which actions are legal and enforceable, and which ones are not?

Entrepreneurship, Crime, and Bureaucracy

In Russia the few successful entrepreneurs face antagonism. This reaction has a number of sources and a long tradition.[25] The entrepreneurs' success is explained either by close contacts with the powerful bureaucracy, whatever they call themselves now, or with criminal elements.

The typically heard scenarios run something like this: an entrepreneur tries to go on his own, whether with a small store or a small enterprise. If he succeeds, he attracts the attention of some neighbors, who try to open a similar store or enterprise. If the new entrants succeed too, fewer accusations are heard. But if they fail, then one hears about the bureaucracy putting obstacles in their way, and that the successful undertaker benefited from his contacts rather than his talents or his ability of daringly taking risks and overcoming them. Such perceptions are frequently accurate, and they lead Russians to demand stronger enforcement of laws and recentralization of power, and also to harbor cynical attitudes toward competition.

Russians view criminal elements as venturing into the void left by institutions that enforced law and order. They also think that criminal elements and the nomenklatura use cooperatives and joint ventures to launder earnings and deposit profits in banks in sufficiently large amounts to buy up additional property formerly belonging to the state.[26] In farmers' markets the criminal intervention is viewed as taking a different form: they are said to control distribution and fix prices.

Shanker (1991a, b) describes recent episodes that show how competition, bureaucracy, and crime are linked in a complex maze. A woman who for seven years was a physics teacher decided at the age of 29 to open a small cooperative in May 1990 with three friends. They leased from the city bureaucracy in charge of arts and cultural activities for children an empty storefront in a suburb of Moscow. Soon after the opening, a group of tough young men "came into the cafe, and once they learned we were a cooperative and did not have a big state trading agency or a foreign firm as a partner for protection, the bargaining began." The racketeers offered "assistance and help," assigning guards at night, finding scarce food items, doing odd repair jobs—for 25 percent of the gross.[27] For several months, the arrangement worked to both sides' satisfaction. But one day an officer of the city cultural department from which they had rented the place came and said that although they had a five-year lease, they would have to break it. It turned out that the restaurant was "the prize in a razborka, or turf battle, between two rival mobs. Her original patrons, the guardians, lost."[28] The bureaucrat's compensation for intervening is not mentioned. Thus, it may well be that the Russian Mafia now has greater or more visible power. But there is no doubt that the nomenklatura cooperates with it, or that those who suffer now are those who suffered under communism—those without the contacts, even if they have skills.

The solution to lawlessness would *not* be to enforce the still-existing bad laws that prevented trade from flourishing, but to decriminalize much that was and still is illegal. No attempt should be made to rewrite every commercial law from the top; institutions and law should emerge through experience, as it has in all places where trade flourished legally or illegally, as shown in the previous chapters. Yet there is no reason to be optimistic about such policies any time soon, since the nomenklatura has no incentive to introduce them.

Contracts and Interpretation of New Laws

Whereas in the West oral contracts are rare, in the Soviet Union's black economy (as in black economies everywhere), such contracts were the rule. They were based on trust, ostracism, and punishment from the informal network if violated.[29] But apparently, before Gorbachev's time, only rarely was a "Mafia" type enforcement applied (although, due to the close interaction between the legal and black sectors, a criminal prosecution occasionally followed breaches of oral contracts in black markets).[30]

When Gregory Grossman asked black marketeers in the Soviet Union how large and complicated operations can be carried out by relying on the spoken word only, "the answer has been 'trust,' sometimes followed by 'after all, we are businessmen, not *apparatchiks.*'"[31] These businessmen operated on the same principle as their Western counterparts, the recognition of property rights, which, as Grossman notes, was enforced by "the customary law of the Soviet underground, nurtured by a philosophy of live and let live, and even with its adjudication arrangements; the informal networks plus corrupt patronage by officialdom; [and the] widespread corruption all around."[32]

Yet instead of legalizing much that was illegal and letting the black market's customary law serve as the seed of the new legal system, one of the first laws of the *perestroika* was the May 1986 law *against* "nonlabor" income. Its aim was the black market, and as one would expect, it eventually turned out to be ineffective. Nobody knew the meaning of "nonlabor" or how it would be interpreted.[33] Would the incomes of hardworking "construction gangs" be considered illegal, since they got their supplies from the black market? Would winnings from state lotteries and interest on state bonds be viewed as illegal? Would high-paid, lazy, unproductive bureaucrats be fired?[34] Would *anybody* with relatively high incomes be accused of earning them "illegally"?

Though the enforcement of the law started with much enthusiasm, the consequences were not as expected. A few high-paid bureaucrats lost their jobs, which was a welcome, though unexpected, interpretation of the law. But food and medical services disappeared from the customarily tolerated "markets," since the enterprising people were afraid that the law would be used against them. Thus more food than before was sold through the black market's channels. The black marketeers, now taking on bigger risks, sold their merchandise at higher prices. The results were increased shortages and higher black market prices. The outcry led to a decision to relax the enforcement of the law, and everything returned to normal, that is, to the pre-1986 situation. By now this whole episode is known in Russia as "the excessive zeal of July."[35]

Despite these experiences, in November 1990 Gorbachev ordered the creation of worker vigilante committees with power to monitor the food industry and punish people involved in theft and "speculation." These committees, elected at workplaces, were given authority to shut down guilty enterprises and demand both the dismissal of personal and criminal proceedings. Also, under Gorbachev's instructions a special KGB unit was instructed to combat black markets, and the police were ordered to collaborate with the workers' committees.[36]

These have not been the only steps that delayed the transition to trade during the six years of Gorbachev's rule and since his fall. In addition to the nomenklatura's unwillingness to allow trade, many fail to understand that such freedoms require more than regular declarations on freeing prices. Here again Western economists may be at fault; they talk about "freeing prices" without mentioning that such declarations are meaningless unless they come with the freedom to adjust institutions. Larisa Piyaseva, a Russian economist participating in a conference on the "Transition to Freedom," remarked that with all the laws passed during Gorbachev's six years in power, "There has been not one step toward a real free market. . . . Gorbachev says he favors the co-ops, but he continues to support legislation that works against them [like a 75 percent tax rate the moment they become profitable]. There is no independent wholesale market for retailers. And since the ruble is not convertible, retailers cannot buy on world markets."[37] The next episode shows how the passage of a law creates a far broader uncertainty, slowing down institutional adjustments.[38]

Laws and Their Interpretation

The new Law on Cooperatives, not by name but in content, came close to defining a system of private property (depending on the interpretation); Gorbachev's Minister of Finance, in preparing it, proposed a tax on cooperatives and their members. The tax rose to 90 percent for a highly paid cooperative worker's income. The proposal was quickly passed by the Presidium of the Supreme Soviet, apparently without any discussion, and the decree stayed in force for a few months until public outcry led to discussions and its demise.

Yet the same Minister of Finance, Boris Gostyev, was again put in charge of preparing the new plan for taxing such enterprises. Eight months later he came out with a similar high-tax plan, after which, as Aganbegyan puts it, he received "*direct instruction* to formulate it in such a way as to encourage the development of cooperatives."[39] Such events could do little to change deeply held beliefs about the bureaucracy's continuing power, about arbitrariness, about how much control Gorbachev actually had and for how long. (Note: This part of the text was written in 1989, before Gorbachev's downfall.)

Mr. Aganbegyan's turn of phrase is particularly revealing. The words "direct instruction" may seem meaningless to Western readers, but they reveal much about how the Russian system still works.

In a society with a tradition of casually disregarding laws and decrees, writing additional ones meant little more than keeping bureaucrats busy. How seriously Gostyev took the instructions to write his plans, we do not know. The fact that he was neither fired nor even reprimanded at the time, but instead was assigned to rewrite the plans, could have been interpreted in a number of ways. Gostyev was too powerful, which was not a good sign since it showed how powerful the old apparatus was (its members would have been hurt most by the new law). Or Gorbachev himself could not be trusted. He himself wanted to sabotage the shift toward such quasi-private enterprises. In this case the whole public discussion was a game to please the West, not a comforting explanation either.

The most comforting explanation is that Gorbachev took the new law seriously, and Gostyev wrote his high-tax plan only because he interpreted the instructions from above according to the custom of such regimes: if either the West or the Russian public wanted new words, beautiful laws, they could have them on paper, but another decree would be written to keep things as they were. Because "direct instruction" was given, the minister should have realized that, for a change, the leader was serious about his plans. So there was hope that the last explanation was the valid one, but one had to doubt the general direction of events.

With good reason: even after the 1991 coup, the approved "privatization" still does not mean the same thing in Russia as it does in the West, or even in Hungary and Czechoslovakia. In fact, the Soviet parliament made clear during the six years of indecision that collective ownership and leasing arrangements took priority over private ownership and foreign investment, privatization being expected to permit "equitable" competition with enterprises still owned by the state.

Combine such vague instructions with the lack of any independent institutions interpreting them, with the fact that both the republics and city councils pass their own rules and laws, and last but not least, with the fact that there is now (in 1992) a 28 percent value-added tax, and a 32 percent business profits tax, and it becomes more understandable why entrepreneurship failed to flourish during the six years of *perestroika,* or at least declared entrepreneurship. Enforcement today is arbitrary, as the following evidence reveals.

In 1990 Boris Korobochkin arranged a barter deal by which a Singapore company would get 50,000 tons of Soviet-manufactured mineral additives for livestock feed. In return, the company promised to supply the Soviet side with 1,200 personal computers, a number of photocopiers,

telefax machines, and other equipment. The KGB called the deal "contra-
band," interrogated Korobochkin, presented nine volumes of evidence
against him, and arrested him on October 4, 1990.[40] The daily events on
the Ukraine-Poland border crossing provide additional evidence of arbitrariness. Russian petty traders wait six days in hundreds of dilapidated
buses, stretching two kilometers, to sell merchandise in Poland. The latter
relatively abounds with hard currency, and salaries average $300 in con-
trast to $10 in the new commonwealth. There are no hotels, but recently
buses were converted into buffets, discotheques, and brothels in the midst
of the muddy landscape. The traders then face the worst hardship: the
border guards and custom officials, who are bribed regularly and who also
confiscate goods since there are no rules. In spite of all these hardships,
people come from as far as Kirghistan, near the Chinese border, to trade.[41]

Emerging Institutions

Russian entrepreneurs tried to deal with this uncertain state of affairs by
various means. Middlemen appeared, claiming to know the sympathetic
bureaucrats who, unlike most others, could get the necessary papers. The
bureaucrats probably hedged their bets: if the Russian leaders will really
allow their people to trade, they may imitate the Czechs, in which case
these new contacts may provide them employment. The Czechs forbade
any previously high-ranking official and member of the Communist Party
from holding any position of importance in the government for five years.
     The Leningrad Joint Venture Association, a nonprofit organization,
represents another adaptive phenomenon. It tries to do the same thing as
the middlemen do, only in a more organized way and pursuing a broader
objective. First it helps entrepreneurs and foreign investors find loopholes
in the maze of conflicting union, republic, and city legislations. It also
helps find that sympathetic, well-connected bureaucrat who can give even
a temporary approval for a venture. But it does not stop at this stage. Once
it succeeds in getting the right papers, the association tries to establish a
precedent and then lobbies the authorities for a truly official recognition. It
hopes that such recognition, once given, can be discarded less easily than
would the word of a bureaucrat, which after the fact can be dismissed as an
errant interpretation.
     In very broad lines, this was the typical atmosphere facing a Soviet
citizen who wished to start up a small business in 1992. Those who try to
set up larger businesses, be they Western companies, or Western com-

panies collaborating with Russian partners, face a different set of problems. Representatives of the Western companies try to establish direct contacts with top officials and avoid dealing with low-level bureaucrats. They are not always successful, as the small number of such ventures reveals. Although more than 5,000 joint ventures between Soviet and foreign companies have been announced, only 600 operated in 1992. The rest were delayed or indefinitely postponed due to the continuing political uncertainty, the lack of fundamental reforms, the non-convertibility of the ruble, and the joint efforts of ministry bureaucrats, secret police, and apparatchicks.

The Laws of the Land

If laws concerning private enterprises were vague and subject to the whims of bureaucrats, so too were the 1991 land laws. One would have thought that the Russians could have started with land reforms following China's spectacular success and increased food supplies. They did not.

According to the latest drafts, Soviet peasants can lease land from the government for ten years, for agricultural purposes only and without the right to pass it along to anybody else during the ten years. City dwellers, however, can lease the land only if they move to the farms and commit themselves to farming. According to Ukrainian regulations, however, even that may not be enough: the local authorities have the right to decide if the migrant can become a farmer.

What will happen after the ten-year lease is not clear. How much will people pay for the land? According to the plans, the center—which is Moscow, or at least it was until the summer of 1991—will determine the price according to the "place" and the "quality" of the land. Quality for producing what? Apples, avocados, wheat, corn, flowers, grapes, cabbages? When this question was raised before the Moscow bureaucrats, even before the self-declared Yeltsin people at the Privatization Committee linked with the Russian Republic's Council of Ministers, one could not get a straight reply. The stories one heard informally suggested that successful farmers, like successful entrepreneurs in the city, were having many difficulties. Not only were they being given the worse land, but if they succeeded despite all the obstacles put in their way by the small-time local bureaucrats, their leases were not renewed.

The land reforms were opposed continuously by Gorbachev, who continues to oppose them even now, out of office. He revealed that much during a March 1993 panel, on which I was asked to participate. Though Gorbachev kept repeating that policies should be based on scientific principles and evidence, he was unwilling to look at the fact that Japan's, Taiwan's, Korea's, and most recently China's spectacular successes started with such reforms. (In Japan they were initiated by Wolf Ladejinsky under the MacArthur occupation.)[42] Why didn't Gorbachev look at such evidence? Contradicting himself, he seemed no longer willing to consider scientific principles—that is, discovered regularities about human behavior that are independent of artificial boundaries. Instead, he referred to the Russians' unique sentimental attachment to Mother Russia. I did not have the chance to ask him how this view is compatible with the fact that many Russians would leave behind not just their land but everything else—if only the West would let them in.

According to the latest reforms, passed February 1, 1992, deadlines were set for local governments to determine farm sizes and other standards for the collectives' workers who want to shift to private farming. Heavy fines are to be imposed on bureaucrats for red tape. In the past, such orders on paper failed. It is also important to note that even the new reforms do not promise privatization in the Western sense of the word. Ownership cannot be passed on through inheritance, retirement, or movement from one farm to the other.[43] It also remains to be seen whether farmers will be ready to produce and sell more when the ruble is not stabilized or convertible to dollars. Why would anyone sell food for pieces of paper, even if he/she owns land?[44]

One reason for dealing at such length with the legal-regulatory environment is that it not only shows how trade depends on a complex maze of institutions, but it also leads to a better understanding of the links between monetary policy, government finances, trade, and the meaning of giving "purchasing power" to a currency.

Inflation: Past and Present

One can already infer from the previous descriptions that neither official prices nor official aggregates gave information on standards of living under communist regimes, nor do they in 1992. Extensive black markets, long waiting lines before stores, lack of heating and light (in Romania), and years of waiting for apartments, cars, and household appliances, continue to imply that nominal prices and wages have little meaning as indicators of purchasing power and prosperity.

Calculating any weighted average based on the quoted numbers and calling it a "price level" has little meaning either. What does it matter that a pound of meat costs a few pennies when one cannot find it in the stores or at best can get it only after staying in line from five to eight o'clock in the morning? Or, what does it mean to take into account rental values when people have to wait years before finding an apartment, if they find one at all? Spare parts for cars and appliances were produced illegally, and the repairs were made illegally too. Home repairs, home decorations, and, in some areas, construction of homes was an almost entirely private (and illegal) affair, the prices of which did not appear in any official index.[45]

The fact that prices did not rise in spite of scarcity and increases in the money supply (comparable to conditions during wars in some Western countries, when price controls and rationing were introduced) only meant that the statistical measures concerning price indices and real wages became useless.

People in the communist countries knew that and never paid much attention to official figures, be they price levels or other aggregates. As noted in chapter 1, Romanian, Hungarian, and Russian statisticians and economists all admitted that the official data for the last decades were pure fiction. It was known that what was produced was not always declared; what was declared was not always produced; and the "price" of what was sold was much higher than the one acknowledged (taking into account bribes, waiting, and black market prices). In addition to these problems were the significant ones concerning the counting of military, secret police, the gulags, hospital treatment for political opposition,[46] or even abortion, a big industry there because contraceptives were not available.[47]

A few numerical examples can give a vague idea how much higher the "true" price level was relative to the official one. O'Hearn (1980) summarizes a large number of estimates concerning the size of the USSR's black economy and the prices charged there. One-quarter to one-third of the Soviet citizens' consumption of fish and alcoholic beverages came through the illegal economy, and the ratio of official to black market prices was 3:14.[48] Neither these weights nor the higher prices appeared in the official indices, of course. An estimated 80 percent of muskrats are caught and sold privately. While state hunters received up to three rubles per muskrat, poachers got fifteen. While Herodotus' *History* sold for ten rubles, the official price was about three rubles (but the book could not be found in the stores). While Dumas's *Three Musketeers* sold for twenty-five rubles, the official price was about two rubles; prices of records sold in black markets were high, and many of them, like books, were not legally available. For years Georgian farmers sold the fruits and flowers they produced (and during the winter season Georgia was among the few republics that could have such production) in the open markets rather than to the state, as required, at a fraction of the price. In the summer of 1991, there were no carrots in the stores, but one could buy five tiny ones for fifteen rubles (the average monthly wage at that time being about 300 rubles).

Assume then that such a country wishes now to change its ways and abolishes rationing and price controls. Measured price levels will jump; the degree depends on the expected tightness of the country's monetary policy. However, such a rise does not necessarily mean that standards of living will drop significantly, even if the numerical measures show such a drop. The scarcity of products and the fact that much was bought on black markets implies that the price level was largely underestimated and real wages largely overestimated. That is why most people under such conditions accept a once-and-for-all recorded inflationary jump without too many complaints. Their real standards of living—in contrast to the statistical one—might not be falling at all.[49] Also, since production in the state-owned factories could no longer be subsidized either, production declined. However, just as the increased statistical inflation should not necessarily be taken as a signal of increased misery, neither should the recorded decline in production. The state-owned factories were producing less of these commodities that people were unwilling to buy for a long time anyway. People start to complain, however, if the freeing of prices is not accompanied by other freedoms, which diminishes their hopes for the future.

This means that the once much-talked-about fear of the ruble's "overhang"—the term used to describe "surplus currency" in Soviet-type economies[50]—was unjustified. The increased money supply of the last few years was *already* reflected in both higher black market prices and higher nominal bribes, as well as less production in the legal markets (due, in part, to the uncertain value of the ruble and the resulting hoarding and bartering).[51]

However, once inflation is let into the open, the difference between a Western country restoring itself after a war, and a reforming, previously communist one, becomes great. In the former the abolishment of controls implies that production will expand in old firms and new firms will be established. However, in Russia this did not happen because new firms were not allowed to emerge, nor could existing ones expand. Thus, whereas the inflationary episode linked with the decontrol of prices is warranted and may turn out to be little more than a statistical artifact, whether such an episode leads people to expect a better future depends on policies that have less to do with the effects of inherited policies than with the uncertain legal-regulatory-fiscal environment discussed before, and with the prospect that the government's deficits will be monetized, a problem we examine next.

The Reforming Governments' Budgets

Between 1981and 1985 the Soviet Union's official, misleading deficits hovered around 2 percent of the officially estimated GNP.[52] Between 1988 and 1989 they increased to more than 14 percent of the estimated GNP, a consequence not of increased expenditures but of diminished revenues.[53] The increased deficit was financed by an increased supply of rubles, while prices were still controlled.[54] The budget deficit in 1991 was estimated to be anywhere between 200 and 400 billion rubles, which were financed during the first eleven months of this year by printing 102.5 billion rubles, 4.4 times the monetary growth of 1990.

The central bank continued to print rubles partly because the monetary system's role in the communist countries was to lend money to state enterprises at zero or low interest rates to buy the inputs they needed to fulfill plans, once the parliament approved the payments.[55] The consequence had been what Kornai called a "soft" budget constraint.[56] The shift toward the partial cut of subsidies and toward decontrolling prices, without introducing either bank reforms or bankruptcy laws, and the fact that the parliament was still controlled by the 1990-elected old guard who approved payments, made things worse. Without the emergence of a significant private sector, there was no commerce on which tax could be imposed and thus no rise in government revenues, and the parliament's actions prevented its expenditures from diminishing significantly.[57]

Other reasons for the governments' lack of control over their budgets is that even the reforms carried out were not coordinated.[58] In 1989 the USSR's Prime Minister, Mr. Ryzhkov, still spoke of five-year plans, and he postponed the reform of retail and wholesale prices (*Pravda,* December, 15, 1989). Also, in 1989 Gorbachev still promised that "basic" food prices, which include fish, milk, eggs, bread, etc., were to remain unchanged for three years. Such promises implied expectations for further uncontrolled "soft budgets" and inflation.[59]

The Russian governments' other expenditures were not under control either during the first years of the *perestroika*. The official statistics divided expenditures into three main categories: the national economy, social and cultural expenditures, and defense. These statistics showed that each represented a stable 55 to 57 percent, 33 and 5 percent of the GNP for 1981 through 1987.[60] But these classifications and the numbers are not revealing. Even Gorbachev suggested that expenditures on the military represented 20 percent of the GNP.[61] Rowen and Wolf (1990), however, suggest that 30 percent of the GNP was being spent on the military.[62] How can Russia establish credibility in its currency under such conditions?

Central Bank's Credibility

After the Second World War and before the 1948 currency reform, Germany had a high inflation rate, empty shelves, a large black market, and a high rate of absenteeism (estimated at 15 percent), and firms paid their workers in kind—symptoms similar to those of the Russian economy today. However, just ten days after a credible monetary-fiscal reform was announced, the goods appeared on the shelves, and the German miracle was on its way.

Germany's 1948 currency reform had two essential characteristics:

- the printing of the new notes was strictly the Allies' responsibility. To ensure the accuracy of the amount of printed notes, the complete operation of the printing plan was placed under the control of the United States, Britain, France, and the USSR;
- to ensure that a sensible tax program was followed, the new currency law contained a provision that all governmental budgets on current account (to distinguish from capital account) must be balanced, and that borrowing for operating deficits would not be looked upon favorably.

Can just these two features of the German reform be replicated in the new commonwealth? To suggest that representatives of central banks with good reputations (the German, Swiss, Japanese, New Zealander) should come to the new commonwealth, establish a currency board, impose monetary stability and credibility, and teach the skills necessary for a central bank's management in a market economy, seems at first sight far-fetched.[63] Moreover, as discussed before, the problem is not so much a lack of technical skills in managing the country's money supply but the political struggle that prevents it.[64]

Yet even if institutions were established to maintain monetary discipline, that by itself would not guarantee prosperity, as emphasized in the previous chapters. Currencies acquire "purchasing power" when trade flourishes, and the conditions that induce such flourishing develop over time. Let us examine how this process can at least start.

From War Economy to Prosperity: Reestablishing
Purchasing Power

The USSR's economy can still be compared to that of an economy at war. Although official statistics admitted that less than 10 percent of the GNP was spent on the military, the CIA estimated the figure at 20 percent. However, in recent years Russian politicians admitted that, since the GNP stood at maybe half the one estimated by the CIA, military expenditures represented 40 percent of the GNP (although, as noted before, American researchers estimated them at 30 percent).

Whereas the transition toward "war" economies in general, and in the USSR in particular, is achieved through state power, the opposite transition must rely on people's willingness to make efforts and invest. However, since people's savings were wiped out through the inflation of the last years, the expectations of three-digit inflation in the future do not induce savings, and Russians are still prevented from having access to financial markets, what can they invest? How can they start to trade?

Consider the situation of a fired secretary, teacher, state worker, or member of either the bureaucracy or the military, who might contemplate opening a small shop, sewing dresses, let us say. With either savings or access to financial markets, and the ability to buy a sewing machine, materials, buttons, etc., they could give it a try. Once a dress, a coat, or a hat is made, the farmer decides to trade for those items with food, rather than hoard it. (Why would he sell it for paper money, which buys him only nuclear arms and bureaucracy?) The money now has gotten some purchasing power in terms of "cloth" and food.

The same scenario holds true when somebody ventures into the baking or construction business. Savings and credit enable one to buy machinery and inputs, and start baking or building. The farmer now sells food for money that acquired "purchasing power" in terms of food, cakes, clothing, apartments. Such expectations, based on trade, give currencies a backing—their "purchasing power"—which the ruble lacks today, since the production of all desired items is unreliable. As long as this is the case, the farmers will either hoard or sell food for foreign exchange.[65] If the Russians continue to spend a large amount on defense or on enterprises that continue to produce products nobody wants to buy, statistics may show anything statisticians will measure. The measures will continue to be meaningless and will not give the currency purchasing power. The measures will not raise government revenues either; without commerce to tax, governments have revenues only by selling resources to foreigners or by centralizing, in which case one is back at square one.[66]

Envy, Ambition and Trade

Anatoly A. Sobchak, the mayor of Leningrad, recently told Hedrick Smith that:

> Our people cannot endure seeing someone else earn more than they do. Our people want equal distribution of money, whether that means wealth or poverty. They are so jealous of other people that they want others to be worse off, if need be, to keep things equal. We have a story: God comes to a lucky Russian peasant one day and offers him any wish in the world. The peasant is excited and starts dreaming his fantasies. "Just remember," God says, "whatever you choose, I will do twice as much for your neighbor as I do for you." The peasant is stumped because he cannot bear to think of his neighbor being so much better off than he is, no matter how well off he becomes. Finally he gets an idea and he tells God, "Strike out one of my eyes and take out both eyes of my neighbor." Changing that psychology is the hardest part of our economic reform. That psychology of intolerance toward others who make more money, no matter why, no matter whether they work harder, longer or better—that psychology is blocking economic reform.[67]

Nicolai Shmelev made similar observations in a speech before the Congress of People's Deputies (and repeatedly emphasized this point at a conference in Rome where fractions of this chapter were presented), saying that:

The blind, burning envy of your neighbor's success has become the most powerful brake on the ideas and practice of perestroika. Until we at least damp down this envy, the success of perestroika will always be in jeopardy.[68]

Alexander Zinoviev shares these views. According to him, Soviet society became a "web of material dependence, servility toward superiors, and mutual support adulterated by mutual jealousy and supervision. . . . Their inescapable result . . . is 'a tendency to make everyone mediocre. Be like everyone else: that principle is the very cornerstone of a society in which communal laws are paramount. . . . A person who can live in society independently of a primary collective is a threat to the very foundations of society.' "[69]

Such torments and attitudes are destructive, and it is not surprising that since ancient times envy—the impulse behind them—has been declared one of the seven deadly sins, the condemnation being an attempt to counteract its effects. In communist and other regimes, when envy has been coupled with fear and a belief in arbitrariness, it has brought about a deeply ingrained sense of injustice, frustration, and nihilism, and led to continuous attempts to undermine people's success, even when the stakes are small. The reactions described before are not part of a national character, of an unchangeable Russian mentality. The reactions and the mentality are the consequences of the political regime and its institutions. Such human impulses can be checked, and can even be transformed into a sense of striving that becomes a valuable basis of culture—called "ambition." But the transformation cannot be achieved by moralizing. How can it be achieved?

Instead of envying other people's successes and brooding over them, one may try to emulate them.[70] Instead of doing everything in one's power to lessen others' financial or professional achievements, one may use the achievements themselves as a source of information, as revealing possibilities for future courses of action that may not have crossed one's mind. If this is the reaction of some people who were suddenly outdone by their fellows, envy is indeed transformed into ambition, and becomes, as Bernard de Mandeville said, "a minister of industry."

The opportunity to leapfrog through trade allows this transformation.[71] Denying leapfrogging through trade, making it dependent on the arbitrariness of rulers and those with connections, brought about the destructive attitudes. When the rules of the game could be arbitrarily changed, becoming richer was dangerous, even if one had the talent and the drive needed. Accusations against achievers could always be invented. That is how top Russian scientists—Kapitsa, Medvedev, Engelhart, and numerous others—found themselves committed to the gulag and to mental institutions, leading one of them to congratulate the state's psychiatrist for having discovered a new illness, "the Leonardo da Vinci syndrome."[72] When Vladimir Kebanov, a coal-mining engineer, established the first independent trade union in Donbass and began protesting violations of the legal rights of employees, most of the union's members were detained, and Klebanov himself was confined to a mental hospital.[73] Korobochkin, the bartering entrepreneur, whose case was mentioned earlier, suggests that what would pass for routine commercial transaction in the West was still defined as late as 1990 as "sabotage" and "speculation."

Envy does not disappear in trading societies. But in such societies, since property rights are better defined and protected, people's envy, anger, grievances, fear, resentment, and revenge is channeled into less harmful activities. Recall that Lavoisier (the famous chemist) was condemned to the guillotine in no small part due to Marat, whose work in chemistry was refuted by Lavoisier, and who ever after envied Lavoisier's success. But Marat could carry out his revenge only during the lawless times of the French Revolution. The success of minorities like Jews, Huguenots, Indians in East Africa, and other successful trading minorities has led to outbursts from parts of the majority. Yet not in all societies did the mediocrity's envy lead to discriminatory legal changes against them, allowing confiscation of property and worse.

Tempting as such measures were for individuals, fragments of the population, and politicians, they had to be resisted, or societies came into being where envy, malice, and hate were subsidized, where talent and ambition were taxed, and where, as a result, the stakes became smaller. Talented people decided not to stick out their necks, and resigned themselves to lives of sad but safe mediocrity. In obscurity and passivity lay safety. With the adoption of such attitudes, these societies fell further and further behind others where arbitrariness and lawlessness were allowed to prevail to a lesser degree.[74]

How do societies arrive at such a system? And why does it persist? These two broad questions are dealt with in the concluding section. The answers are linked with issues raised in previous chapters about security threats, the roles of government, and the way chaos and crises lead to social orders in which rulers, the military, and intellectuals (or priests in the past) shape institutions that transform and eventually freeze ideas of the moment into lasting, harmful myths.

Security Threats and Governments' Power

How could a state that appeared to be a sea of tranquility, order, and obedience in 1985 arrive at such a state of disorganization in 1991?

A partial answer to this question has been given. The tranquility and order were only on the surface. Below it was a turbulent, corrupt, declining state, whose coffers were empty, whose black markets thrived with the bureaucracy's collaboration, and whose torture and threats kept people obedient but did not turn them into communists.[75]

Another question is: If this was the case, why did it all come unraveled now, and so quickly, after seventy years of communism?

Nobody could have predicted the precise timing of the last empire's fall, even if historical experience tells us that the inability of a government to secure credits has led not just to its downfall, but to significant political changes, a regularity discussed in the next chapter. (Necessity—lack of money, that is—is the mother of invention in political matters too.) Still, the role of leaders, their particular outlook, their willingness to take some responsibilities and not others is undeniable, the views of Marxists or of Tolstoy (in *War and Peace*) notwithstanding. Gorbachev did what no one else would have, at least not in the same way and not at the same time. The importance of a leader cannot be underestimated, and his decisions represent, in part, what some like to call the element of "chance" in history.[76] Yet many signs since the seventies suggested that constraints and opportunities had changed, and that Russian leaders would have to react and depart from their routines.

So let us open a parenthesis and look at the picture from a broader perspective.

Much has been written about what caused the unexpected, revolutionary happenings of the last few years. There have also been renewed discussions on just what made the Western experience so different from the Russian one. To say that history made them different is meaningless: the question is what features of their history made Russians, as well as some other nations, obedient for so long to rulers whose follies were evident to most Western eyes.

A glance at the history of Russia shows that, since its origins, security threats—many very real, though some imagined—have shaped its institutions. Defense always leads to centralization, and persistent centralization leads to abuses.[77] In addition to security threats, historians and legal scholars go back to the Gregorian Reformation and the Investiture struggle to explain some of Russia's features. In the West, the church became a political and legal entity separated from the secular political institutions— though only after prolonged struggles. The clergy was freed from the domination of lords, kings, and emperors, something that did not happen in Russia (as has not happened yet in most Muslim countries). Harold Berman has pointed out that this separation gave rise to the formation of the first modern Western legal system, the new canon law of the Roman Catholic Church, and "eventually to new secular legal systems as well— royal, urban, and others."[78] For a long time it turned the Church into the only institution capable of resisting royal and feudal authorities, preventing abuse of monopoly power.

In contrast, for two centuries before the October Revolution, the Russian Orthodox Church was already governed by principles set down by Peter the Great in 1721 (the Ecclesiastical Regulation), whose overall goal was to catch up with the West. According to them the Church ceased to be an institution independent of government, and its administration became a function of the state, Peter's explicit goal being to abolish any "further danger from a second competitive focus of power in the land."[79] He achieved this goal and, as Robert Massie concludes, the state's control over the Church had an injurious effect on Russia. The church occupied itself with private spiritual matters and did not stand up against governments on behalf of Christian values in questions of social justice. Alexander Solzhenitsyn may be right in declaring that Russian history would have been incomparably more humane and harmonious in the last few centuries if the Church had not surrendered its independence, if it had continued to make its voice heard among the people, as it did, for example, in Poland.[80] But the relevance of such counterfactual contemplations, or what economists call "simulations," is not clear. Russian history would also have been different if the Mongols had never threatened them, if its priests had been more heroic, or if Stalin had not succeeded in outwitting Trotsky.

This was not the only harmful inheritance of Peter the Great's years in power. Upon his return from a long stay in Western Europe, he brought with him Swedish and Dutch advisers, and instituted reforms in 1698. He tried to imitate Western patterns of social organization; his domestic policies were all shaped by the goal of catching up with the West.[81] But he distorted these patterns. If the West—the Dutch republic in particular, as we saw in chapter 3—could succeed by allowing social mobility, why not *force* such mobility on Russians from the top?

This is what he did. He relied on the rank and file of the Guards Regiments (a special army unit he had created) and also forced nobles' sons to enter as privates. If they proved themselves, they were promoted to higher tasks in the diplomatic, military, judicial, or administrative service. This pattern of guiding social mobility from the top and keeping those who get to the top on their toes remained a special characteristic of Russian history, Stalin being among those who practiced it with a vengeance.[82]

Peter the Great left another inheritance. Even before communism, Russia had a tradition of peasant collectivism, based on communes and cooperatives (*obshchina* and *artels*) because of regulations introduced by Peter (concerning taxation and representation before authorities). Only in 1861, with the abolishment of slavery, were steps taken to create peasant proprietors, which, however, did not go quickly or far enough. This was at the root of the 1905 unrest. Reacting to it, P. A. Stolypin, a Tsarist minister, decided to speed up the process. By 1915, 2 million got titles to individual plots, and 1.7 were allowed to break up the communes. But these numbers were small; in 1913 there were 103 million peasants.[83]

Still, this decade of privatisation before the First World War saw trade, industry, and agricultural productivity rising quickly, and peasants investing in new technology. Then the war broke out, taking the peasants away from the fields and requiring the remaining ones to produce much more to support the war effort. There were shortages and price increases. During wartime, the government took food away from the peasants by force, which brought renewed agrarian rioting. Peasants without plots parceled away estates. Although the government was committed to land reform, it was unable to execute it because of the war or convince the peasants of its continued commitment. Since the government needed more food for the army during the war, it passed a decree on March 25, 1917, allowing confiscation of one's entire crop. The result was more revolt. Briefly, and very broadly, these were essential features in the history of "private property" in Russia just before Lenin's appearance on the stage.

These events—the confiscation of food in particular—turned out to work in his favor, although up to this point Lenin neither had nor sought the peasants' support. Many peasants came to believe that the opposition would give the lands back to the owners, whereas the Bolsheviks would not. This combination of bad luck, bad timing, and mistaken policies of repeated property confiscation, when in the two decades before the war the seeds of developments that characterized the rise of the West were sewn, explain in part the Bolsheviks' early success.[84]

In 1921 Lenin announced his New Economic Plan (NEP), which would allow peasants and small traders to buy and sell freely. Only banks, factories, foreign trade, and transportation would remain in state hands. The fact that Russians could accept living with such constraints should not surprise us: after all, just ten years ago François Mitterand confiscated the banks in France,[85] and many means of transportation in Western countries still belong to, or are strongly regulated by, the state. However, Lenin's policy was abandoned by Stalin, who emerged as his successor in 1927. The compulsory collectivization of the 1930s caused not only the deaths of millions but severe crisis and starvation, created by Stalin on purpose. Stalin gathered food and raw materials from the farmers by force. He did so in order to support workers building dams and factories, and opening mines—the Five Year Plan, the whole enterprise carried out like a military campaign. Not surprisingly, the official statistics in 1932 showed rapid industrial expansion.

Why did the majority of Russians put up with these policies? Starvation, torture, deportations, and killing of tens of millions, which reached their apogee in 1937, give a partial answer. But let us remind ourselves of the images filtered to the Russian public from the West during the thirties. They heard about the 1929 Great Crash and its aftermath: 30 percent unemployment in some parts of the world, and hyperinflation and unrest in others during the 1920s. They might also have heard about the National Recovery Administration (NRA), which, by regulating wages and prices for two years (before the Supreme Court struck it down in 1935 as unconstitutional), might have suggested that the two systems of government were getting closer. This was the world in which Russians, even those on the top who could have opposed Stalin, shaped their opinions on the options.

By the late thirties Germany was rising, and the Second World War coming. When one's life and home are threatened, even if he/she does not stand wholeheartedly behind the government, he/she may accept the constraints of military organization. During such times, people become more obedient and make greater efforts, even with meager monetary compensations.[86] After the war, Russians were continuously taught about the threat to their country and the necessity of accepting hardships. They were also told that, once they caught up, a better life awaited them, and that even the

West would correct its errant ways. And what did Russians see in 1958? In a way, they had caught up. They, rather than the United States, were sending the Sputnik into the skies.

However, a significant change in policy, carried out by Khrushchev, had unexpected consequences, diminishing the Communist party's hold on society. He stopped Stalin's regime of terror. With this, however, as Martin Malia (1989, 321, signing his article as "Z" noted, "he gave away his leverage against the apparat and thus his own safeguard." Khrushchev gave the *apparatchiki* "not only security of their persons; he inadvertently gave them life tenure in their positions as well. . . . Brezhnev and his allies prudently drew from Khruschev's fate the lesson that this group's privileges must forever remain inviolate."

The accidental result of the reform was the triumph of the nomenklatura—and here we arrive at the point where this chapter started. Under Brezhnev, the security police was brought under the party's control too, and it could no longer control members of the party as before. Although the beneficial effect was that the ruler's power diminished, the unanticipated impact was that the additional power now became vested in the bureaucracy, leading to the "stability of cadres." "This policy was," Malia concludes, "the origin of the extraordinary gerontocracy, led by Brezhnev himself, Suslov, Andropov, and Chernenko, who dominated the Soviet scene in the last decade before Gorbachev and whose longevity compounded the arteriosceloresis of all other aspects of Soviet life."[87]

By the seventies it also became clear that the costs imposed by the "Star Wars" program could no longer be borne. Innovations in communication helped change perceptions and showed Russians that they were being used and abused by party members with monopoly power, that they had been far outdone by those living under the system that was supposed to collapse. Such innovations also did something else. When I was growing up in communist Romania, rumors about people trying to strike and to demonstrate on the streets, reached people in other localities months after such demonstrations took place. It was thus much harder to coordinate actions and mobilize people, something that the communist regime tried to prevent.[88] This too changed significantly in the seventies and eighties with technological innovations spreading information quickly.

The system collapsed because all these factors combined served to empty the government's coffers; it could no longer keep up militarily with the West, spend more on internal enforcement, and continue to distribute goods and services at their traditional levels. The West outdid the communist countries by far, and the changes became more visible than ever before.[89] It became far more difficult to rationalize, to ask ordinary Russians to accept hardships, and to continue with vast expenses on the military. In the name of what idea? The idea for which people were asked and forced to accept sacrifices was wrong; that fact became far too evident. It also became evident that, behind the slogans, the system benefited a small group possessing monopoly power. Thus patriotism was no longer sufficient to propel people and sustain their efforts. The results showed up everywhere, from workplaces to the government's books, where revenues were collapsing and expenditures rising.[90] The taxing machine called government broke down, and since the rulers could no longer secure their own population's or outside credit, the system was beyond repair.

Some Soviet commentators give other explanations for today's situation. They suggest that Stalin perverted the revolution and Lenin's NEP; that Brezhnev destroyed Khrushchev's reforms, leading to corruption; that mismanagement and too much centralization is the problem (according to Gorbachev). None of these arguments stand up to closer scrutiny. It was the system that tolerated Stalin and his followers. Mismanagement and corruption have not been "mistakes," but resulted from a system in which trade was outlawed. The system is fundamentally flawed because it reflects the idea that one can rule from the top, limit initiative, responsibility, and discussion, and yet encourage innovations. This is its major flaw, leading any state that adopts its features to fall behind.

Last but not least, one may ask why no significant decentralization occurred during the six years Gorbachev was in power. Gorbachev gave one answer. He repeatedly emphasized that he still believed in a government that centralizes many decisions. The model that he and others had in mind seemed close to the one Franco practiced in Spain, only based on a communist ideology and vocabulary rather than a fascist one. It is too early to judge if he was sincere in his opinion or if there was something more hiding behind it. He might have recognized that a move toward decentralization would inevitably lead to the end not only of the nomenklatura but of the Russian empire. Expecting decentralization to succeed, Russian leaders might have been painfully aware that the center's claims to authority would eventually be denied, and the days of Russia as a major military superpower would be numbered. The potential rise of nationalism in the republics and the dismantling of the country, rather than just the protection of the large bureaucracy, might have held reforms at bay during the six years. The mistake was assuming that the dismantling could have been prevented.[91]

Let us conclude this chapter with a brief speculation about the future. (This paragraph was written long before the March 1993 power struggle between Yeltsin and the parliament). Since the nomenklatura does not wish to give up power, though it now tries to become richer through trade deals with foreigners, Russia will follow the uncertain political and economic path of many Third World countries. The path is uncertain, because in the absence of tradition or any institutional anchor, the role of leaders, their character, and their opinions are crucial and unpredictable.[92] This is the same point made in the previous chapter on central bankers, although the context there was narrower. The next and final chapter elaborates on this point by discussing the links between policies and politicians on one side, and political institutions to control them on the other.

Chapter 6

Policies without Dogmas

Alfred North Whitehead was asked "Which are more important, facts or ideas?" The philosopher reflected for a while, then said: "Ideas about facts."

—Lucien Price, *Dialogues of Alfred North Whitehead*

Many economists wrote on the difficulties with conventional national accounts, Robert Eisner among them. Yet he not only argued that they should be retained in spite of their errors but advocated revising and expanding them. His argument was that even conventional historical series offered "enormous value for economic analysis," suggesting that the expanded series could be of even greater value.[1]

Conventional historical aggregate measures have never been of great scientific value, nor will his suggested revised series turn out to have such value. On the contrary, the conventions helped establish bureaucracies and harmful myths about prosperity. We still use these myths' misleading languages in public debates, which at times lead to disastrous policies. Throwing more money at institutions that sustain these myths only leads to persistence in error.

One such myth was that counter-cyclical policies based on the use of measured aggregates sustain prosperity. Politicians and macro-economists paid no attention to the success of Northern Italy, Spain, Taiwan, Hong Kong, Singapore, nor the recent successes of Southern China, pockets in former Eastern bloc countries, or Switzerland (not to mention all the historical evidence discussed in previous chapters); these countries either had no reliable national aggregate data when they succeeded or were never polluted by macroeconomic ideas. Moreover, macroeconomics never paid attention to the rise of centers of growth, to the fact that some regions within national borders thrived, whereas others languished. This could have suggested that national statistics are of little relevance for shedding light on the process they called growth.[2]

Macro-economists and politicians had strong incentives to keep such evidence out of sight and mind. The success of cities and regions that did not depend on "national" macroeconomic policies could not only raise doubts about the relevance of this field of study but also diminish the importance of political leaders. If regions can prosper without politicians' favors or languish in spite of receiving them, the belief in politicians' ability to solve problems may be shaken. People may impose stronger constraints on their range of actions. Neither macroeconomists nor politicians would like that. The first group would protest in the name of science, the second in the name of public welfare. Neither notion should be taken on face value.

It was exactly the aforementioned countries', regions', and cities' experiences that initially led us to raise the questions examined in the first chapters. Was it possible that countries could do quite well without having access to aggregate numbers or pursuing any conventional, so-called fine-tuning, macroeconomic policies? Was it possible that only interest groups—farmers, social engineers, politicians, government bureaucrats, macro-economists—wanted these numbers initially?[3] And if so, was it possible that the aggregate numbers were in fact useless in smoothing the way toward prosperity, that using them for political reasons did more harm than good? Briefly, could it be true that macroeconomics and the beneficial effect of macroeconomic policies were just myths? The answers to all these questions were positive.

To reach this conclusion, we need not contradict the observations that low aggregate saving rates, large and misspent money resulting in budget deficits, and foreign trade deficits may at times have signaled that something was wrong. This happened when the deficits and debts resulted from the mistaken idea that development and growth could be based on government expansions, funded through domestic and foreign borrowing. Yet even in this case, aggregate figures about debts, deficits, government expenditures, and saving rates could neither reveal the source of troubles nor help find remedies. Worse still, focusing on them shifted our attention from sickness to symptoms, from what governments were doing with the money and what was wrong with political institutions, to abstract fractions and the arbitrary categorization of expenditures.

In this book I have tried to discard the obscure language, the scientific masks and pretensions, and to use simple words to discuss matters that economists and politicians made look technical and scientific. I have also offered remedies. This chapter sums up the picture from additional, broader angles and discusses in detail the fundamental remedy offered in this book: relying far more on the political institutions of referendum and initiative, rather than on experts and politicians, to make decisions about the government's role in the economy, its taxing and spending powers in particular. These institutions provide the flexible key to some of the great political problem of modern times:[4] How can an increasing number of people practice popular sovereignty? What institution can best approximate the ancient practice of town meetings in small communities? How can the persistence of erroneous policies be avoided?

These are the fundamental problems and questions. After all, whatever the solutions the economists and social scientists come up with, correct or incorrect, and even if politicians and the public adopted the incorrect ones, the question remains: Are there political institutions in place to prevent *persistence in error*? I emphasize these words because, as already mentioned in previous chapters, the issue is not the committing of errors. That is unavoidable. People make mistakes, and they learn by making them. The question is, are the institutions of society flexible enough to allow speedy correction? And if not, how do the institutions of referendum and initiative make the political system more flexible? The second part of this chapter answers these questions. The first part looks at the meaning of prosperity from one additional, broad angle, complementing discussions in the previous chapters, and then leading to the political issues discussed in the second part.

Sustained Prosperity

> No matter how refined and how elaborate the analysis, if it rests on the short view it will still be . . . a structure built on shifting sands.
> —Jacob Viner, *The Long View and the Short,* 1958

Sustained prosperity results from people's willingness to take chances, to court risks daringly, and to successfully overcome them, which then results in the commercialization of knowledge. Governments can provide the framework within which these activities can thrive best, but as shown in the previous chapters, this is easier said than done.

In a world marked by large and unexpected demographic changes, significant changes in security threats, and governments trying to correct consequences of mistaken policies, providing a "stable framework" is a complex task. It becomes a pragmatic art. The art is obscured today by the masks of science, the use of the macroeconomic language and the myths of scientific policies, which in turn are based on numbers whose changing meaning over longer periods of time has never been closely examined.

(Although there are even economists who claim to have discovered statistical regularities not just over decades, but even over centuries, the so-called Kondratieff cycles.[5] Fortunately, except for a few academics, nobody takes such claims seriously.) So let us take a long and broad perspective and evaluate some familiar figures to see what light they shed, if any, on prosperity.

Trust and Trade

Family and kin, religious and ethnic groups, play a major role in the allocation and distribution of resources in industrial societies today. In the past and in the less developed societies today, they have played and continue to play a far greater role. The way in which members of societies with smaller and less mobile populations have interacted, and the implicit contracts that regulated their behavior, stand in sharp contrast to today's legally binding contracts and trade among strangers.

When populations were smaller and less mobile, people got to know one another through participation in ceremonies, religious or otherwise, and decided how much they could trust one another. Trust is not only a tenet of civil society but an investment that facilitates trade. People learn to establish norms concerning contingencies, to settle feuds, and to enforce contracts, skills that serve beyond a single transaction.[6] As long as people traded within a relatively small and stable community, norms established through kinship and religion and ethnic ties guided people's expectations and offered mutual protection.[7] When people traded with strangers, market institutions (formal contracts, warranties, insurances, etc.) as well as governments took over these roles, although even today some industries in the West rely on trusted institutions inherited from distant pasts, and not just in their black markets.

Murray Schumach (1981), in *Diamond People*, describes the mainly Jewish, New York–centered diamond industry of the twentieth century and shows how social and religious bonds diminish the costs of contracts. Trade is based on complex rules that go back a thousand years. Contracts are still based on codes of honor whose roots can be traced to the Old Testament, the Talmud, and the teachings of the Maimonides. A handshake and a Hebrew-Yiddish expression of "Mazel and Brucha" (Luck and Blessing) complete contracts of a million dollars, rather than lawyers (and if the parties contest a contract, they seek the rabbi's advice).

In other words, when and where people trade with smaller, less mobile, more homogeneous groups, they resort to what we today call "noninstitutional" arrangements for both enforcing contracts and providing security. Moreover, friends and kin provide both collateral and social security.[8] Simon Kuznets (1979) emphasized that:

> Perhaps [the] most far reaching aspect of the investment in children is that of security—not merely or primarily the economic security of parents who, in their old age, have to rely on the help of surviving children, but much broader, encompassing protection against natural and social calamities, protection not provided by the government or other non-blood-related organs of society. The pressure in many preindustrialized societies . . . for larger families and a wider blood-tie group has been associated with the weakness of the government and the need to rely on family ties for security of the individual numbers. As long as governmental and non-blood-related organizations remain weak, an adequate increase of those related by protective blood ties will be a high priority goal. (43–44)

It is not surprising that in Japan business is done differently than in the West. The percentage of merged households (two adult generations living together) is 50.2 percent there, but only 2 to 3 percent in the United States and the United Kingdom, and 9 percent in France.[9]

The existence of these complex institutions means that growth, reforms, and trade are not a simple matter of political announcements, of "shock treatments," of "freeing prices," of mechanical ways of catching up. "Markets" do not exist in a void, and political announcements will not create them. Trade is based on complex information and trusted institutions, customary, legal, or other, about whose elusive origins and functioning economists know very little, and macro-economists nothing at all (judging from the content of their "scientific" writings). No recipes will instantly create trust or the institutions necessary for trade. These emerge through learning and through trial and error, when people are allowed to look for and exploit opportunities. Such learning takes time.[10]

Trust and Prosperity

What happens when the population with whom one trades increases (because of increased mobility, increased population, or freer trade)?[11] Such changes lead to less frequent exchanges between any two individuals and to increased probability of fraud.[12] As a result, the costs associated with trade, which just rely on existing arrangements based on customs, kinship, and religion, increase.[13] However, as shown by the evidence presented in previous chapters, people invent new arrangements and institutions to lower these costs—unless political institutions stay in their way. When that happens, the interpretation of changes in aggregates over longer periods of time becomes more difficult because new, complex institutions rise to substitute for the flawed political ones, trying to find ways to re-link people and generate trust. The increased strength of religious institutions in Poland, Latin and South America, and many Third World countries during decades of dictatorial and corrupt rule is a symptom of such adjustments. When even such adjustments are under constant attack, as happened in the Soviet Union, a tenet of civil society is significantly weakened. The loss of trust significantly retards the society's recovery once the political regime changes, which then gives rise to nationalist sentiments as the means to re-link people who have lost trust one in the other.[14]

These are the broader implications of taking trust into account; they show how this resource interacts with a society's political life and prosperity. These observations also have narrower implications for interpreting aggregate figures, over longer periods of time or when comparing various societies.

A society, which is less homogeneous and its population larger and more mobile, will have a greater measured wealth when trade is allowed to flourish. This is so because the output of institutions that substitute for trust is measured in the society with the greater population, but the same output is not measured when produced by shared beliefs and informal institutions. Yet the "wealth" of the two nations could be the same.[15]

The fact that there were 624,000 practicing lawyers in the United States in 1984 (one per 375 individuals),[16] and roughly 60,000 in Japan in 1982 (one per 1,968 individuals), and whose incomes appear in the respective GNP figures, does not necessarily imply that the difference in the incomes of the legal sector in the two countries reflects an addition to "wealth."[17] Perhaps the lawyers in the United States are involved in property rights questions arising from innovations in new fields: biology, genetics, intellectual property. Perhaps more innovations occur in the United States than in Japan. In this case their output contributes to wealth.

Perhaps the number of lawyers increased because the United States has more divorces, and the flaws in its legal and political process have made tax laws and regulations more complex.[18] In this case trade was taxed and wealth diminished, though changes in aggregates cannot distinguish between the two possibilities.

Even without taking these two possibilities into account, the difference in figures still does not necessarily imply that the Japanese are better off without the extra lawyers. In Japan, religious personnel may fulfill the same roles as lawyers and psychologists do in other societies. They may be paid less, but maintaining temples and adhering to custom does not come cheap, and it is not clear how the output of this sector is being counted.[19]

These arguments have additional implications concerning the interpretation of numbers over longer periods of time or across countries.[20] In one society children and other family members may be viewed as providing insurance against old age, illness, or rainy days in general. In other societies, with different institutions, children may be expected to play these roles to a lesser extent or not at all. In the latter case, parents may view expenditures on children as "consumption" more than "investment." The interpretation becomes even more problematic if parents in the same society still view their children as investment, while others view them as bringing pleasure, that is, as consumption. If some standardized aggregates are computed in these societies, none of them will influence anybody's decision, or provide any information on possible future changes in the economy; if they are used to compare societies—as is done routinely today in the standardized accounts of international institutions—one will get statistical illusions and little else.

Let us illustrate this last point with the help of additional, detailed, and recent demographic figures.

Government Expenditures and Aging Population

During the 1960s and 1970s the age structure of the U.S. population changed significantly and unexpectedly.[21] The number of children younger than 15 fell by 7 percent, and the number of elderly people 65 or older grew by 54 percent.[22] It has been estimated that in 1983 older people got $217 billion in Federal funds, whereas the outlay on child-oriented programs was $36 billion. Since children outnumbered old people, the expenditure per child was less than a tenth of the expenditure per older person.

This expenditure pattern cannot be explained by the fact that children were becoming better off than the elderly. In 1982, 23 percent of children lived in poverty, compared to 15 percent of the elderly. In 1970, 16 percent of those under 14 lived in poverty, compared to 24 percent of the elderly.[23] If one is worried about investment in the future of the United States, these numbers should be cause for worry, and not the total expenditures on either children or the elderly.

The relative improvement in the elderly's situation is attributed to the various increased monetary transfers, be they in the form of Social Security benefits or health care: 69 percent of medical bills for people 65 or older are paid for with public funds.[24] Many economists view expenditures on health as an investment in maintaining one's "human capital" and thus raising society's productivity and future prosperity. This interpretation of medical expenditures, however, is open to debate too.

Mortality rates improved in all age groups between 1968 and 1980, but reductions in mortality have been concentrated for those aged 60 to 75, who had a four-year gain in life expectancy.[25] Keeping these numbers in mind, can one say that the Medicare outlays estimated at $112 billion in 1988 can all be counted as investment? Or should part of this figure be viewed as consumption, in the sense that it did not significantly affect the future productive capacity of the economy? The medical expenditures on the unexpectedly increased number of elderly resulted in increased taxes. Can, then, one say that the Medicare outlays were a bad investment, since increased taxation of the younger generation diminished their incentives and opportunities (even if they expected to live longer)?

One cannot answer any of these questions by relying on theoretical arguments or on aggregate figures. However, one may try to answer them by looking at some additional, detailed demographic figures. One can argue that the elderly's longer life expectancy can be more than mere consumption. If they are in better health, they may decide to stay longer in the labor force, and the younger generation may also plan to stay longer in the labor force with a longer life expectancy in mind. Or, if the older generation decides not to stay longer in the labor force, they still can help their grown-up children by staying with their grandchildren or otherwise helping out. Such help could also increase the younger generation's number of hours and efforts at work, since they will know their children are being taken care of and less work may be waiting for them at home.

Of course, the opposite may happen too: the grown-up children may find themselves taking care of not only their children but their parents too, and for a longer period of time than they expected, which would increase their burden. Thus, whether or not the Medicare outlays were an investment or not depends on whether or not the older people stayed longer in the labor force, whether or not they provided the aforementioned services, and how longer life-expectancy effected the younger generation's plans.

There is not much information on the type and extent of services that grandparents provide, although the numbers are suggestive. Recall that the percentage of merged households (two adult generations living together) is 50.2 percent in Japan, but only 2 to 3 percent in the United States and the United Kingdom, and 9 percent in France. Taking into account this drastic difference in housing arrangements, it well may be that the same expenditures per capita for the health of the elderly may be a good investment in Japan, but less so in the United States and the United Kingdom.[26]

As for the older people's participation in the labor force, it did not increase. In the United States 83 percent of all men and 92 percent of all women over the age of 65 are out of the labor market, even though three out of five have no disability preventing them from work. Among those aged 55 to 64 the retirement rate has doubled in the past twenty years. Only 32 percent of men aged 60 or over are in the labor market, compared with 45 percent twenty-five years ago. Why this change took place does not concern us here. These additional detailed numbers show one more time why aggregate data about total government expenditures, deficits, saving rates, expenditures on health, and others provide no insights to recommend any particular fiscal policy; they also suggest that counting expenditures on health as investment may be inaccurate too. As for the costs of such government expenditures, one cannot know much either, since we do not know the public's perception of foregone opportunities.[27] When governments provide the service—old-age insurance, or health in the previous example—nobody knows their appropriate level under the current political institutions.

With these observations we are back at the subjects raised in chapter 2: is it a problem today that the government spends "too much" on Social Security benefits, health care, education? Or is the problem linked to the fact that expenditures on "education," "health," or "investment" are in fact misspent on a growing bureaucracy? Or that, even if the government spends the money wisely and prudently on health care, the protection of the environment, education, the arts, and other "worthy" causes, society is just not rich enough to pay taxes for all these causes? Or that, if interest groups passed programs funded by governments, the resulting increased taxes diminish incentives to work and invest, and make the country poorer (regardless of what is being measured)? Or do the increased debts and deficits reflect the more fundamental problem of drastic demographic change of aging populations to which regulations and institutions (age of retirement and many social programs, for example) have not been adjusted?[28] Maybe health care worked in Canada not because it was well-designed and well-administered but, by sheer luck, because the population was much younger?

None of the aggregate figures gives answers to these questions. Calculations about the value of entitlements (for Social Security or other items) are relevant only in the sense that they give vague estimates of commitments. But the emphasis on the calculations misses the essential question: are there flexible political institutions in place that can prevent *persistence in error* when governments make too many commitments? And if not, can some be devised? The next sections answer these questions.

The Political Remedy

> The people have spoken—the bastards.
> —Dick Tuck, loser in the 1966 California state senate race

The institutions of referendum and initiative, practiced by the Swiss, have prevented persistence in error as far as government policies are concerned.[29] These institutions have done so by diminishing political power directly, rather than indirectly, as federalism does. Being aware of such an effect is sufficient reason for politicians and lobbying groups to oppose their introduction and invent arguments against them. This raises the question of how they can be introduced in a society, a question that will be answered at the end of the chapter.

In principle, a democratic, federal system already insures competition among political organizations. The allocation of powers between state (or provincial) governments and the mobility of people across state lines reduce the dangers of grave mistakes and abuses of monopoly power by local governments. Therefore, there are benefits to provincial governments that share power within a federal state rather than one central government.

If taxes were raised in one state or province but not in another, or if living in one province was not to their liking, people could move to another. Such mobility within a federal state ensures more competitive checks on governments at the provincial level than between sovereign governments, since migration from one country to another is more difficult than across provincial lines.[30] Federalism also encourages experimentation with different methods of providing government services, each being adapted to local conditions, on state or provincial levels. Through trial and error, in their own community or elsewhere, people can learn the best ways of providing services.[31]

These are the principles. In practice, central governments severely restrict provinces and states in federations in the ways they can compete.[32] More important: the question remains, how can the federal government be controlled when the federal institutions that decide on taxes and spending are not separated? An overlooked feature of Swiss federalism—the constitutionally guaranteed institutions of referendum and initiative—show that there is a way to diminish such interventions and resulting centralization of powers on both the federal and local levels—if people really do not want them. The Swiss federal solution may not be perfect (what political solution is?). Yet I know of no better arrangement that allows citizens to express their ideas and correct them if they are proven costly and wrong. Concerns that such a system leads to the rule of mobs and threatens individual and human rights are unfounded. It has not happened. Nevertheless, if this is feared, the risk can be diminished by restricting the range of subjects on which initiatives and plebiscites can be held, which would exclude fundamental rights.

Referendum and Initiative

"Referendum" means that laws and resolutions made by representatives must be submitted to the people for acceptance or rejection. "Initiative" means that people have the right not only to vote on proposals but also to *initiate* the enactment of new laws or constitutional amendments, and alter or abolish old ones, if a certain number of people so request.[33]

The second feature is important, and it distinguishes the Swiss system from others, where politicians rely occasionally on referenda.[34] Whereas in Switzerland these institutions act through regular channels, entrenched in their constitution, they are used arbitrarily in other countries (and can be misused by ambitious politicians during periods of upheaval). The same term is used to describe two very different practices, but one should not confuse the occasional plebiscites with the constitutionally guaranteed institutions. The latter system provides a way for systematically correcting mistaken decisions through initiatives, whereas the irregular one does not.[35]

Nor should the institution of initiative be confused with petitions or lobbying. Politicians in other western democracies can disregard petitions at their leisure. They can also respond far too easily to lobbying. In contrast, when the institutions of referendum and initiative are in place, politicians have more difficulty in subverting the people's will since their actions can be nullified.

It is no accident, therefore, that politicians have limited roles in Switzerland, and one does not hear much about them. Nor is it accidental that no significant differences divide the policies of the parties.[36] Through these two institutions, proposals are considered in separation, which significantly diminishes the range of the politicians' "business" and power and of pork-barrel politics.

In recent years the Swiss have voted separately on issues like having extra air pollution devices in motor vehicles, lawful abortion, the introduction of VAT (value-added tax), and increasing grants for universities and research. All these initiatives were voted down. Other initiatives, concerning consumer protection and equal rights for women and men, and recently the purchase of airplanes for the military, were accepted. Altogether, of the 216 amendments proposed between 1874 and 1985 on both the federal and the canton level, 111 were accepted and 105 were rejected. Of the 111, 8 were popular initiatives and 14 were counterproposals.[37] Frey (1992) notes that on the federal level alone there were 147 obligatory referenda (on constitutional issues), and 103 optional ones (on laws), and 104 initiatives between 1848 and 1990. Among the latest was the referendum on closer ties with the European Community. The Swiss decided against: the majority voted against it in twenty-three cantons, and for it in only seven.

Here is a sample of topics on which referenda were held, on which the government and parliament already agreed, but which the voters later rejected (see Frey, 1992):

- Politicians rejected the idea of proportional voting for parliament. Nevertheless citizens adopted the idea in 1918, and the Radical-Democratic party lost 40 percent of its seats;
- A popular initiative in 1946 succeeded in making "urgent" federal laws subject to obligatory referendum within one year, though government and the parliament were against it;
- Seventy-six percent of the Swiss rejected joining the United Nations, though government and parliament wanted to join.

This means that people vote on both important and marginal issues separately, preventing painful compromises during elections, when they could strongly agree with some of their potential political representative's opinions but strongly disagree with others.

The options of referendum and initiative thus diminish the importance of politicians' opinions, theirs and bureaucracies' power, and incentives for lobbying groups to organize. The institutions impose stricter controls on government's expenditures and enable a quicker correction if an erroneous policy has been chosen. These combined effects imply a greater correspondence between political decisions on publicly supplied goods and the voters' preferences, though it does not necessarily imply either less taxation or fewer regulations. This is indeed what Swiss researchers found when they looked at the evidence concerning publicly supplied goods across the Swiss cantons.[38]

Consider then how such a system would solve minor and major recent issues in the United States. The Corporation for Public Broadcasting is asking for 50 percent increase in government funding for 1993 through 1996, bringing it to about $1 billion (about 17 percent of its budget). George Will, a columnist, is the most visible and vocal opponent of the subsidy, and the former chairman of the corporation, Sharon Percy Rockefeller, is its advocate, each claiming to represent the "common" man and woman. It is hard to know how the Congress will vote on the issue because of the usual package deals of pork-barrel politics.

The alternative under the referendum and initiative system would be simple: ask people what they want. (Much as I love opera, my guess is that the majority would say "no" since today there are plenty of cheap substitutes for the CPB, like cable, videos, and ordering of programs by phone.) In the same vein, the far more weighty issues of government expenditures on R & D, health, schooling, and even Social Security could be decided.

Consider the funding of large-scale R & D programs, which economists frequently put forward as a necessary role of governments, since the private sector would not undertake them. Yet in a recent book, Linda Cohen, Roger Noll, and their co-authors (1991) find that federal R & D programs have hardly been a success:

> On the basis of retrospective benefit-cost analysis, only one program—NASA's activities in developing communication satellites— . . . can be regarded as worth the effort. But that program was killed. . . . The photovoltaics program made significant progress, but it was dramatically scaled back for political reasons. . . . The remaining four programs were almost un-

qualified failures. The supersonic transport (SST) and Clinch River Breeder Reactor were killed before they produced any benefits, and Clinch River, because of cost overruns, absorbed so much of the R & D budget for nuclear technology that it probably retarded overall technological progress. The space shuttle . . . costs too much, and flies too infrequently. The synthetic fuels program produced one promising technology . . . but billions were spent on another pilot and demonstration facilities that failed. (365)

The title of their book—*The Technology Pork Barrel*—summarizes the source of failure. Once again, referendum and initiative could provide a remedy. People would be acquainted with the facts and their various interpretations, and be less impressed with the opinions of experts relying on abstract, general theories about the role of government in subsidizing R & D, or on the importance of sustaining failing programs. Even if people would accept government interference with such projects, they might initiate votes on specific programs; to stop spending on failed experiments and to prevent shutting down the successful ones because of political games.

Thus the referenda and initiatives on separate issues would lead to a far closer relationship between fact and measurement, between actual well-being and the data that are supposed to reflect it. When people approved public spending on education, on antipollution devices, or on particular R & D projects, they would reveal their preferences and also correct more easily those situations when preferences or the government's relative efficiency in offering a service changes.

In Western countries today we have no idea what we are measuring when looking at governments' vastly increased expenditures on even health and education. Much of it may reflect the costs of maintaining a large bureaucracy and the power of lobbying and interest groups, rather than providing higher quality health care or education. How can one otherwise explain the fact that in Denmark (with a population of 5.1 million) 50 bureaucrats supervise about 180,000 teachers, whereas in Quebec (with a population of 6.9 million) 50,000 bureaucrats supervise 90,000 teachers? (With predictable results: Quebec has the highest high school drop out rates in Canada, close to 40 percent). Thus measurement bears less relationship to well-being, and the system is not flexible enough to correct for mistaken fiscal and regulatory policies adopted in the past.[39]

The typical objection to adopting the Swiss schemes in other countries is that people must first become Swiss before agreeing to them. This may be funny, but it turns out to be just another play on words. Closer inspection reveals that the Swiss were not so "Swiss" before agreeing on the widespread use of these institutions. Rather, these institutions turned them into the calm, civilized, prosperous, peaceful Swiss that we are accustomed to today.

Until the beginning of the nineteenth century they had their share of religious conflicts—like all other Europeans. In the 1830s there were protests against the aristocratic governments, and in 1831 serious conflicts arose in the Cantons of Basel, Schweiz, and Neuchâtel—on grounds similar to those in the rest of Europe. In 1847 twelve and a half cantons joined the Federal cause, seven joined the Secessionists (one and two half-cantons remained neutral), and the Swiss fought their Civil War of 1861–64. The Secessionists lost. The subsequent constitutional reforms led to the 1874 document that identifies the Swiss political system today.[40] This document, and the rules it delivered and enforced, forged the federation of people speaking German, French, Italian (and the small number of Romansch) into the current Swiss tribe.[41]

Additional objections could be raised against emulating features of the Swiss federal system. One can say that the institutions of referendum and initiative are far too costly to operate in more populous countries. This is not a serious objection. Innovations in communication technologies—the option of electronic highways—have lowered the costs of operating such institutions. At the same time, the costs of large governments and persistence of mistaken policies—which might be eliminated by shifting toward referenda and initiatives—have increased.

Another objection to emulating features of the Swiss system is its impracticality. As noted, these drastic institutional innovations are not feasible: the politicians on whom their introduction depends have no incentives whatsoever to introduce them. Referendum and initiative strike a blow against lobbying, the selling of fiscal and regulatory loopholes, and dependence on political maneuvers. It deprives politicians of their role as favor brokers. It also weakens the believers in the centralized, all-problem-solving state and undercuts the bureaucracies established by them; they can never be sure of what they will be allowed to do in office or how long they will be allowed to stay there.

There is also less money in pork barrels, since taxpayers have the option to vote on every transaction involving their own money. The

institutions diminish adherence to party lines or even to the sharp definition of such lines, since the referenda on separate issues diminish incentives to form inflexible alliances. Once in place, these institutions diminish
the importance of politicians, although each individual now has a greater
stake in political life. No one should be surprised that no politician can be
expected to advocate institutional changes permanently curtailing his/her
own power.[42]

Nevertheless, one of the significant political changes of 1992 was that
many important decisions in various parts of the world were decided by
referenda. In March 1992, white South Africans voted for reform. In June,
Danes defeated the European Community's Maastricht treaty. In September, the French approved the treaty, though barely. In October, Canadians
overwhelmingly vetoed a wishy-washy, mish-mash document that politicians tried to pass off as significant constitutional reform but that only
promised to suffocate every loudly whining group with commitments. A
few weeks later, voters in different parts of the United States responded to
69 ballot initiatives—more than at any time since 1932.[43] If voters in
Colorado refused to approve special rights for homosexuals in a November
1992 referendum, Oregonians rejected a measure to declare homosexuality
"wrong, unnatural and perverse." On June 2, 1992, a nonbinding referendum on the division of California into two states appeared on the ballots. It
was approved by 55 percent of the voters: in 27 out of 31 counties the
proposal gained majority. In fact, in California any issue can be put now to
a statewide vote if 615,958 signatures are collected.[44]

In Ireland, people voted on the issue of abortion. In June 1991, 96
percent of the 63 percent of Italians who went to the polls voted yes in a
referendum designed to reduce corruption in elections. The referendum
was initiated by Mario Segni, a dissident Christian-Democrat, and was
opposed by the leaders of the big parties. Another referendum scheduled
for 1993 would change the voting system for the Senate. President Boris
Yeltsin of Russia held a referendum on April 11, 1993, for Russians to
decide on the allocation of powers between president and parliament.

The fact that all these referenda took place and that many others are
planned does not mean that politicians suddenly favor giving people more
power. People have always wanted greater control over their political
institutions. Already a survey on February 12, 1913, in Canada showed
that 3,982 answered Yes and only 62 No to the following question: "Are
you in favor of having the Initiative, Referendum and Right of Recall
placed upon the Statute of Books of your own province?" In spite of such

overwhelming opinion in their favor, the institutions were not introduced.[45] So why do we see this sudden shift in 1992? One answer is that
politicians have decided to rely on referenda not because they want to see
them become a permanent institution, but to win approval of bold departures and embarrass the opposition (and gain more power, as in Yeltsin's
case), or to evade the responsibility for a difficult decision (Ireland's
abortion case).

In spite of this skeptical reservation, there is reason now for cautious
optimism that significant changes in political institutions may be on their
way. It may happen not because politicians want to use them, but because
the governments' coffers are empty.

What Happens When the Governments' Coffers Are Empty?

A serious objection to drastic change in political institutions is that, since
the United States and Western countries have performed reasonably well,
we should not fix something radically unless it is broken. This objection
does not stand up to closer scrutiny either; it is exactly this idea that caused
the stagnation or downfall of many once-successful firms and societies
when they failed to adapt to a significantly changed environment.[46] They
were leapfrogged by newcomers unburdened with traditions of the political culture of their firms.[47]

Historical evidence from all fields of human activity—in science,
technology, or political affairs—suggests that radical innovations have
rarely been carried out by insiders or during normal times. Although the
ideas were offered during such times, they were shelved, discarded, or
ridiculed, executed finally because of outside pressures. Unless a crisis
destroyed traditional alliances, drastic innovations were not executed in
any domain, in the political sphere in particular.[48] Keeping this regularity
in mind, we can see greater chances that such innovations will be carried
out today because the coffers of many governments are empty, and the
economies of these same governments are falling behind others for a
variety of reasons.[49]

Joseph Schumpeter (1991) was among those who noticed that, when
rulers' or governments' coffers were empty, the existing political institutions crumbled, and new ones replaced them, though nobody could have
predicted their precise nature. It happened in the distant past when the
Parliament in England and the Cortes in Spain acquired greater powers,

leading in the English case to the Glorious Revolution in 1688, the triumph of the Parliament, and prosperity.[50] European observers of the seventeenth century noticed that the Dutch had significantly low interest rates in florins on municipal and provincial loans, and some thought erroneously that low rates could be achieved through regulation. They failed to notice that rates were low because the Dutch were the first northern people to maintain confidence in Amsterdam's and the province's fiscal responsibility at a time when most European governments were bankrupt (Spain and Austria) or on the verge of bankruptcy (Stuart England and Bourbon France).[51]

"Fiscal responsibility" meant that investors believed in the government's ability and willingness to cover commitments with future revenues. Whereas the English war effort in 1666 against the Dutch was hindered by lack of funds, the Dutch had no difficulty raising them. After the Glorious Revolution, the English did not face this problem. A century later, French commentators saw the origins of British financial success in the transfer of power from an absolutist to a constitutional monarchy at a time when the French monarchy was no longer able to secure new loans based on anticipation of future revenues. This was the problem the French rulers faced, not the magnitude of outstanding debt. Britain too was in debt then, and the per capita tax burden in Britain was three times heavier than in France. By 1782, the 70 percent of public revenue consumed to service Britain's debt was far greater than its French equivalent.[52] Yet, whereas Britain could secure loans, France couldn't. In his book about the French Revolution and the events leading to it, Schama (1989) emphasizes that fiscal and political, as well as military policies (which the fiscal policies financed to prevent France's military decline), brought the monarchy to its knees.[53]

This sequence of events is similar to those that took place on the North American continent at that time. The finances of the new nation became chaotic after the peace of 1783, and the government authorized expenditures without having the power to tax. The financial and political system broke down in 1786 when, in spite of the new country's potential, the government could not secure loans abroad or at home. This crisis led to the Constitutional Convention of 1787 and the new nation two years later.[54] The shift to referenda and initiatives in California, briefly mentioned in the previous section, were also consequences of repeated fiscal crises in that state. It now faces a deficit of $11 billion—which its constitution prohibits. It is no accident that in the Japan of the 1870s, the Meiji revolution came about when the old Tokugawa tax system crumbled and the treasury was empty.[55]

Though we know that the Soviet Union's government had large deficits—in part, once again, because of its attempt to prevent its military power from declining—time will tell whether the resulting fiscal and political policies brought the communist rulers to their knees. If they did, the fall of the USSR would fit into a well-known, long-identified pattern.

If a regularity behind the causes of regimes' downfalls can thus be simplified, the causes of the emergence of specific institutions, in particular referendum and initiative, cannot. The end of communism, or the inability of some Western governments to secure loans, do not by themselves induce a drastic change in political institutions, such as the constitutionally guaranteed referendum and initiative would require. The historical evidence suggests only that the governments' cash-flow and credit problems led to significant political changes *when* people despaired of the system and no longer saw the fiscal problems as consequences of wars, accidents, or corruption. This is, in fact, the definition of fiscal crisis, a crisis that Western European countries, the United States, and Canada are facing now. The evidence presented in the previous section suggests that the option of referendum and initiative is available today and, if properly introduced, would provide solutions to the fiscal crises of the "tax states."[56] The next, concluding section discusses an additional issue that might be solved by these institutions.

The Politicians' Character and Ideas

> Government remains the paramount field of unwisdom because it is there
> that men seek power over others—and lose it over themselves.
> —Barbara Tuchman

Why is the character of political leaders so important today? Why do people expect to solve many problems by electing strong leadership figures? Why did it matter that George Bush lacked "charisma" and Bill Clinton remained an "enigma"—to quote typical newspapers headlines of the 1992 elections?

Laws, constitutions, and federal structures serve as insurances against abuses of power, but they are not sufficient. Without tradition, laws and constitutions are little more than pieces of paper. However, even when traditions have been established, the recent decades have shown that parliaments, congresses, and presidents in Western democracies have found ways to circumvent laws and abuse their positions because the institutions responsible for taxing and spending were not separated. This experience has led during the recent decades to the public's intense and justified scrutiny of politicians' character. People expect that politicians with special skills are, to some extent, the answer to today's flawed political institutions, which are characterized by intense lobbying and strong bureaucracies driven by fads and ideologies.

Thus the scrutiny is justified, as is the public's cynicism. The cynical attitude is justified since today's political institutions cannot insure that even strong and politically skilled people will succeed in withstanding lobbyists' pressures and preventing the persistence of mistaken policies. The scrutiny is justified since the public is aware that there are no institutions in place to insure against persistence of erroneous policies. This explains why voters judge candidates by their strength, discipline, and willingness to accept responsibility. The leaders' views and character are a substitute and an insurance for better governments.

Referendum and initiative could provide a far better insurance by dissecting the elected politicians' ideas; by insuring against the politicians' excessive ambitions, lust for power, and strongly held views; and by making the process far less personal. Consider the 1992 elections in the United States.

President Bush personally opposed abortion, except in cases of rape, incest, or when the life of the mother was at stake; Governor Clinton was pro-choice. On capital gains, Bush offered a tax rate of 15.4 percent on all gains; Clinton advocated a 50 percent exclusion from taxation for long-term investment in new businesses only, but would not provide them for securities or other investments. Bush opposed industrial policies that promoted specific industries, whereas Clinton favored them. One can go on and describe their different ideas and positions on regulation, health care, environment, foreign policy, defense spending, welfare, and so forth. Voters had no other option but to buy a package deal and vote for either Bush or Clinton.

Consider now the option the voters would have if they could rely on the institutions of referendum and initiative. If a voter were pro-choice but favored low capital gains tax, and had no a priori objection to promoting particular industries, he could vote for either politician, since he could later express his view on each idea in separation and change either his views or the policy by starting an initiative. The voters' power is enhanced, whereas the politicians' is diminished. The politicians' particular ideas, their strength in opposing lobbying groups, and their ability to negotiate deals with the bureaucracy all become less relevant. Once the two institutions are firmly in place, the issue of politicians' character would diminish also, because people harboring excessive ambition and desire of power would not make politics their career choice but would turn their energies and ambitions to other fields.

Many of the problems we face today happen not because bad people are in charge or because "experts" come up with bad ideas. But today's political institutions have the capacity to turn virtues into vices, and fail to prevent persistence in error even on those rare occasions when the error is admitted. Bad ideas continue to be executed with impunity and escape the financial measuring stick. There are fewer occasions to reconsider, to weigh, to deliberate whether or not the expenditures made sense. Referendum and initiative would induce such debates, teach responsibility among voters, prevent the persistence of error, and thus destroy some myths[57]—a condition to finding the ways to prosperity—and create new ones.[58]

Whatever they turn out to be, they will not matter as much as myths do today. There will be more faith in institutions and less in principles. Considering the disasters to which ages of faith in principles have led, an age of belief in both principles and institutions giving citizens more powers would be a relief.

APPENDIXES

Underground Economies and the Measurement of Wealth

Underground activities refer to:

1. Legal activity that yields income that is not reported to the tax authorities. The reasons for the lack of reporting may be the following: paying less tax; receiving unemployment or social security benefits and other public assistance, which would be denied if incomes were declared; being illegally in a country;
2. Illegal activity that yields income.[1]

People who carry out illegal activities may not necessarily evade taxes. If they believe that their income declarations are kept secret and will not be used by other government agencies for prosecution, they may tell the truth. If this is the case, then the only reason for the under-declaration of revenues would be to pay less taxes and get greater welfare benefits—activities identified in the first category only.

People do not seem to have such trust in their governments, and thus both types of underground activities result in an underestimation of incomes. People seem unwilling or unable[2] to tell the truth about their incomes even when told that the surveys will be used for scientific inquiries only.[3] Hessing et al. (1988) found no correspondence between people's self-reports of tax evasion and the officially documented behavior.[4] This total lack of correlation was obtained despite the fact that all government claims against the people filling the reports had been settled and people knew that the accuracy of their self-reports could be checked against their tax records.[5]

A 1971 Social Science Research Council survey of second job holding also found that, as the questions asked about second jobs became more detailed, the response rate declined, possibly for fear of being incriminated before tax authorities.[6] Indeed, Keenan and Dean (1980), examining peoples' attitudes toward both taxes and tax surveys, conclude that an adequate response rate could only be achieved by guaranteeing and demonstrating the complete anonymity of the replies, by conducting the survey in public places (rather than at home), and by asking respondents to place their written (and completely anonymous) replies in a sealed box. Nobody has ever done such survey anywhere.[7] Thus it is hardly surprising that opinions differ significantly on the reliability of the currently published GNP figures when trying to adjust for their "hidden economies" only.[8]

This brief survey leads us to consider more general problems linked with the measurement of aggregates. Whether one looks at the income, the expenditure, or the output methods for calculating the GNP, one encounters problems due to non-response, lies, or underreporting. Since the reasons and sources of the discrepancies are different, proper double-checking is not feasible. On one hand, estimates of the expenditure measure of the GNP are derived mainly from a wide range of surveys designed specifically for statistical purposes.[9] These estimates, as noted, may be biased because of non-response or conscious understatement.[10] On the other hand, the income-based measure of the GNP may be biased because the data are collected through the respective revenue services in the various countries. Wages and salaries are calculated from tax reforms filled out by employers, whereas income from self-employment is based on those reported by the self-employed themselves.

Thus, unsurprisingly, there have been fluctuating differences between these two measures of GNP (varying between 1 to 5 percent),[11] which have been attributed not only to the problems mentioned until now but also to inflation (which, when it is in the range of 10 percent or more may, because of the timing discrepancies, lead to problems in comparing the numbers obtained through the two methods). Also, in countries where pay freezes were imposed,[12] there has been a growth in other forms of remuneration (such as payment-in-kind) that go on undeclared. The discrepancies were also attributed to the introduction of new taxes (the value-added tax in Europe), which, in order to be evaded, led to underreporting of business activities by the self-employed.[13] Bureaus of Statistics solve such discrepancies between the various accounts in a totally arbitrary manner, adding billions in one place or subtracting billions from another.

Mismeasured Aggregates,
Models, and Policies

In order to compare easily the views and conclusions discussed in the text and in the standard rational expectation literature, I use the same notations as Sargent and Wallace do in their 1975 paper.

Suppose that a variable y_t, which the monetary authority is interested in controlling, is described by the stochastic difference equation:

(1) $y_t = \alpha + \lambda y_{t-1} + \beta m_t + u_t$

where u_t is a serially independent, identically distributed random variable with variance $Var(u)$ and mean zero; m_t is the rate of growth of money supply; and α, λ, and β are parameters. y_t may represent either the unemployment rate, or the deviation of real GNP from the potential one.

Assume that the goal of the monetary is to minimize the variance over time of y_t around a desired steady state level, y^*. But, although both the monetary authorities and the public know that y_t is not properly measured, the monetary authorities shape their policies by looking at the measured figure, y^m_t, whose relationship with the real one is given by:

(2) $y^m_t = y_t + \varepsilon_t$

where both y_t and ε_t are random variables. The error term, ε_t, refers to both the undeclared output and to measurement errors due to innovations. Thus, neither $Cov(\varepsilon_t, u_t)$ nor $Cov(\varepsilon_t, u_{t-1})$ nor $Cov(\varepsilon_{t-1}, u_t)$ can be assumed to equal zero. The first two covariances are not equal to zero because innovations lead to mismeasurements, whereas the third reflects the fact that the fraction of undeclared output at time $t-1$ (depending, let us say, on the rate of marginal tax rate at time $t-1$), has an effect on innovations at time t. But, as in Sargent and Wallace's model, let us assume that ε_t, the measurement errors, are identically distributed with $Var(\varepsilon)$ and mean zero.

Consider now their first, "Keynesian" model and assume that monetary policy is set by choosing the parameters g_0 and g_1 according to this feedback rule:

(3) $m_t = g_0 + g_1 y^m_{t-1}$.

Substituting for m_t from (3) and (2) into (1) gives:

$$(4) \quad y_t = \alpha + \lambda y_{t-1} + \beta[g_0 + g_1(y_{t-1} + \varepsilon_{t-1})] + u_t$$
$$= (\alpha + \beta g_0) + (\lambda + \beta g_1) \, y_{t-1} + \beta g_1 \, \varepsilon_{t-1} + u_t.$$

From this equation one gets the steady-state mean of y:

$$(5) \quad Ey = (\alpha + \beta g_0)/[1 - (\lambda + \beta g_1)]$$

and the steady-state, conditional variance of y_t, y_{t-1} around y* (assuming, as in Sargent and Wallace, that they are equal), is given by:

$$(6) \quad \text{Var}(y) = (\lambda + \beta g_1)^2 \, \text{Var}(y) + \beta^2 \, g_1{}^2 \, \text{Var}(\varepsilon) + \text{Var}(u) + 2\beta g_1 \, \text{Cov}(\varepsilon, u)$$

or

$$(7) \quad \text{Var}(y) = \frac{\text{Var}(u) + \beta^2 g^2{}_1 \, \text{Var}(\varepsilon) + 2\beta g_1 \, \text{Cov}(\varepsilon, u)}{[1 - (\lambda + \beta g_1)^2]}$$

The monetary authorities within this model can choose an optimal policy, g_1 (as in Sargent's and Wallace's model), so as to minimize the variance of y, and then choose g_0. But here the solution also depends on $\text{Var}(\varepsilon)$, the variability of the measurement errors, as well as on the covariance between the realized "real" shock, u_t, and the measurement error. In terms of the evidence presented in the chapter, this would imply, for example, that monetary authorities take into account that innovations lead to misestimating the real GNP, as do increases in population, since the shift from the consumption to investment and speculation as far as housing is considered is not being taken into account.

In practice, the figures concerning the variability of measurement errors and the covariances have rarely been calculated, and if they have been and corrections were made, they were done with a long lag. Thus, even if this Keynesian-type model gave an accurate description of the way policy could be thought about to affect output, the question that lingers is: What happens if, in practice, monetary authorities react by taking into account the measured variables?[1]

Then, the authorities behave as if the variance of output is given by:

$$(8) \quad \text{Var}(y) = \frac{\text{Var}(u)}{[1 - (\lambda + \beta g_1)^2]}$$

which is minimized by setting $g_1 = -\lambda/\beta$. But if this policy is pursued, the realized variance will be:

$$(9) \quad \text{Var}(y) = \text{Var}(u) + \lambda^2 \, \text{Var}(\varepsilon) - 2\lambda \, \text{Cov}(\varepsilon, u)$$

and thus different from the one predicted, which simply equals $\text{Var}(u)$.

Assume that although monetary authorities believe in the model of the economy presented here, they realize that in practice, the errors not being known, the best they can do is to either set policies at $g_1 = -\lambda/\beta$, or give up and pursue a fixed monetary rule, i.e., $g_1 = 0$. If they choose the latter strategy, the variance of output becomes:

$$(10) \quad \text{Var}(y) = \frac{\text{Var}(u)}{1 - \lambda^2}$$

This monetary rule should be preferred if:

$$(11) \quad \frac{\text{Var}(u)}{1 - \lambda^2} < \text{Var}(u) + \lambda^2 \, \text{Var}(\varepsilon) - 2\lambda \, \text{Cov}(\varepsilon, u)$$

Recall now the measurement problems and magnitudes discussed in the text, which are caused by fluctuations in the size of "black markets," by innovations, and by unreliable price indices. They all suggest that both the variance and covariance terms might be relatively large: Mankiw and Shapiro's estimate of just the acknowledged errors in GNP growth rates gives a lower bound of the errors involved. Thus, one must not necessarily be a monetarist to be in favor of a monetary rule rather than "discretion."[2] Notice also the fact that fluctuations in what is being *measured* may or not diminish if a monetary rule is pursued, because what is being measured depends on the covariance term, about which little is known, as shown in the text.

Mismeasured Aggregates and Aggregate Supply Functions

In light of the evidence and discussion in this chapter, it is hard to justify an aggregate supply function postulated in Sargent and Wallace and the "rational expectations" literature, which is the following:

$$(12) \quad y_t = \xi_0 + \xi_1(m_t - E_{t-1} \, m_t) + \xi_2 \, y_{t-1} + u_t$$

where ξ_0, ξ_1, ξ_2 were fixed parameters, and $E_{t-1} \, m_t$ was the public's expectation of m_t as of time $t - 1$. When price indices are built the way they are, the monetary authority's attempt to target nominal interest rates based on the mismeasured figures, may bring far greater surprises than the difference between the realized and anticipated money supply.

It should be emphasized, however, that in extreme situations, when money supplies have been either growing or diminishing relatively fast, the model described in Sargent (1986)[3] may capture the way in which anticipations concerning the relationship between the price level and the realized and expected money supplies are formed.[4] But within Sargent's model, used to explore hyperinflations, there is no discussion on the relationship between *output* and monetary surprises, but only between the price level and the government's constraints on the ways in which its expenditures are expected to be financed. Indeed, in general, it would be hard to justify a relationship reflected in (12). During hyperinflations output diminished, and people shifted to barter, gold, and foreign currencies. The unsatisfied increases in nominal demand resulted in these extreme circumstances in empty shelves, long queues or black markets, and diminished production.[5] This evidence implies that, in some circumstances, firms do *not* increase production in response to nominal shocks facing them.

Yet there is nothing that contradicts such behavior with an assumption of profit maximization. Consider features of Lucas's (1973) model, on which Sargent and Wallace's equation, referred to in (12), was based. Lucas explored implications of behavior when a confusion was made between nominal and real shocks. In order to reach the conclusion that the confusion *always* leads to an increased output, Lucas makes a number of assumptions. One is that at time t producers know only the price in their own market. The other is that in response to an increased demand, they always adjust their output, though by how much depends on the relative variability of nominal and real shocks.

The persistent evidence that, when the variance of nominal shocks is *high,* producers adjust to the increased nominal demands by adjusting prices and waiting (or even diminishing production—so shelves become empty and lines longer) implies that firms do not always react according to the supply function assumed in the model. Does the different reaction reflect a non-optimal behavior (even within Lucas's own model)? The answer is no.

Lucas assumes, as noted, that producers only know the price in their own market at time t. But rephrased, this same sentence can also be read as follows: "producers *know* at time t that at time t + 1 they will know both the extent of the nominal shock, as well as everything else that happened at time t." Thus, when adapting to a shock at time t, one does not contradict the assumption of profit maximization by stating that the firm has two options:

- to adjust output, as in Lucas's model, or
- to postpone production, wait until time t + 1, and then decide if an increase in output is warranted.

If firms pursue the strategy Lucas assumes, they will make the mistake of confusing nominal for real changes, and profits (for producers) and leisure and welfare (for workers) are being reduced. If the second strategy is pursued, the firms' mistake will be of *not* increasing output when the increased demand was in fact due to real changes taking place.[6] As noted, during periods of rapid inflation, the evidence suggests that producers pursue the second rather than the first strategy, trying to distinguish temporary from permanent changes.[7] In this case, one cannot easily justify a supply function as in (12), though in the case examined next one can.

Aggregate Supply and Inflation within Limits

What happens when inflation is relatively low and measurement problems prevail?[8] Then, as argued next, Lucas's assumptions seem sound and the confusion between nominal and real shocks can be rationalized on the grounds that everybody is aware of the severe measurement problems, of price indices in particular (though see discussion in chap. 4).

Recall Lucas's assumption that people observe price changes in their own markets only at time t, but they have to predict the "price level" from previous information. Formally, this statement was translated as:

(13) $p_t = P[p_t/\Omega_{t-1}] + \xi_t$

where p_t is the average economy-wide logarithm of price, $P[.]$ the projection of p_t on information available at time $t - 1$ and ξ_t a random variable, the surprise part of the aggregate price level, which cannot be predicted from information Ω_{t-1}.

This same relationship, however, can be interpreted differently: the "surprise" part of the price level can be due to measurement errors, discovered with a lag. Thus, even if there is no monetary surprise at time t, the confusion between real and nominal shocks will occur when there are measurement errors in price indices, and the results in Lucas's model follow.[9]

In his recent survey of macroeconomics, Mankiw (1990) emphasizes that although some critics have argued that the confusion about the price level cannot plausibly be so great as to generate the large changes in output and employment observed over the business cycle, no compelling evidence explains why this approach has been so widely abandoned. The evidence and arguments presented here and in chapter 4 may revive this interest: not only can the confusion be put on a sounder footing than just reliance on monetary surprises, but one can also understand the severe impact of the confusion. Two cases are discussed in chapter 4: first, when central banks misread the changes in the CPI, interpreting them as being due to monetary shocks, and pursued a policy of high nominal interest rates, which the bank viewed as being low real ones but the public viewed as high real ones. Such policy can have significant and lasting impacts, as Blinder already showed. The second episode also concerns the impact of a mismeasured CPI, when a significant fraction of the government's expenditures have been linked to the mismeasured index.[10] One impact of such a mechanical policy, as will be discussed in chapter 4, has been an unexpected increase in government spending, giving rise to expectations of either higher taxes, higher interest rates, or higher inflation rates in the future.[11] In all these cases, the confusion due to mismeasurement has large and lasting consequences.

The aforementioned distinction between the effects of unexpected low and high inflation rates can shed light on the fact that one observes a Phillips curve–type relationship at times, whereas at other times, one does not. Moreover, the rigidity of nominal contracts, which according to some models explains the Phillips curve, can be linked to the existence of measurement errors. D. H. Robertson made this point back in 1935 in his comments on Keynes's *General Theory*. He argued that "the unreliability of index numbers . . . [was] quite sufficient reason for working people to think, *within limits,* in terms of money" (italics added).[12] Though Robertson does not elaborate on this point, or define what determines the limits, the arguments and evidence presented here support his view and also define the limits. When there is, let us say, a 3 to 5 percent stable growth in the money supply, and there are also innovations, demographic changes, the price indices will reflect a mixture of real and monetary changes, and contracts will be made in terms of money. However, when the stable monetary rule is abandoned, contracts will become indexed—as shown in chapter 4.

The arguments presented in this appendix formalize part of the arguments in the text and show the following:

- during "normal" times, measurement problems may be sufficiently important to undermine the effectiveness of discretionary monetary policy;[13]
- when measurement errors are important, one can favor rules even if one happens to be a Keynesian.
- if one gives the term "discretion" an interpretation *different* from the one now being given in macroeconomic models—reacting to specific changes and events rather than reacting mechanically to changes in aggregates—one can favor discretion without relying on Keynesian vocabulary and arguments. See discussion in chapter 2 and chapter 4.

Demography and Savings

Reuven Brenner, Marcel. G. Dagenais, and
Claude Montmarquette

It is thrifty to prepare today for the wants of tomorrow.
                    —Aesop, *The Ant and the Grasshopper*

As this prudent economy, which some people call Savings, is in private
families the most certain method to increase an estate, so some imagine
that whether a country be barren or fruitful, the same method if generally
pursued (which they think practicable) will have the same effect upon a
whole nation, and that, for example, the English might be much richer
than they are, if they would be as frugal as their neighbours. This, I
think, is an error.
                    —Bernard de Mandeville, *The Fable of the Bees*

Chapter 3 showed that the emphasis on private savings or national savings is mis-
placed, if one's goal is to understand growth and formulate policies to sustain it. What
is being measured as "national savings" is another mismeasured aggregate, and not
only for the reasons mentioned in chapter 1. By using the standard macroeconomic
methods, this appendix shows that aggregate savings are mismeasured, and that by
looking at the official figures one does not know how much is "invested" in the
economy.[1]

This is the case because measured savings depend not only on traditional
economic variables, but also on other factors such as the abrupt rise in the divorce rate
that occurred during the 1970s and 1980s in the United States, and the increase in
women's participation in the labor force, both of which resulted in women's greater
investment in education, formal or informal. The smaller financial savings that resulted
from this greater expenditure on education is measured as declined savings rather than
increased investments. Moreover, expectations of more predictable incomes for women
are not even captured, although the diminished savings result from the changed
expectations.[2]

Thus, the reason for linking these additional variables with the measurement of
savings is simple. As long as marriages were relatively stable, women's financial
insurance was based on their husbands' earnings and the family's assets, which

177

included financial savings. With the abrupt rise in the divorce rate during the 1970s and 1980s, women could rely far less on such assets. The abrupt changes can be linked with a legal innovation in 1970. California passed the first law in the Western world to abolish any requirement of fault as the basis for marital dissolution, and later it was adopted elsewhere. For this as well as for additional reasons, women decided to study more and stay longer in the labor market. Instead of saving in the form of financial assets, women came to expect that education and experience in the job market would provide "savings" and enable them to adapt to the decreased reliability of marital agreements.

Yet neither women's increased expenditures on education (financed implicitly by government subsidies to educational institutions) nor their greater experience in the labor market are counted in national statistics as either "savings" or "investment." Thus one could predict that increases in divorce rates, in the participation of women in the labor force, and in their years of study would contribute to a significant decline in *measured* saving rates. The U.S. data examined here fail to falsify these predictions. If this is the case, the meaning of changes in national savings rate is even more blurred than usual.

Savings Defined

Whatever monetary income is not spent is, by definition, saved in the form of a financial asset. Even without taking into account the possibility of foreign investments, this definition does not imply that investment in a society equals the amount saved in either financial assets or traditionally measured investment goods.

If people decided to spend more money and more of their other resources on health, education, or gaining experience in the labor market (through formal or informal on-the-job training), such sums[3] represent additional investments too.[4] Buying more consumer durables—be they cars, diamonds, gold, or works of art[5]—also represent, in part, savings and investment. And, although in the United States they are not counted as such, a government's increased expenditures on roads, schools, and even on the military may at times represent additional investments rather than "consumption" or "waste." Thus, building arguments based on static relationships (or even on their more sophisticated versions) expressed in Keynesian symbols as

$$Y = C + S \; ; \; Y = C + I \to I = S$$

where Y stands for income, C for consumption, I for investments, and S for savings, and which imply that ex-post savings equal investments, are not illuminating when significant changes take place in what people view as "consumption" and "savings." What can be and has been measured as either "consumption," "savings," or "investments" does not correspond to the theoretical definitions of these terms. Thus one can hardly expect to produce the desired effects by recommending policies based on the various figures dutifully published by bureaus of statistics today, since they do not capture people's changed perceptions of what constitutes savings, investment, and consumption.

How Are Savings Measured?

In public policy debates in recent years, much has been written about the facts that saving rates are too low, being in the range of 3 to 6 percent in the United States, the United Kingdom, France, and other countries, which prevents "adequate" investments, but relatively less was written on the ways this figure is calculated in the National Income and Product Accounts (NIPAs) in the United States, or in accounts under other names in other countries. Holloway (1989) and Boskin (1988) are among the exceptions.[6] They give detailed accounts of how savings are calculated and show the formidable limitations of the methods being used, as summarized in chapter 1.[7] Yet their reservations and many others' are important if one wants to measure the correct level of savings in an economy. That is not the goal of this appendix. Its goal is to show what happens to *measured* savings when drastic demographic changes take place. This will suggest not only that national savings are not properly measured but also that relying on changes in the measured aggregates to shape policies would be a mistake. As shown in chapter 3, it is the flow of credit that counts, not static notions.

A Demographic Model of the Determinants of Savings

Suppose that, because of the increased probability of divorce, both married and unmarried women decided to study more, enter the labor market, and stay there longer. All these reactions would lead to: a) diminished savings in the form of financial assets for a household; b) increased investments in women's "human capital," in the form of on-the-job training or longer years of formal education. Moreover, the anticipation of increased incomes by women in the future would lead to diminished financial savings in the present. Thus, although the measured savings may diminish, the decrease does not imply that the economy will be in bad shape: women's greater education and experience is an investment (in the formal, measured economy).[8]

The following facts demonstrate the correspondence between the theoretical model capturing these arguments and the situation in the United States. One-half of all new marriages are now expected to end in divorce, and in the past, women and the minor children in their custody experienced, on average, a 73 percent *decline* in their standard of living in the first year after divorce.[9] The U.S. Census Bureau estimated that 59 percent of all children born in 1983 are likely to live in a single-parent family before they are eighteen, and the National Institute of Child Health and Human Development projected that two-thirds of the children born in wedlock in 1980 will experience the disruption of their parents' marriage by age of 17.[10] The 1972 Consumer Expenditure Survey revealed that families with working wives have lower saving rates than families with non-working wives, *ceteris paribus*,[11] and Johnson and Skinner (1986) found that women who divorce, increase their labor supply in the three years prior to the separation. In other words, anticipation of divorce was found to increase the women's labor supply.[12] Indeed, the increase in women's participation in the labor force between 1960 and 1980 was dramatic. In 1960, 32 percent of the working population were women, and 60 percent of all wives contributed no cash earnings to their households. In 1980 the first proportion increased to 42 percent (and to 44.3 percent in 1987), whereas the second diminished to 40 percent.[13]

These drastic changes can be linked to the change in divorce laws and the resulting expectations of diminished financial security. Recall that, as late as 1966, New York's law permitted divorce only upon demonstration of adultery.[14] But in 1970, California was the first state where the legal *innovation* of "no-fault" divorce went into effect. In 1971, Iowa was the second state to adopt the law. By 1974, as Jacob (1988, 80) remarks, "the year in which the National Conference of Commissioners on Uniform State Laws and the American Bar Association had promulgated the Uniform Marriage and Divorce Act with its no-fault provisions, the more authoritative listing of state divorce laws declared that forty-five states already possessed a no-fault procedure," middle America being added to the list in the late 1970s.[15] In 1985, South Dakota became the last American Jurisdiction to repeal an exclusively fault-based statute.[16] The following numbers give an idea of the changes that took place: divorce rates per 1,000 mid-year population were 2.00 in 1940, 2.55 in 1950, and 2.18 in 1960. The rate increased to 3.51 in 1970, reached 5.19 in 1980, and was 4.96 in 1985.[17]

Let us take now a closer, detailed, look at our results. The decisions of having or not having another child, of entering or reentering the labor market, of studying or not studying more, of how much to save and in what form are taken simultaneously.[18] This implies that women's rate of participation in the labor force depends on expectations of returns to education, on fertility decisions, as well as on evaluations of the probability of divorce. In turn, the anticipated divorce rate itself will be affected by the increased participation of women in the labor force (since women would have less incentive to stay locked in unsuccessful marriages), and by fertility decisions (since fewer children may mean less commitment to marriage). Therefore, a simultaneous equation model is required to explain these phenomena, changes in measured savings being just one of the equations in the model.[19]

Five equations describe the model used here. The first one concerns the women's labor force participation (FLP), which is assumed to depend on: the anticipated divorce rate (DRA), and lagged values both of this participation rate (FLP_{-1}) and of indicators reflecting being either a part- or a full-time student (WSR_{-1}). All three explanatory variables are expected to have positive signs: education and work in the past indicate an ambition to be in the labor force, whereas anticipation of divorce indicates fears of being forced by changed circumstances to do so in the future. Incentives for entering the labor force and for investing in human capital are thus enhanced by precautionary motives. Our first equation is, therefore, expressed as follows:

(1) $FLP = F(\overset{+}{FLP}_{-1}, \overset{+}{WSR}_{-1}, \overset{+}{DRA})$.[20]

But DRA—the anticipated divorce rate—is not observable. We assume that anticipation on the divorce rate for the coming year is unbiased and that, therefore

$$DRA = DRF + \varepsilon$$

where DRF is the divorce rate observed in the subsequent year and ε is a random anticipation error.

One may argue that the causal relationship between the divorce rate and female labor participation is in the opposite direction. That is, the changed participation of women in the labor force *led* to the legal changes that increased the divorce rate. But reading the history of the "divorce revolution" does not suggest that this is the case. There were demands for changing the law, but the "no-fault" concept of divorce, introduced in California in 1970, was an *innovation* whose impact, concerning the significant decline in the divorced women's standard of living, was not anticipated. On the contrary, advocates of the legal change expected that the divorced women would become better off.[21] Thus it seems more plausible to assume that in this specific historical context the relationship as defined in the first equation is the right one.

The second equation presents the relationship between the women's decision to be either a part-time or a full-time student (WSR) and other variables. This decision is assumed to depend on: a) decisions of the same nature made in the past, that is, the lagged variable (WSR_{-1}), since completing studies takes time; b) the number of children less than five years old in the household (P5T); and c) the probability of divorce, the indicator of which is the anticipated rate of divorce (DRA):

$$(2) \quad WSR = W(\overset{+}{WSR}_{-1}, \overset{?}{P5T}, \overset{+}{DRA})$$

The reason for the two positive signs is as explained above. The reason for the question mark for the "young children" variable is that, on one side, their presence could delay plans to study, since reentry in the labor market might not be planned yet. On the other side, to study part-time could be an attractive opportunity for women with young children.

The third equation describes the fertility decision, represented here by the same variable as used in the previous equation, P5T, indicating the number of young children at home. The explanatory variables in this case are: a) WSR_{-2} (i.e., WSR lagged two periods), the variable indicating here the "return-to-school" decision; b) FLP, indicating the labor force participation of women; c) DRC, the current divorce rate, which is the same as the DRF variable, but lagged by one period (the higher this rate is, the smaller the family size should be); and d) URT, the urbanization rate (raising children in a city being more costly than raising them in rural areas):

$$(3) \quad P5T = P(\overset{-}{FLP}, \overset{-}{WSR}_{-2}, \overset{-}{DRC}, \overset{-}{URT})$$

The fourth equation describes the determination of DRF (and hence DRA, the expectations about divorce rates):

$$(4) \quad DRF = D(\overset{?}{FLP}, \overset{-}{P5T}, \overset{+}{DRC}, \overset{+}{DRD}, \overset{-}{DRDC})$$

A new variable in the equation is DRD, a dummy variable that accounts for the changes in the divorce laws during the seventies.[22] This variable, as well as the one indicating the current divorce rate, DRC, is expected to have a positive sign, whereas the one indicating the number of young children is expected to have a negative one. DRDC is a cross variable: DRD × DRC. It suggests that the effect of changes in divorce laws declines as the current divorce rate increases. The effect of increased participation of women in the labor force (FLP) on the divorce rate is not clear: on the one hand, possessing marketable skills may hasten the decision to divorce. On the other hand, the increased participation may delay decisions to marry, and if there are fewer marriages, there will also be fewer divorces.

The fifth equation represents the decision to save in the form of physical or financial (rather than human) capital. SRH represents this decision, as measured by the rate of household savings. It is supposed to depend on the following variables: a) IGR, the growth rate of real income per capita; b) PAT, a demographic variable indicating the fraction of elderly (more than 74 years old) in the total population; c) SSV, indicating Social Security payments as a percentage of the Gross Domestic Product; d) INR, the annual inflation rate; e) PTT, the number of children between 5 and 15 years old in the household; f) FLP, the already defined labor force participation of women variable; and g) P5T, the young children variable.

The reason for using two variables for children, one endogenous and the other exogenous (or at least predetermined), is similar to the one Johnson and Skinner (1986) gave in their analyses of the determinants of the labor force participation of women. Though they admitted that a complete model of household behavior would include decisions about having children as an endogenous variable simultaneously determined with labor supply and divorce probabilities, they emphasized that *"past* decisions about children and labor supply will also clearly affect current labor supply and divorce probabilities."[23] The estimated fifth equation is therefore

$$(5) \quad \text{SRH} = S(\overset{-}{\text{FLP}}, \overset{-}{\text{P5T}}, \overset{+}{\text{INR}}, \overset{?}{\text{IGR}}, \overset{-}{\text{PTT}}, \overset{?}{\text{PAT}}, \overset{-}{\text{SSV}})$$

The reasons for the expected signs are the following: Modigliani's (1970) life cycle model suggests that the sign of the real income per capita growth rate should be positive and the one representing the aging population should be negative. However, in a recent survey, Hurd (1990) refers to a literature on the bequest motive and the risk-averse elderly to suggest a consumption trajectory practically flat over the life cycle.[24] The female labor force participation variable, viewed as a substitute for the precautionary savings of the household, is expected to have a negative sign. According to Feldstein (1977, 1980), the private savings rate should decline with an increase in the provision of Social Security,[25] whereas the annual rate of inflation is expected to have a positive effect on the savings rate (see Jump 1980, Dagenais 1990). Unanticipated inflation, which is usually accompanied by rises in real interest rates,[26] reduces the real-market value of personal financial wealth and induces households to increase their savings to make up for the losses, especially if unanticipated inflation is considered a signal that tough times lie ahead.[27]

Data and Results

To test the dynamics of households' decisions and to assess the role of divorce rates on the savings behavior, particularly during drastic changes in divorce laws that occurred in the United States between 1970 and 1985, we use the aggregate time series data for the U.S. economy covering the period 1960 to 1985. Data for the five endogenous variables of the model are obtained in the following way: the savings rate (SRH) is derived from aggregate data; the time spent by women in the labor force is approximated by the female labor force participation rate (FLP); the percentage of women enrolled in part-time or full-time studies at universities (WSR) is used as a measure for pursuing such studies in general (not necessarily at a university); the ratio of population of children aged five or less in the total population measures fertility (P5T); the anticipated divorce rate is measured as explained in the previous section (DRA).

Three exogenous demographic variables are used in the model: the ratio of the population between the ages of 5 and 15 over total population (PTT); the ratio of population over 74 years of age over total population (PAT); and the ratio of urban population over total population (URT). The other exogenous and predetermined variables are of three types. There are lagged values of the endogenous variables FLP, WSR, and DRA, namely FLP_{-1}, WSR_{-1}, WSR_{-2}, and DRC. There are purely exogenous variables, namely: a dummy variable related to the timing of changes in divorce laws (DRD); the growth rate of real per capita disposable income (IGR); the annual rate of inflation (INR); a Social Security variable (SSV); and, finally, the variable DRDC, a cross variable of the predetermined variable DRC and the exogenous variable DRD. Table 1 presents descriptive statistics on the principal variables of the model. The system of equations that describe the model and a summary of the hypotheses are presented at the end of the first appendix to this chapter, whereas the descriptive statistics are summarized next, in table 1.

Table 2 presents the estimates of the model (obtained by iterated three-stage least squares).

The numbers in these tables show that, in general, the estimated model fails to contradict the predictions made. The reported R^2's are high and most coefficient estimates are statistically significant. The numerous relationships among the endogenous variables fail to falsify the simultaneous model. The negative sign of the female labor force participation variable in the last equation suggests that labor force participation may be viewed as a substitute for the household's precautionary financial savings.

The results also support Modigliani's life cycle model of savings since the coefficients of the demographic variables, P5T and PTT, as well as the coefficient of the income growth rate variable, IGR, are all significant and of the expected signs. One result that contradicts Modigliani's model prediction concerns the sign of PAT, the variable indicating the fraction of elderly in the population.[28] The effect of inflation rate, INR, is positive, which, as explained in the previous section, reflects the assumption that unanticipated inflation reduces the real value of the financial personal wealth, gives a signal that tough times are ahead, and induces people to save more. Many empirical studies in a number of countries obtained this result. Horioka (1986) found that, in Japan, increases in the inflation rate increase rather than diminish real savings in financial assets, and both Jump (1980) and Dagenais (1990) found the same phenomenon for, respectively, the United States and Canada. The increased inflation represents such pessimistic expectations, for it implies that the government is unable to cover its expenditures by its revenues. This raises the prospect of a downward revision of the value of social security and other benefits in the future, inducing increased savings today. (Feldstein's social security variable was dropped from the savings rate equation since the coefficient estimate was found to be insignificant. Once again, this

TABLE 1.   Demographic Model of the Determinants of U.S. Household Savings Rate: Descriptive Statistics

Symbols	Definition	Mean Deviation	Standard Deviation
SRH	Savings rate of U.S. households (% income)	7.10	1.17
FLP	Women's labor force participation rate	37.96	3.76
WSR	Percentage of woman students enrolled in universities (part time and full time)	44.50	5.57
P5T	Percentage of the population aged less than 5	8.60	1.56
INR	Annual inflation rate of the CPI (1980=100)	5.20	3.50
IGR	Annual growth rate of real per capita disposable income	3.17	2.36
PTT	Percentage of the population between the ages of 4 and 15	18.14	2.32
PAT	Percentage of the population older than 74	3.91	0.51
DRF	Divorce rate at time t+1	4.00	1.19
DRC	Current divorce rate	3.89	1.22
DRD	Dummy variable for changes in divorce laws: = 0 for 1960–67 = 0.1 to 0.9 for 1968–76 = 1.0 for 1977–85	0.52	—
URT	Percentage of urban population	76.15	2.27
SSV	Social Security as % of GNP	4.97	1.55

Sources: WSR: UNESCO, *Annuaire Statistique,* 1960–77; 1979–85; URT: World Bank, *World Development Report,* 1960, 1965, 1975, 1980–85; P5T, PTT, PAT: United Nations, *Demographic Yearbook,* 1961–66, 1979; *Current Population Report,* Washington: U.S. Bureau of the Census, Series no. 1022, no. 721 no. 441; SRH, SSV, IGR: *National Income and Product Accounts, 1929–82,* Washington: U.S. Department of Commerce, Bureau of Economic Analysis; *Survey of Current Business,* Washington: U.S. Department of Commerce, Office of Business Economics, July 1983, 1987, 1988; DRC: United Nations, *Demographic Yearbook,* 1950–84; FLP: International Labor Office, *Yearbook of Labor Statistics,* various years; INR: IMF, *International Financial Statistics,* Washington: 1984, 1988.

result is not very surprising since a large number of empirical studies in a number of countries got similar results (Horioka's 1986 analysis of Japan, for example).

Most variables of the model are expressed in terms of ratios so that the coefficient estimates of table 2 are comparable. The overwhelming results point to the women's labor force participation rate variable as a good candidate to explain the relative decline in the U.S. rate of savings, as the women's labor force participation rate has increased from a value of 31.78 in 1960 to 43.10 in 1985. Over the same period, as illustrated in figure 1, the inflation rate and the growth rate of real per capita disposable income explain the fluctuations in the savings rate. Finally, the percentage of the population aged less than 5 has decreased and the percentage of the older population has increased, both *contributing* to increases in the measured savings rates.

In conclusion: the female labor force participation rate seems to play an important role explaining the decline of the savings rates of U.S. households. The fact that the female labor force participation rate has steadily increased over time is reflected both by the positive coefficient of the lagged variable FLP_{-1} in the female labor force

TABLE 2.   A Simultaneous Equation Model of the Determinants of Savings

Variables	SRH	FLP	WSR	P5T	DRA (DRF)
Endogenous					
SRH					
FLP	− 3.3966			− 0.66526	− 0.01782
	(1.29)			(0.0987)	(0.01049)
WSR					
P5T	− 2.3663		0.66355		− 0.24415
	(0.788)		(0.451)		(0.0476)
DRA (DRF)		0.2381	1.6505		
		(0.0877)	(0.716)		
Lagged Endogenous					
FLP$_{-1}$		0.84352			
		(0.0731)			
WSR$_{-1}$		0.05781	0.83204		
		(0.0410)	(0.0497)		
WSR$_{-2}$				0.34644	
				(0.0468)	
DRC (DRF$_{-1}$)				− 0.39347	0.57670
				(0.163)	(0.135)
Exogenous					
INR	0.36313				
	(0.0869)				
IGR	0.21508				
	(0.0812)				
PTT	− 0.70835				
	(0.490)				
PAT	14.083				
	(5.538)				
DRD					1.5039
					(0.433)
DRDC					− 0.21539
					(0.0637)
URT				− 0.19764	
				(0.03732)	
Const.	111.58	2.8379	− 4.3203	35.006	4.2964
	(43.31)	(0.947)	(5.754)	(3.216)	(0.891)
Other statistics					
R^2	0.6153	0.9976	0.9904	0.9834	0.9977
ρ	− 0.05	− 0.19	− 0.23	− 0.11	− 0.27

Note: Standard errors are in parentheses; ρ is the autocorrelation coefficient of the residuals.

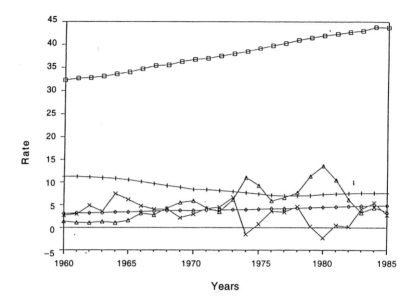

□ = FLP: Women's labor force participation rate
+ = PST: Percentage of the population aged less than 5
◊ = PAT: Percentage of the population older than 74
Δ = IGR: Annual growth rate of real per capita disposable income
x = INR: Annual inflation rate of the CPI

Fig. 1. Selected variables

participation rate equation, and by the one corresponding to the lagged variable representing the percentage of woman students enrolled in universities. A key variable explaining the increased rate of participation in the labor force is the anticipated divorce rate, DRA, as in Johnson and Skinner (1989). In turn, the current divorce rate, DRC, and the evolution of divorce laws in the United States determine the anticipated divorce rate. According to our estimated coefficients, without these laws the measured savings rates would be, on average, 2.2 percent higher each year. The anticipated divorce rate variable is negatively influenced by the female labor force participation rate, with the percentage of total children in the population variable having, as expected, a strong negative effect. Figure 2 illustrates the timing of the emergence of the divorce laws as well as the decline in the U.S. savings rates.

The equations reflecting the determinants of the decisions to attend school and to have children complete the model. The percentage of woman students enrolled in universities (part time and full time), WSR, is explained by the lagged values of this variable, and is positively and significantly influenced by the anticipated divorce rate,

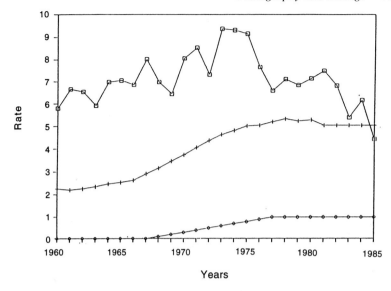

□ = SRH: Personal savings rate
+ = DRF: Divorce rate (at time t + 1)
◊ = DRD: Dummy variable for changes in divorce laws

Fig. 2. Measured savings and divorce rates

DRA. As expected, young children at home may induce confined mothers to resume schooling, most probably on a part-time basis only, although the positive coefficient of this variable, P5T, is not highly significant. Finally, the women's labor force decision variable, FLP, the current divorce situation, DRC, and urbanization, URT, all affect negatively the women's decision of bearing children, as expected. The significantly positive influence of the lagged values or the attending school variable, WSR, suggests that educated women may consider a pause for childbearing shortly after school and before entering permanently into the labor market.

Other Research on Savings: A Comparison

The traditional research on savings followed Modigliani's (1970), who examined differences in private saving rates between the years 1952 and 1960 for thirty-six developed and less-developed countries. His explanatory variables were those suggested by the life cycle model: productivity growth, population growth, and the age structure of the population.[29] As the data in the previous section suggests, there was no reason for either Modigliani or his followers to even think about introducing divorce rates in either their models or their empirical analyses, since those rates were relatively stable during the years covered by their research.[30]

In recent years the most influential research on savings surrounded the issues raised by Feldstein (1977, 1980) about the relationship between the provision of social security and private savings. He concluded that lower labor force participation of the elderly significantly raises the private saving rate, whereas greater social security diminishes it. Both his model and his findings have been challenged, and, as noted, in some empirical analyses the social security variables did not turn out to be significant, and even the labor force participation of the elderly reversed its sign.[31] This reversal led to renewed interest in the question of what explains the large discrepancies in private saving rates both across countries and over time. Mismeasurement, as shown in the previous chapter, is one answer. But others were given too.

Blades and Sturm (1982) introduced variables representing institutional differences across countries, as well as various definitions of saving and income, to explain the large differences in saving rates across countries. They succeeded in obtaining somewhat better results, but significant differences still remained. Graham (1989) introduced in his empirical examinations the labor force participation of women too (in addition to traditionally introduced variables like the one representing the changing age structure of the population, social security, and others), though not for the reasons mentioned in this paper. He introduced it in order to capture differences in the labor supply of the working age population (25 to 64 in his analyses) across countries.[32] One of his conclusions, however, was similar to one of ours. Graham emphasized "that an increase in the labor force participation rate of (female) workers may lower household saving rates calls for additional research." (1523).[33]

Kotlikoff (1989), who has done the most extensive research on savings in recent years, reached a similar conclusion and emphasized that:

> Despite the importance of demographic change to savings . . . there has been limited research on this subject. Research by Barro and Becker (1987, 1988) and several other researchers has just begun to link fertility decisions and long-run savings behavior. Research by Noguchi (1986) has begun to explore the interactions of non-altruistic bequests and demographic change. . . . But little or no work has been done on the more subtle influences of demographics on savings. For example, no one has yet considered how changes in family size influence family insurance and thereby the extent of precautionary savings. No one has explored how increases in divorce rates affect saving behavior. (32)

In this appendix, we have tried.[34]

Conclusion

There is little doubt that the accounting relationship between financial savings and investment is accurate, and that if more was invested that also means that more was saved. But why is such an ex-post relationship of any interest? If one finds that investments have diminished—something that we presently do not know, since not only education (and health) but also other expenditures on "durables" are not counted as such—one may worry about the prospects of future prosperity. But even if this was the case, the remedy can be found not in subsidizing savings (since the subsidies mean that a tax is implicitly imposed on something else) but only by increasing the incentives to invest. As far as a society's future prospects are considered, one should focus not on how to change people's decision to save, but on how to change their incentives to take risks. Why can't one simply change incentives to save unless one also changes incentives to take risks? Suppose that revenues from interest on one's savings are taxed, and one recommends eliminating such taxation in order to increase savings. If the government, however, does not reduce its expenditures, the diminished receipts from this source of revenue will have to be compensated for by increasing taxes on other activities. But such taxes diminish the incentives to take risks, and so total investment and saving may not change, although their composition will. As we have already seen, what will be measured is still another issue.

This appendix suggests that innovative divorce laws have changed these incentives and, as a consequence, changed the composition of "savings" and "investments" in society, moving away from investments in financial assets to investment in education and more continuous participation in the labor force. What happened in the "aggregate," i.e., to total investment in society, we do not know. This fact, combined with the evidence and arguments presented in the text, suggests that by just relying on some official aggregate figures, a recommended change in policy to affect the level of savings would be hard to defend. It would be far better to change tax laws and regulations that would have a direct impact on incentives to invest. When one gets the added incentives to invest, the additional credit and savings will come. Then, of course, one will observe a positive correlation between measured savings, and measured output and productivity. But correlation is no causation.

The Model

Suppose that, because of increased probability of divorce, both married and unmarried women decide to study more, enter the labor market, and stay there longer. All these reactions may lead to: a) diminished savings in the form of financial assets for a household; and b) for women, increased investment in their own "human capital," be it in informal on-the-job training, or longer years of formal education. Moreover, the anticipation of increased incomes by women in the future may lead to diminished financial savings in the present. Thus, although the measured savings may diminish, the decrease does not imply that the economy will be in bad shape: the women's greater education and experience is an investment (in the formal, measured economy).

A simple two-period model illustrates how measured savings can decrease and human capital and woman labor force participation can increase when demographic changes take place.[35] Consider a representative working married woman with children, and assume that her expected utility depends on present and future consumption. The level of expected utility is also an increasing function of the time that she spends attending to her children or in leisure activities. The woman's objective is

(1)   max E $U(C_1, T_1^c, C_2, C_2^d, T_2^c)$

where

U denotes the utility function;

C_1 denotes the consumption level in the first period;

C_2 denotes the consumption level in the second period, if there is no divorce;

C_2^d denotes the consumption level in the second period, if there is divorce;

T_1^c is the time spent in period 1 for attending to the children or for leisure;

T_2^c is the time spent in period 2 for attending to the children or for leisure; and

E is the expected value operator.

The first period wealth constraint is :

(2) $C_1 = (1 - s)[(1 - l_1)T_1 w_1 + V_1]$

where T_1 represents: total time available (T) minus a fixed amount (T_1^c) spent on children's attendance or on leisure in period 1. l_1 is the proportion of T_1 spent in acquiring human capital through course attendance, for example. w_1 is the wage rate in period 1 and $(1 - l_1)T_1 w_1$ is the woman's labor income during period 1. V_1 is her nonlabor income, which may come in part from sharing the husband's income, and s is the saving rate.

The second period budget constraint is uncertain. If there is no divorce, then, with probability $(1 - p)$, the budget constraint becomes

(3) $C_2 = s[(1 - l_1) T_1 w + V_1] (1 + r) + l_2 T w_2 + V_2$

where r is the rate of interest and w_2 is the wage rate in the second period. This rate is an increasing function of $l_1 T_1$ [$w_2 = g(l_1 T_1)$]; it depends on the amount invested in education during the first period. l_2 is the proportion of available time spent on the labor market in period 2. In this second period, the woman shares her time between the labor market ($l_2 T$) and children's attendance or leisure [$T_2^c = (1 - l_2)T$]. V_2 is the nonlabor income accruing during period 2.

However, if there is a divorce (and the woman has the custody of her children), then, assuming that a part $(1 - b)$ of the financial savings is lost in the separation process, the budget constraint becomes, with probability p,

(4) $C_2^d = b s [(1 - l_1) T_1 w_1 + V_1] (1 + r) + l_2 T w_2 + V_2^d$

where b is a fractional term $(0 \leq b < 1)$, and V_2^d is the nonlabor income during the second period, if there is divorce. Given that it has been widely observed that the economic condition of women with children deteriorates notably after a divorce, it is reasonable to assume that $V_2^d < V_2$.

For the sake of simplicity, let us assume a separable utility function,

(5) $EU = U^*(T_1^c) + U(C_1) + (1 + i)^{-1} \{(1 - p) [U^*(T_2^c) + U(C_2)] + p[U^{**}(T_2^c) + U(C_2^d)]\},$

where U(.) corresponds to the utility associated with the consumption level and $U^*(.)$ corresponds to the utility associated with child attendance or leisure. $U^{**}(.)$

represents the fact that, in case of divorce, the household production function changes significantly, thus altering the indirect utility function.[36] i is the subjective discount factor.

Assuming that T_1^c is constant and that the marginal utility of both time spent with children and consumption are declining, the first order condition for optimization can be derived as

(6) $Y_1 = Y_2$

where

(7) $Y_1 = U'(C_1)$

and

(8) $Y_2 = k\{(1 - p)[U^{*\prime}(T_2^c) + U'(C_2)] + p[U^{**\prime}(T_2^c) + U'(C_2^d)]\}$,

U' denoting the derivatives of the utility functions with $k = (1 + i)^{-1}$.

The decision variables are s, l_1 and l_2 [note that $T_2^c = (1 - l_2)T$]. Before period 1 starts, women are assumed to decide what share of their time, T_1, will be devoted to acquiring human capital, and what proportion of their income of period 1 will be saved. Women are also assumed to decide what share of their time will be spent on the labor market in period 2. This decision affects the type of training that will be acquired in period 1, since some types of skills are more appropriate for part-time employment than others. Finding optimal levels for the variables s, l_1, l_2 within a general framework is not very illuminating. Simulation results are more revealing. They test the coherence of the model and reveal its main features. To carry them out, equation (5) is specified as:

$$EU = \beta\ln(T_1^c) + \alpha\ln(C_1) + (1 - i)^{-1}(1 - p)[\beta\ln(T_2^c) + \alpha\ln(C_2)] + p[\delta\,\beta\ln(T_2^c) + \alpha\ln(C_2^d)],$$

where C_1, C_2, and C_2^d are as defined in equations (2), (3), and (4).

The logarithmic utility function implies a constant relative risk aversion parameter equal to 1. To calibrate the model, we assume that the total (non-sleeping) time available, T, is 112 hours per week, and the time spent in period 1 for either attending to the children or for leisure, T_1^c, is 72. T_1 equals 40 hours. This is the time allotted to acquiring human capital and working in the first period. The coefficient α, the weight of the utility of income, is set arbitrarily at 1. The weight for the utility of time, β, is fixed at 1.75, such that in period 1 the marginal utility of working the 41st hour (at an hourly wage rate of w = 25$) is equal to the marginal utility of the 72nd hour of leisure.[37] The coefficient δ increases the utility of leisure for the divorced woman. This coefficient in our simulations varies between 1.1 and 1.3. The proportion of the savings retained by the divorced woman, the coefficient b, varies between 0.35 and 0.65. The rate of return on savings, r, is set at 30 percent. It is based on an annual real rate of return of 4 percent under the assumption that the period 1 lasts ten years. The actualiza-

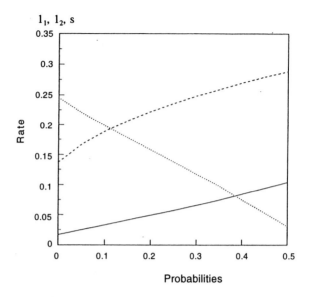

Fig. 3. Optimal decision parameter values as a function of divorce probabilities

tion rate, i, is equal to r for simplicity. w is arbitrarily set at 25$. w_2, the wage rate in the second period, is a function of the time spent in acquiring formal human capital in period 1:

$$w_2 = 0.66 \ w \ \{1 + \lambda[(l_1 T_1)^k]\}.$$

With no investment in human capital in period 1, $l_1 = 0$, and $w_2 = 0.66w = 16.70$$. For any savings to occur in period 1, the hourly wage rate for the unqualified labor force must be smaller than w_1. The assumption that $w_2 < w_1$ for the unqualified worker is justified in our model since period 2 includes retirement time. It takes into account indirectly the fact that the spending of households with children increases through time, a dimension that otherwise is not being taken into account. For the qualified worker, $l_1 > 0$ implies that w_2 increases in the ranges given by the parameter λ, that varies between 0.1 and 0.25 in different simulations and the parameter k, that varies from 0.4 to 0.8.

V_1, the nonlabor income in period 1, is partly attributed to the spouse and is fixed at 500$, or about half the labor income. V_2 is set at 333$, smaller than V_1, for the reasons discussed previously for w_{2c}. Nonlabor income in case of divorce, V_2^d, is set to 1, enhancing a well-established fact that the standard of living of divorced women falls considerably, on average, due mostly to unpaid alimonies.

Many simulations were run with these specifications with values for the probability of divorce, p, ranging from 25 to 50 percent. In almost all cases, the results show that an increase in the probability of divorce increases schooling and labor force participation and decreases savings. A typical result suggests an increase of 50 percent in l_1, 15 percent in l_2, and a drop of 70 percent in s, when p jumps from 30 to 50 percent. A specific case is illustrated in figure 3.[38]

The Econometric Model

The complete model and a summary of the hypotheses are described by the following system of equations, having this general form:

$$(I - B)\ \underset{\sim}{Y} = \underset{\sim}{\Gamma} \underset{\sim}{X} + \underset{\sim}{E}$$

Y is the vector of endogenous variables:

$$
\underset{\sim}{Y} = \begin{bmatrix} SRH \\ FLP \\ WSR \\ P5T \\ DRF \end{bmatrix} \text{ and } \underset{\sim}{B} = \begin{bmatrix} 0 & \bar{B}_{1,2} & 0 & \bar{B}_{1,4} & 0 \\ 0 & 0 & 0 & 0 & \overset{+}{B}_{2,5} \\ 0 & 0 & 0 & \overset{?}{\bar{B}}_{3,4} & \overset{+}{B}_{3,5} \\ 0 & \bar{B}_{4,2} & 0 & 0 & 0 \\ 0 & \overset{?}{B}_{5,2} & 0 & \bar{B}_{5,4} & 0 \end{bmatrix}
$$

The predetermined variables are

$$\underset{\sim}{X'} = [FLP_{-1}, WSR_{-1}, WSR_{-2}, DRC, INR, IGR, P5T, PAT, DRD, DRDC,$$

URT, SSV, const]

and

$$
\underset{\sim}{\Gamma} = \begin{bmatrix}
0 & 0 & 0 & 0 & \overset{+}{\gamma_{1,5}} & \overset{?}{\gamma_{1,6}} & \overset{-}{\gamma_{1,7}} & \overset{?}{\gamma_{1,8}} & 0 & 0 & 0 & \gamma_{1,12} & \overset{-}{\gamma_{1,13}} \\
\overset{+}{\gamma_{2,1}} & \overset{+}{\gamma_{2,2}} & 0 & 0 & 0 & 0 & 0 & 0 & 0 & 0 & 0 & 0 & \gamma_{21,13} \\
0 & \overset{+}{\gamma_{3,2}} & 0 & 0 & 0 & 0 & 0 & 0 & 0 & 0 & 0 & 0 & \gamma_{3,13} \\
0 & 0 & \overset{-}{\gamma_{4,3}} & \overset{-}{\gamma_{4,4}} & 0 & 0 & 0 & 0 & 0 & 0 & \overset{-}{\gamma_{4,11}} & 0 & \gamma_{4,13} \\
0 & 0 & 0 & \overset{-}{\gamma_{5,4}} & 0 & 0 & 0 & 0 & \overset{+}{\gamma_{5,9}} & \overset{-}{\gamma_{5,10}} & 0 & 0 & \gamma_{5,13}
\end{bmatrix}
$$

I is an identity matrix, and E a vector of error terms. It is assumed that the elements of E have a multinormal distribution and are independent between observations. The nonzero elements of B and Γ are the model coefficients to be estimated. Table 2 presents the estimates of the model obtained by iterated three-stage least squares.

Adjustments to Demographic Changes

Broadly speaking, there are two options open when scarcely populated societies suddenly start growing (be it because of suddenly diminished epidemics and wars, or technology invented in one society being transferred to another).[1] One is to stay an essentially agricultural society with little hierarchy and a government fulfilling minimal functions.

This remains a choice when there is both sufficient land and other "natural" resources to replicate the existing, traditional organizations, spreading them over larger and larger territories, *and* no outside threats.[2] Because of geographical reasons (being relatively isolated and less accessible), some groups had the option to pursue such a strategy for a longer time than others: the case of the United States. From ancient times Russia, for example, could not make this choice. Outside pressures (from the Mongols on) required the organization of armies and greater concentration of population, by regulation if deemed necessary.[3] As argued and shown in chapters 2 and 3, military competition combined with population growth blurred the meaning of aggregate statistics.

As population continues to grow, people can no longer photocopy the traditional structures and superimpose it on new locations. The continuing outside pressures, be they population or innovations of any type, military ones in particular, and the resulting threat of falling behind, also lead to the recognition that maintaining one's place in the world requires a social organization encouraging innovations. Societies diverged radically in their search for such organization for a number of reasons, some accidental, others not.[4]

Whether an increase of population made a country richer or poorer depended on the opportunities given to the additional people within the institutions that these societies had stumbled upon.[5] Some societies recognized that the kind of existence people had been accustomed to could no longer be maintained, and that the "property" of the additional people—the young and poor—was the option of keeping them healthy and developing their skills. Such "natural" endowments could be unlocked and turned into wealth only if institutions were adjusted, and property rights reallocated. This is where the roles of governments discussed in chapters 2, 3, and 5 became evident, though totally unrelated to any attempt of carrying out macroeconomic policies. When people's abilities and willingness to take risks were *not* unlocked,

196 Adjustments to Demographic Changes

population growth led to pollution, poverty, political instability, and decreases in what John Hicks called "true national income"—even if conventional numbers measured magnificent increases.[6] Policies favoring trade, along with a political and fiscal system that gave the poor and those falling behind a stake in the system, were necessary conditions for sustained prosperity, as already explained in chapter 2.

Notes

Preface

1. See Arnold Beichman's *Anti-American Myths* (New Brunswick: Transaction Publishers, 1992), which discusses in detail this and the next example in this paragraph.

Chapter 1

1. See Giavazzi and Spaventa (1988, 19) and "The Italian Economy," *Economist,* February 27, 1988. One cannot exclude the possibility that there was a political motivation too behind the revisions. The European Community requires its members to reduce the deficit/debt to GNP ratio to lower levels. If such reasoning played a role in the revisions, it suggests one should be even more skeptical of the aggregate numbers. Spaventa (1988) notes that the revised sectorial accounts are not available; there are no data for sectorial disposable income, savings, and expenditures.

2. These figures were given without even taking into account contributions made by drug smuggling, but taking into account estimates that showed that 54 percent of civil servants had second jobs and 33 ran other businesses during official working hours (without declaring their respective incomes), and the possible impact of tax evasions in the manufacturing sector.

3. In Britain the definition of unemployment has been changed thirty times since 1979, due to political manipulations. Not surprisingly, twenty-nine of these adjustments caused improvements in the figure.

4. "Even Richer than They Seem," *Economist,* March 19, 1988, gives examples concerning Taiwan's economy. Since financial services are tightly regulated, small, illegal operators provide services that banks and brokers cannot. Thus, although one cannot make a legal currency swap, a working currency swap market exists. The same is true for commodity futures, especially gold. One impact of the regulation is that Taiwan is one of the world's biggest consumers of Reuter screens, which make the operation of the small financial bureaus feasible. Surveys in Taiwan also suggest that 15 to 20 percent of export earnings are uncounted because of double invoicing, and 7 to 8 percent of manufacturing output is undeclared.

5. See Park (1981). The United States Internal Revenue Service (1979) estimated it in the range of 6 percent, although recent private estimates put it anywhere between 2 and 25 percent. See Murray (1985).

6. See Feige (1980), O'Higgins (1981).

7. See Stournaras (1989) on Greece. Also see Brown et al. (1984).

8. See Ethier (1986), Smith (1986), and "Shadow Economy," *Economist,* September 19, 1987. See "Black Economies in Latin America: Safe as Houses," *Economist,* November 12, 1988, and Moffett (1989). Why data in Peru are totally unreliable is discussed in detail in de Soto (1989). Why data in planned economies are unreliable is examined in Winiecki (1988) and, later, in chapter 5.

9. In the long run the latter change in policy makes society better off: there are greater legal opportunities to exploit, and there is less bribery and corruption. Thus there are less "transaction costs" for carrying out trade.

10. See Morgenstern (1963, 19). On Spain see, "Shadow Economy." On the unreliable unemployment figures, see Gutman (1979 a, b). As for the problems linked with illegal transactions in international trade, see Bhagwati (1974). Further details on the measurement of underground economies can be found in appendix 1.

11. Heckman (1989) notes that "Largely anecdotal evidence on the underground economy [in the United States] suggests that it is large and growing. It is estimated that more than 25 percent of male ghetto dwellers derive their income from illegal activity. Studies of ghetto youth reveal that illegal activities—principally drug dealing—constitute the greatest source of market income for young men. Criminal activity is linked to opportunities in the mainstream economy. We should not be surprised to find that many participants in the underground economy are making sizable incomes—certainly larger than they could have earned in the conventional economy. Although the source of the growth would be disquieting, proper measurement of uncovered activity might reveal greater growth in relative earnings of minority workers than is reported in official statistics. It is naive to assume that all persons in the inner city who are undercounted [and more than 25 percent seem to be] are poor. As things now stand, we can only guess about the earnings and activities of uncovered persons. Until we make more concerted efforts to discover the unmeasured, the old adage 'out of sight—out of mind' applies." But Heckman does not explain why.

12. The reason is that quarterly data are published when information on two months is available; statisticians extrapolate for the third. In this case, there was an unexpected increase in exports that led to the significant change in the growth rate figure.

13. See Brookes (1987).

14. See "Counting the Ways," *Economist,* December 26, 1992–January 8, 1993, 16.

15. Solomou and Weale (1988) argue that much of the economic history of late Victorian and Edwardian economies is misleading because the data are wrong. The use of the "compromise estimate" of GNP (i.e., an average of the income, expenditure, and output estimates) in most macroeconomic interpretations of the period has given rise to a number of results that are no more than statistical artifacts. They also take note of the large tax evasions between the years 1856 and 1907, ranging in some categories between 11 and 57 percent. Sayers (1976, 317–34) notes the unreliability of balance of payment figures in England between the two world wars and before the first. Yet policies were defended just as aggressively then on the basis of such figures as they are today. Before 1914 there were no official statistics on balance of payment figures in the

United Kingdom, and Sayers (315) notes that it is still impossible to know the impact of the First World War on the United Kingdom's external position.

16. See Wriston (1989). The numbers do not seem to become more reliable. On the contrary: Stout (1989, A1) notes that "In April, the growth in new jobs was estimated at a mere 117,000; after the statistics mills had gathered more information, however, the figure was nearly doubled to 206,000. Similarly, the May total was raised from 101,000 initially to 207,000, and June's from 180,000 to 250,000. . . . The annual rate of growth was revised upward a full percentage point, to 2.7 percent from 1.7 percent."

17. When the mean of the "true" growth rate is 2.4 percent, and assuming normal distribution.

18. By December 1991, only Germany and Japan paid attention to the GNP. Other governments started looking far more closely at the GDP. The difference between the two measures is this: GDP measures the value of all goods and services produced in a country. GNP equals GDP plus net factor income from abroad; that is, profits, investment income, and workers' compensations. Since the difference is volatile, the GDP may give a better indication of what is happening within the national borders. In 1991 in West Germany, the GDP grew by 3 percent, whereas the GNP grew by 1.9. The difference is due to the large number of eastern Germans who work in the western part (the figures for the Germanies are not yet integrated), but send their wages to the east. See "Grossly Distorted Picture," *Economist,* December 14, 1991, 79.

19. Retail sales account for a third of the United States economic activity.

20. See Brookes (1987).

21. In May 1989, the U.S. government reported a fall in retail sales of 0.1 percent, only to discover that they had overlooked $1.4 billion in sales. The revised numbers showed a 0.8 percent increase. The mistake was also included in the GNP statistics. When the correction came, the Federal Reserve had already cut interests for fear that the economy was heading into a recession. See Crutsinger (1990). Similar reports about bad data appeared in Canada. See Beauchesne (1990).

22. Quoted in Koretz (1988).

23. In order to correct, in part, for such distortion, one should use the so-called chained price index. When used, it gives 0.5 percent less real growth than the alternative, fixed weight index. See Koretz (1988). Boskin, quoted in Stout (1989), also notes that deregulation of many American industries in the 1970s and 1980s "obliterated the reporting of reams of information to regulatory agencies. Import figures are harder to come by as well. 'As we've progressively reduced tarrifs, all the data that came in with them are much less available.'"

24. This is just one example that shows the arithmetics behind the misleading statistics of manufacturing output. McMillion (1992, F13) pointed out recently that "Even Commerce Department officials who assign values [in this sector] admitted—in the Survey of Current Business last year—that 'only substantial research effort over many years holds any promise of overcoming . . . formidable statistical problems' with these figures. The rapid pace of technological change makes it virtually impossible to measure 'constant' output over time."

25. Michael Harper, chief of productivity research at the Bureau of Labor Statistics, gives a simple example showing why. "Do higher premiums, which tend to

boost an insurance company's revenues, also serve to boost its productivity? . . . Or are higher premiums merely a signal of higher policy risks?" Quoted in Malabre and Clark (1992).

26. See Malabre and Clark (1992).

27. See Malabre and Clark (1992).

28. See "Garbage In, Garbage Out," *Economist,* June 4, 1988.

29. "Garbage In, Garbage Out," *Economist,* June 4, 1988.

30. The sources and methods of National Accounts statistics in the United Kingdom are described in Maurice (1968). The rather arbitrary way of dealing with numbers comes to the fore in a number of places. On pp. 223–26, for example, Maurice describes the "arbitrary," "uncertainly" adjustments made to the Inland Revenue profit data.

31. The editorial "Counting the Ways," *Economist,* December 26, 1992–January 8, 1993, notices that "Official statistics have also failed to keep up with the rapid expansion of foreign investment. In the past decade, direct investment overseas has grown five times faster than world output and more than three times faster than trade. As a result, crude trade figures are becoming less useful as a guide to economic health. Trade balances are losing their meaning. One third of American exports go to American-owned firms abroad; goods shipped by the American subsidiaries of foreign firms to their home country account for another third. If net sales of American overseas subsidiaries are added to America's trade balance, then America has a big 'trade surplus,' not a deficit. This growth in intra-firm transactions has blurred the very idea of international trade."

32. Produced by the Bureau of Economic Analysis (BEA) in the United States.

33. Boskin (1988) summarizes the critical literature on the subject. Obstfeld (1986, 82) also notes that "since national product figures represent the nominal value of goods and services produced by a country's factors, as measured by realized financial flows, exchange-rate induced redistribution of wealth between nations do not enter into the NIPA definition of national income or saving. Also ignored are the changes in the real value of net external debts due to inflation." Bradford (1990) argues that more attention should be paid to measures of national wealth at asset market values. But he does not discuss the problems linked with the measurement of savings and wealth. See Brenner (1983, chapter 2) on the relationship between demographic changes and what we may be measuring. On problems linked with the measurement of consumption, see Wilcox (1988).

34. See Boskin (1988, 25). This has posed a particular problem since the 1960s, when the ratio of house prices to average earnings in the United States, United Kingdom, Denmark, and other countries increased significantly, from about 2.5 to 5.5. Also in the NIPAs (National Income and Product Accounts), for example, savings reflect: 1) resources freed for investment, *but* where investments are defined as purchases of fixed capital goods only—structures and equipment—by private business and nonprofit institutions.; 2) the value of the change in the physical volume of inventories held by private business; 3) the changes in net claims of U.S. residents on foreigners. Also, the guideline used in the NIPAs is to measure investment as business expenditure, which is not charged to current expense. But, as Holloway (1987) notes, some expenditure by business, like those on R & D, although they may represent

"investment," are treated as current expense. Moreover, whereas capital formation by households in the form of housing is treated as "business activity," expenditures on durable goods other than houses are *not* capitalized (and are all counted as consumption). (Expenditures on education or health are not counted as investment either.) Finally, capital formation by government, as argued in the next chapter, is not recognized either. Holloway (1987) also discusses the rather arbitrary ways in which private and public pension funds are treated.

35. The relationship between savings and government accounting is raised in Boskin et al. (1987a, b).

36. See *The Consumer Price Index Reference Paper* (catalogue 62–553), occasional, February 1985, 50.

37. See *The Consumer Price Index Reference Paper,* 19.

38. See Segal (1977).

39. Not until 1988, when the report on the CPI was written. When such a long time elapses between two surveys, a number of serious problems might arise, not only for domestic comparisons but for international ones too. Segal (1977, 51) notes that in 1974, 83.4 percent of all retail sales in Canada were made through Combination Stores and only 5.4 percent through Grocery Stores. Segal thus recommended that smaller stores not be included in the sampleb Casual observation, however, suggests that the importance of both "superstores" (Loblaws in Toronto, Super Carnaval in Quebec— neither is in the sample of outlets on page 23 of the *Evaluation Report*) and smaller stores has increased significantly, in part because of the massive increase in the participation of women in the labor force and the fact that the smaller stores were open on Sundays. For this same reason there has been a large increase in enterprises specializing in "home delivery"; one wonders about the way they were included in the sample.

40. The Geneva report emphasizes the problematic treatment of quality changes but notes that the only thing that the participants could agree upon was "the need to take [such] changes into account when measuring price changes" (*Report of the Seminar on the CPI,* 7). But there was no agreement on how: some argued that prices of seasonal products and new fashion lines should be all excluded from the calculation of the CPI. (How "real" would fashion-conscious women and men consider such an index to be?) Others said they should be included, but then attention must be paid to discounts. There was general agreement only on the fact that if such items are introduced, it should be done in such a way as to give a "representative picture of the year . . . and that the methods used be generally understood and accepted by the public"(7). But how to do that is of course the question, to which there was no clear-cut answer.

41. The Geneva participants also discussed the issues of officially fixed prices, leading to quality deterioration—the case of postal services in the United States and Canada (and of medical services in Canada) fit into this category. They decided that the hidden changes should be taken into account.

42. See *Evaluation Report,* 28. More about price indices is said in chapter 4.

43. In Japan and in France, however, no weight is given to mortgage interests.

44. Though there are no reasons to transfer the method since the tax treatment of mortgages is different in the two countries.

45. See Peter deVries and Andrew Baldwin (1985, ix).

46. The Canadian treatment of homeownership costs has no logical foundations. Ownership housing is not treated as a capital good (which would result in the "rental equivalence approach" now used in the United States). Nor does it reflect a user-cost approach. The Canadian approach is designed to detect the impact of price changes on homeowners' specific costs of shelter, as opposed to tenant's specific cost of shelter. The U.S. approach in contrast is designed to answer the question: "How much rental income do the owners of housing units forego when they choose to occupy the units themselves instead of renting them out?" The owned accommodation costs by components is calculated according to these weights: repairs, 9.2 percent; property tax, 20.1 percent; insurance premium, 4.7 percent; mortgage interest, 40.2 percent; replacement costs 20.6 percent; other, 5.2 percent. Yet apparently only Canada and the United Kingdom include mortgage interest costs in their consumer price indices. Japan does not, and whereas the United States did for many years, a reform in the early 1980s took these costs out of the index. See the *Report of the Seminar on the CPI.*

47. See Alan Blinder (1980, 564).

48. See appendix 2 for the formalized version of this statement.

49. See appendix 2.

50. They will need to look at more than one index because of the imprecision of such measures, as explained before.

51. See Brenner (1990a, 156–8).

52. See Mankiw (1990, 12).

53. See White (1984, 3), on changed perceptions of the same acts, depending on the circumstances.

54. This is not an abstract, esoteric point. In 1992, when Canada tried to write a law to prevent entry of terrorists, critics of the early draft showed that its wording would have prevented entry to those who fought against Nazi Germany or communist regimes.

55. There are a number of reasons for the confusion besides mismeasurement. If monetary policy is used as a tool of short-run stabilization, then lowered interest rates, let us say, may lead to expectations of further cuts and thus postponed investments. Such a reaction, as Schwartz (1987, 183–4), for example, has pointed out, "complicates the execution of policy, since it means that actions take effect well after they are initiated. Hence a policy of stabilizing short-run fluctuations in the economy implies the ability to forecast the course of economic activity and the subsequent effects of policy actions." Friedman (1960, 93) made a similar point when he wrote, "We seldom in fact know which way the economic wind is going to be blowing, when the measures we take now will be effective, itself a variable date that may be half year or a year or two years from now."

56. The distinction implies that taking away discretion would be good only as long as everybody agrees on what money is. But when the term money loses its traditional meaning due to innovations and specific events, having discretionary power is preferable. To use the previous analogy: when everybody agrees who is a terrorist, discretion should indeed be taken away from policymakers. But when there is no such agreement, discretion is preferable.

57. Though reached here from a different angle, this conclusion is similar to the one reached by Kydland and Prescott (1977). The other policy recommendations that follow from the arguments and evidence presented here also remind one of Friedman's (1969), Friedman's and Schwartz's (1971) and Lucas' (1989), although they are reached from a different angle, and they are the following: a) if governments decide to vary their expenditures, they should do so, but *not* in response to movements in aggregate variables; b) if governments decide to vary the tax rates they may do so but, once again, *not* in response to changes in aggregate variables.

58. See Duncan and Shelton (1978, 84–6).

59. See Morgenstern (1963, chap. 9). I am not trying to belittle the importance of statistics or of econometrics. Figures are very valuable, if they can be trusted. But the question of how to verify comes after the questions, what does one want to verify, and why. Also, as noted, in stable circumstances even bad numbers can make very good predictions. This, however, does not imply that they have the slightest scientific value—recall the very accurate predictions made in Babylon on the positions of stars just by using ingenious mathematical manipulations.

60. See United Nations report (1953, 1, par. 6). See discussion on the flaws of aggregate figures and the process that led to their acceptance in Waring (1988). Though strident, and sometimes inaccurate, it has many valid criticisms concerning the building and use of aggregate figures.

61. This chapter also serves as a reminder of the fact that the widespread use of measures by some influential groups of people is no guarantee that the numbers are even vaguely useful for society. See some professors' cynical attitude when they teach macroeconomics in Colander and Klamer (1990). Also see discussion on the exaggerations that have led to bad policies with respect to gambling in Brenner and Brenner (1990). A reminder of that discussion may be useful. In the 1950s the Kefauver Committee published a $20-billion estimate for the annual receipts from gambling in the United States. How did the committee get the number? Out of a hat: the California Crime Commission said $12 billion, Virgil Peterson of Chicago said $30 billion. The committee made a rounded average. See Singer (1971, 6).

62. Sennholz (1984, 10) notes that in the United States the marginal tax rate for a family of four earning the median income has risen from 17 in 1965 to 24 percent in 1980, and for double-median incomes it rose from 26 to 43 percent. This means that the incentives to make false declarations in order to evade taxes have changed too.

63. Some econometricians have long been concerned that mismeasurement of data leads to spurious results and obscures true relationships, particularly when longitudinal data sets are used. If measurement errors are uncorrelated over time, then statistical problems caused by the mismeasurement of data may be greatly exacerbated when longitudinal data are used to estimate fixed-effects or first-differenced regressions. But if data are consistently misreported, then first-differencing could increase the reliability of longitudinal data. As shown here, although the data are indeed misreported, there is nothing consistent about the source and magnitude of errors. Discussions about measurement errors in various contexts, in addition to Morgenstern's classic book, can be found in Ashenfelter and Solon (1982), Griliches (1974, 1985), Duncan and Hill (1985), and Solon (1987).

64. See Friedman's (1940) earlier criticism on Tinbergen's data and methods. Commenting on an early version of this paper, Friedman (1988) wrote that about twenty years ago the Financial Secretary of Hong Kong revealed to him that he refused to permit the construction of GNP statistics for Hong Kong because, he said, if they were available they would inevitably tend to promote central planning, which he strongly opposed. White and Wildavsky (1989, 71) also concluded that even after fifty years the greatest obstacle to Reagan's vision of the nation was the Great Depression. According to them, the crash and its aftermath of unemployment had dampened Americans' enthusiasm for unfettered capitalism.

Chapter 2

1. If one assumes an open economy, net national savings fall and consumption rises during the first period at the expense of some combination of investment and net exports. As a result, standards of living are higher during the first period but lower in the future compared to what they would be in a world of no deficits. See Gramlich (1989, 23).

2. The issue is more complicated because government borrowing may have an effect on interest rates, exchange rates, inflationary expectations, etc. In a closed economy, the increased interest rate will diminish private consumption and investment. In an open economy, where interest rates are determined by world rates, government borrowing reduces future income because it diminishes the stock of overseas assets and hence the net inflow of investment income. There is nothing new about the argument in the text. Savage (1988, 109), for example, notes that from 1797 until 1820, New York ran deficits every year except for two years. Between 1817 and 25 it financed the construction of the Erie Canal, the first great state-funded public works project. Before it was even finished, the tolls exceeded the interest charges, the cost of freight from Buffalo to New York City dropped from $100 to $15 per ton, the transportation time fell from twenty to eight hours, and the bonds issued for the construction sold at a premium.

3. These conclusions have implicit assumptions behind them, among them that private savings are not affected by government borrowing. Some economists believe in the Ricardian equivalence theorem and argue that it is not possible for governments to alter the balance of consumption over time. If the government borrows more, the private sector will, they argue, reduce its own consumption and save more in anticipation of higher taxes in the future. See Barro (1989). Whether or not one can identify the type of expenditure depends on the way the accounting is done. See Yellen (1989), and discussion later in the text.

4. See model, discussion, and evidence in Brenner (1983, 1985). Also see Lane (1966, part three).

5. This is the opportunity cost of the policy, which is relevant for making the decision. Consider the United States deciding to give more help to Russia today in order to prevent political instability. Also see Fialka (1989).

6. Money that, let us say, they previously held in gold or in a foreign country. This section was written long before the Los Angeles riots in 1992. The arguments can be found in Brenner (1985).

7. This does not imply a "free lunch." Rather, following changes that have led to instability, new policies—call them "social innovations"—are adopted that diminish risks. See formal model and discussion in Brenner (1985, chapter 2), and Brenner and Brenner (1990, appendix 1 to chap. 2), concerning models about the impacts of redistributive policies. In these circumstances the debt is not an intergenerational burden, as Modigliani (1961) suggested in a static model.

8. Or, consider another possibility. Frequently in the distant past workers resisted new machines and new work routines, the example of the Luddites being probably the best known. But the workers' reactions varied, depending on how they felt about future possibilities. Suppose that, when unrest is on the rise, governments pay unemployment benefits or establish funds for retraining workers. Such expenditures, paid initially by either taxation or deficits, may nevertheless promote investments, innovations, and employment if investors now expect less resistance in the form of strikes or other symptoms of unrest. Innovations in law and social programs, just like technological ones, may be beneficial to all parties concerned. Thus, the mere facts of either increased taxation or increased government expenditures does not give us enough information to decide whether they will advance or delay prosperity. The increased taxation or the increased government expenditures should, however, be temporary if indeed the innovation is beneficial.

9. These questions are posed by Eisner (1986, 47), who suggests that, if the numbers about debt and deficits were accurate, one could have such theories without any regard to the historical context or matters of internal and external social stability in particular. The arguments also suggest that cross-section and time series analyses may be inappropriate for examining the data, since the numbers would appear in an ahistorical context.

10. This reservation holds even if one assumes that methods of government accounting do not vary across countries and time, which is not the case.

11. See discussion on relationships between other variables, and the discrepancy between traditional theories and the facts, in Barro (1989), Savage (1988, chap. 2), and evidence on interest rates and deficits in Frenkel and Razin (1988). For example, during the latter part of the 1970s, a rise in the U.S. budget deficit (as a share of GNP) was accompanied by a rise in the interest rate, while in 1986 and 1987, the correlation was negative.

12. It did not surprise those who believe in the Ricardian equivalence idea, which suggests that the method of financing of a given level of government expenditures does not matter, and that the government's fiscal impact is summarized by the present value of the expenditures. See Barro (1989). But notice the difference with Barro's views: here the government can innovate. Also see detailed discussion in chapter 3.

13. See Brenner (1991) and Colander and Brenner (1992).

14. See Savage (1988, 55). He also notes that initially "much of this debate focused not on 'deficits' but on the debt, or 'public credit,' or the use of paper money, better known as 'bills of credit' . . . Deficits were harmful, because, among other reasons, they threatened the federal government's ability to retire the debt. In the proper context, employing paper money technically involved running budget deficits, and debate over bills of credit may be considered to represent more modern notions of deficit spending." One reason for the creation of these "bills of credit" was that the

colonial governments frequently found their supply of gold and silver suddenly diminished when England was fighting one of its wars. The money created was frequently spent on poorhouses, workhouses, widow and veteran pensions, public works, and so forth (see discussion later in the text on poverty and public works). See Savage (1988, chap. 3, 61–62), where he documents expenditures for those falling on hard times.

15. See Savage (1988, 55–56).

16. The reason for this latter belief was that "While speculators, bankers, and the moneyed aristocracy would benefit from the unearned financial leverage and profits derived by financing the national debt, the government would spend its added revenues by promoting an industrialized economy through Hamiltonian policies that resembled those of mercantilist and corrupted England. Once again England served as the model to be avoided, for just as its government was corrupted in no small way due to its enormous debt, English society and its moral values were also corrupted by a system of manufacturing and industry that created vast social and economic divisions" (Savage 1988, 95). These opinions are in contrast with today's; now the federal government's intervention is advocated on the grounds that it may diminish inequality. Savage (1988, 107) also notes that debts and deficits were tolerated at the state but not at the federal level, and quotes at length from a letter Thomas Jefferson wrote in November 1798 calling for a balanced budget amendment.

17. See Savage (1988, chap. 7, 202–4), quoting and summarizing Reagan's speeches.

18. See discussion in Savage (1988, chap. 7).

19. As quoted in Savage (1988, 202).

20. Although the idea of the national debt was new, there was nothing new about governments raising loans in order to finance wars: that has been done for centuries past. But until the later part of the seventeenth century, these had been "short-term loans," raised to meet a particular emergency and repaid out of taxes at the time. What was new in the English case was the setting up of a "long-term" debt to be handed on from generation to generation, the interest becoming a permanent annual change to be paid out of taxation. See Hill (1986, 144–47).

21. See Hill (1986, 144–47). If one deflates these numbers by the CPI (as it appears in Goldstein 1988, 387), the strong trends still persist. The CPI stood at 783.1 in 1696 and at 716.9 in 1713, at 673.0 in 1748 and 716.9 in 1763. Only in 1783 was it at the level of 982.0, and it doubled to 1819.1 by 1815. Not only in England but in the United States, increases in deficits have been frequently associated with wars and expenditures abroad. See Savage (1988, chap. 4 and chap. 5), who notes, for example, that in 1898 and 1899 the federal government had deficits associated with the Spanish American War, and in 1904 and 1905, federal financing for building the Panama Canal led the government into deficit spending for a sum of $65.5 million.

22. In particular see Smith (chap. 1, Book V, 245–55).

23. Smith's definition of "unproductive workers" differs from ours: he included in this category actors, scholars, and lawyers, among others.

24. Schumpeter (1972, 327) notes that public borrowing for nonproductive purposes worried Hume and Smith, but not the French economists, who viewed government expenditures as a factor in national prosperity.

25. Whereas Smith's views on unproductive workers, and the American-born ideas about the evils of federal deficits have survived, the views that one should look at the composition of expenditures, and that deficits on the states' or local levels might be beneficial from time to time, have ceased to play roles in macroeconomics.

26. Although not for reasons discussed by Bernheim (1989).

27. See Fisher (1933, 1934).

28. As did Britain. See Blaug (1976, 162–63).

29. See discussion in Blaug (1976), Brenner (1979, 1985, chap. 5), and Savage (1988, chap. 6).

30. Blaug (1976, 162–63) notes that "no American economist between 1929 and 1936 advocated a policy of wage-cutting; the leaders of the American profession strongly supported a programme of public works and specifically attacked the shibboleth of balanced budget. A long list of names including Slichter, Taussig, Schultz, Yntema, Simons, Gayer, Knight, Viner, Douglas and Y. M. Clark concentrated mainly at the Universities of Chicago and Columbia . . . declared themselves in print well before 1936 in favour of policies that we would today call 'Keynesian'. . . . Orthodox economists had no difficulty in explaining the persistence of unemployment. The government budget in both the United States and Britain was in surplus during most years in the 1930s. It did not need Keynes to tell economists that this was deflationary." Also see Savage (1988, chap. 7).

31. A detailed discussion can be found in Brenner (1979, 1980, 1985, chap. 5).

32. See Marc Bloch (1953, 176), who wrote that "there is hardly one of [Keynes's] books in which he does not, from the beginning expropriate terms, usually pretty well established, in order to decree entirely new meanings for them, meanings which sometimes vary from work to work, but in any case, intentionally depart from common usage." Also see Hutt (1979), the prologue and chap. 2 in particular.

33. See Keynes (1936, 304); italics in original.

34. All dictionaries before and after Keynes still define inflation as "too much money chasing too few goods," which implies a rise in prices.

35. See detailed discussion on this point in Brenner (1979, 1980), and chapter 5 in Brenner (1985).

36. "Fact" according to Keynes, who, however, presented no evidence to support his views. The existing evidence, of his times and ever since, fails to support Keynes's opinion. See discussion and references on this point in Brenner (1979, 1985, chap. 5 and chap. 6).

37. See Keynes (1936, 9), and discussion on this point in Brenner (1979), where I also discuss why Keynes did not advocate reduction of money-wages as a remedy. But, as noted, neither did Keynes's non-Keynesian contemporaries recommend such a policy. See Blaug (1976).

38. As quoted in Brittan (1992).

39. Irving Fisher (1933, 346), for example, wrote that "If [the debt-deflation theory] is correct, it is always economically possible to stop or prevent such a depression simply by reflating the price level up to the average level at which outstanding debts were contracted by existing debtors and assumed by existing creditors, and then maintaining that level unchanged." Ayres (1944, 276) made similar points: "In the event [that the total amount of income . . . somehow fails to flow into

the market] the recreation of money values by deficit financing up to the amount of purchasing power necessary to absorb the product of industry at full employment would only be a salvage of purchasing power already lost by its former owners and so the whole community. It is this circumstance which has led to the recognition of deficit financing by many respectable economists in recent years. . . . Indeed there is no good reason why such a program should not take the form of the outright issue of currency in the amount so indicated." Also see Fisher (1934) and detailed discussion on these points in Brenner (1985, chap. 5).

40. See Robinson (1962) and Leijonhufvud (1968).

41. See Keynes (1936, 315).

42. See Keynes (1936, 129–31); italics in original.

43. For theory and facts related to this view, see Brenner (1983, 1985, 1987).

44. See Keynes (1936, 359) and Appleby (1978, 144).

45. As quoted in Appleby (1978, 144).

46. See Appleby (1978, 153).

47. See Botero in E. Cochrane and J. Kirshner, *The Renaissance* (1986, 241–42). This view also explains, according to Botero, why " . . . in Rome the poor, who made up the fifth class, were not usually enrolled in the militia except for service at sea, which was always held to be less honorable than service on land" (241). Botero noticed possible solutions: "In order to involve their people in the defense of the republic as much as possible, the kings of Rome saw to it that every one of them owned property: the love of their farm, [they believed,] would lead them to love and defend the established order. Lycurgus, as Nabis said to Quintus Flaminius, 'thought that equality of wealth and dignity would make many willing to bear arms on behalf of the republic.'"(243). Margaret Thatcher's idea of encouraging homeownership has ancient roots.

48. Also see McNeill (1974, 76–77) on the role of public ceremonies in Venice. The building of boulevards was part of the numerous public ventures done under Napoleon III, supervised by Baron Hausmann, with the explicit goal to avoid riots and revolutions: the police and the military were expected to control the crowds more easily in broad spaces than in the narrow streets, which Hausmann erased.

49. Jordan (1959, 46) also notes, "We sometimes forget how essentially insecure the Tudor political society really was and how awkwardly ineffective was the central power in dealing with purely local disturbances," of which there were plenty (77). There were rural risings in the South, in Kent, and in Essex between 1549 and 1560; there was the Wyatt's rebellion in 1554, after the enclosures, and in the Midland counties shortly after the accession of James I. It must also be noted that order was induced not only through reforms but also savage enforcement in cases of riots.

50. Botero also noted that one can get rid of the poor by sending them off to colonies, as the Spartans did to the Partheniae (*Renaissance* 1986, 242), or, something that Botero does not note, as the various rulers did when sending them to the Crusades (a period of large population growth). England got rid of its troublemakers by sending them to Australia. In recent decades, Germany and Switzerland have sent home foreign workers during prolonged recession.

51. These two viewpoints are not significantly different from those held in

psychology about the reaction to children. One school has taught that parents must teach children discipline early. Thus picking up a crying child was discouraged, since it trained the child to keep crying. In the fifties, "science" discovered that, unless parents picked up their crying children, the children would become neurotic adults at best, criminals at worst. But "science" was wrong, and we are now stuck with not only a no less neurotic generation, but a whining one. In all this flip-flop, common sense was lost.

52. See McNeill (1974, chap. 6), who remarks that the stability was maintained at the peasantry's expense.

53. Surely, the work employed some people. But then so did the gulags. These examples just show in the extreme why one should reject arguments in the abstract about governments creating employment.

54. These arguments show from yet an additional angle that the aggregate models overlook the importance of historical background. Regulations, laws, taxes that exist in a certain point in time must be taken into account when evaluating the effect of an additional policy. For example: minimum-wage laws and regulations destroy many entry-level jobs for the unskilled, since due to them employment costs grow faster than productivity. How then can young and unskilled workers start learning the many invisible skills that only steady employment provides? And who can correct for such mistaken policies? Tax incentives, subsidies, and public works may correct for them. Such additional government intervention leads to a distant second best. Opportunities would be better if the initial regulations were dismantled to start with. However, as long as they are not, an additional policy may help counteract their negative effect, but it is not a sure thing. If the unskilled unemployed find jobs in the public sector due to "public works," and the private sector may be unwilling to pay the higher wages, then society will be burdened by higher taxes and get deeper and deeper into a confusing, costly maze of complexity. This argument is the same as in the previous chapter and sections, when we saw how discretionary monetary policy may be useful when it corrects for mistaken policies in the past.

55. Recall that the introduction of minimum wages in Canada, for example, had to do with the entry of low-skilled women in the labor force. Authorities feared that they would turn to prostitution if there was no minimum-wage legislation. I am not aware of studies that followed up whether or not the fears were justified. But such fears, justified or not, shaped public debates. It is possible that they were based on myth.

56. See Teitelbaum and Winter (1985, 77) and Brenner (1987, chap. 7).

57. As quoted in Young (1973, 34–35). These statements should sound familiar: just replace the Soviets and the Germans with the Japanese, and England with the United States. See discussions on leapfrogging in general, and its impact in various contexts, in Brenner (1985, 1987), Brenner and Brenner (1990).

58. See McClelland (1979, concluding chapter). De Custine (1989, 231) quoted in 1839 the Empress Catherine saying, "My dear Prince, do not distress yourself because the Russians have no desire for knowledge: if I institute schools it is not for ourselves, but for Europe, in whose estimation we must maintain our standing; but if our peasants should really wish to become enlightened, neither you nor I could continue in our places." Geld (1990) also draws attention to the fact that expenditures on education mean very different things in different countries. He remarks that "while

one of the first things the English-speaking settlers of North America did was establish a broad foundation of community schools, schooling in Brazil was the privilege of a landed, bureaucratic minority. Their motto might have been: 'Education for those in control.'"

59. Simultaneously with the decision to send food, the Germans also contemplated imposing tougher emigration regulations. See "Food is Sent to Soviets to Forestall Exodus," *Wall Street Journal,* November 30, 1990: A11. If food is used for such political goals, can subsidies to the agricultural sector be justified and viewed as insurances? I do not give this example to justify the policy. The alternative of letting people move and become enthusiastic "Americans," "Canadians," or "Europeans," rather than who-knows-what-type of "Russians," may be preferable in the long term. See next chapter.

60. One must also bear in mind that lobbying groups frequently put forward the argument that an industry is essential for defense and should be subsidized. This should not be taken on face value. See Brenner (1987, chap. 7).

61. As the neoclassical or the Ricardian approach would require.

62. See discussion in Brenner (1985, chap. 5).

63. See data on World Military Expenditures in a publication with the same title by the U.S. Arms Control and Disarmament Agency, and *The Military Balance,* published by the International Institute for Strategic Studies. Also see discussion and reference to other sources in Brenner (1985, chap. 5).

64. A question one has to answer before venturing into a line of research following Ricardian ideas or Kotlikoff's (1987) suggestions.

65. See Kennedy (1975).

66. This happens because of the expectations for diminished demands. The notion of "crowding out" and the model behind it are discussed in Brenner (1985, chap. 5).

67. Worrying about the actions of freed soldiers is not new. See Bridenbaugh (1968, 391). Adam Smith (1976, 1: 496) also remarked that when there are abrupt changes, "humanity may . . . require that the freedom of trade should be restored only by slow gradations, and with a good deal of reserve and circumspection. . . . The disorder which this would occasion might no doubt be very considerable." Smith thought that the disorder would be considerable, though less so than generally feared, because the discharged soldiers could find employment. Still, he did emphasize that the transition would not be easy since soldiers have been used to "idleness and dissipation" (492–93).

68. See discussion in Brenner (1987, chap. 6 and chap. 7). I should also point out that the definition of R & D is completely arbitrary, depending on the tax laws. As Vogel (1988) accurately points out, much of the output of the entertainment industry, be it a new movie or a new show, is, properly speaking, an "R & D" project. Yet, although the entertainment industry is one of the United States's major exports, its expenditures are not viewed as contributing to R & D.

69. Federal Express, Purolator, and Facsimile machines have entered into this market only during the last decade.

70. See discussion in Brenner (1987, chap. 6).

71. See sources and discussion in Brenner (1987, chap. 7).

72. See Freeman (1983, chap. 9). Freeman also notes that in the United States, the United Kingdom, and France the aircraft industry accounted for more than a quarter of the total industry R & D expenditure during much of the postwar period, financed by governments.

73. See "Ex-Soviet Scientists Get $100M to Stay at Home," *Financial Post,* February 18, 1992: 8. Also see Brenner (1987, chap. 7).

74. As quoted in Pinson (1954, 241). The 1881 measure introduced insurance against industrial accidents (although this measure failed to pass the Reichstag). The first enacted measure was the Sickness Insurance Act of 1883. In 1884 came the accident insurance bill, and in 1889 came a measure for old-age and incapacity insurance. See Pinson (1954, 246), Craig (1978), Mommsen (1981), and Rimlinger (1982).

75. The fear of socialism was profound, as William I admitted in his message from the throne on November 17, 1881. He stated that "the healing of the socialists is not to be carried out by the regression of the Social Democratic excesses but is, at the same time, to be sought in the positive furthering of the welfare of workers" (Pinson 1954, 445). The goal was to diminish the workers' revolutionary ardor by making social reforms and thus prevent "the entire fabric of society [falling] in the cataclysm and chaos of violent revolution" (Pinson 1954, 446).

76. This remark led historians to conclude that "Bismarck's aim was unambiguously political: in the grim moments of dependency, the lower classes should not have to rely on indigent family, on indifferent employer, or on a socialist party" (Stern 1977, 219). However, Johnson (1983) notes that Bismarck's social legislation gave temporary remedy, at best.

77. As in Auerbach and Kotlikoff (1987), for example.

78. The model presented in its most elaborate version in Brenner and Brenner (1990) shows why one cannot separate the issues of creation and redistribution of wealth.

79. See Brenner (1987, chap. 6).

80. Examples are discussed in Brenner (1985, chap. 1).

81. The fact that one cannot easily categorize expenditures also comes to the fore when one reexamines details in defense contracts, which automatically enter into the category of military expenditures. Ernst Fitzgerald (1972, 159), for example, notes that part of contractors' "inefficiency" can be explained by the fact that they had to provide for such things as equal employment opportunity programs, seniority clauses in union agreements, programs for employment of the handicapped, apprentice programs, aid to small business, aid to distressed labor areas, and encouragement of improvements to plant layouts and facilities. In this case, too, part of the expenditures classified under the military should have been classified under the categories of social insurance programs and education. But how much in each? Nobody knows. In the light of this discussion, the type of calculations done by Musgrave (1980) or Boskin et al. (1987 a, b) are not illuminating.

82. On "scientific" publications, see Colander and Brenner (1992, chap. 1).

83. See "Canadians Believe Ottawa Wastes 47 cents of Every Tax Dollar," *The Gazette,* January 7, 1993: B1.

84. See Watson (1992).

85. See Morgenstern (1963, 243); italics in original.

86. See Friedman and Friedman (1987, 125). The Friedmans attribute the practice to the interests of some groups and the growing bureaucracy.

87. In Romania under Nicolae Ceausescu an estimated 30 percent of the people were employed by the Securitate (the Romanian KGB), full- or part-time. Also recall that dissent was viewed as mental sickness, suitable for compulsory hospitalization—another "service" added to measured output. The institutions of these societies drew attention to the fact that they were there to maintain established hierarchies, insure their members, and maintain monopoly power.

88. See A. Agabengyan (1989, 46–47).

89. One should rather say the lack of either, as shown in Brenner (1990).

90. See A. Agabengyan (1989, 59).

91. See J. Winiecki (1988, 4).

92. See "Workers Plan Strikes to Protest Huge Hungarian Price Increases," *The Gazette,* January 8, 1990: C12, and Dobbs (1990).

93. The potential misuse of statistics by governments was also noted by Josiah Stamp (1880–1941), who, when questioned on the validity of public statistics, said: "Governments are very keen on amassing statistics. They collect them, raise them to the nth power, take the cube root, and prepare wonderful diagrams. But you must never forget that everyone of these figures comes in the first place from the village watchman, who just puts down what he damn pleases." As quoted in Nettler (1978, 57) and discussed in Wright (1985). See also Di Guardi (1987).

94. See "The Black Hole of Money," editorial, *New York Times,* January 17, 1988. Also see Stulz (1986).

95. Although even the evaluation of such data may not give a clear picture: how does one evaluate the impact of increased expenditures on the military? See the discussion in the next chapter. As to the productivity, trade deficits, and international debt figures, changes in which also have been linked to discussions about the problems the United States is assumed to be facing today: if possible, they are even less comprehensible than the deficit figures. See discussion in Morgenstern (1963) and Morris (1989) on the way international trade figures and debt figures are computed.

Chapter 3

1. See Appleby (1978).

2. See Dudley's (1991) summary in chapter 5.

3. This is the last example of the reign of a city unsustained by forces of a unified state, until the recent emergence of Hong Kong and Singapore.

4. See Brenner (1993).

5. See Barbour (1966).

6. Also, geography was such that for part of the year it was easier to defend the city. See Dudley (1991, chap. 5).

7. I mention "society as a whole" because the idea that saving is good for individuals can be traced back to the ancient fable about the industrious ant.

8. The Navigation Act of 1651 is one of them. The Dutch, when it was convenient for them, claimed that they were committed to *mare liberum* ("free sea") and

opposed the British position in having property rights in surrounding seas. See Schama (1988, chap. 4).

9. Amsterdam's emergence (1585–1610) was in no small part due to the immigrants from Antwerp. That city fell to the Duke of Parma in 1585, and its port was closed. See Barbour (1966).

10. Huguenots came from France, nonconformists from England, and Jews from all over Europe. But Amsterdam's rise started with Antwerp's fall. There was a brief period of persecution (1617–19), and some discrimination against Roman Catholics and Jews, but the treatment of the Jews was by far the most tolerant for those times. See Barbour (1966, 11; 16, note 7). Kindleberger (1978, 180–81) notes that Newport, Rhode Island, thrived because, its population being more tolerant, it attracted large number of Jews and Quakers, as did commercial cities around the world.

11. See McEvedy and Jones (1980, 62). They also note that by the late seventeenth century Dutch prosperity was declining under a load of taxation, and population growth stopped, the population staying stable until the beginning of the nineteenth century. According to other estimates, the population trebled between 1550 and 1650. See Schama (1988, 223).

12. See Barbour (1966). In 1514 Antwerp and the Southern part of Netherlands were prosperous, not the North. At the time Amsterdam had a population of 13,500, whereas Antwerp's was 100,000. By 1582, Antwerp's was 83,700, and in 1589 only 42,000. See Dudley (1991, chap. 5), Aymard (1982).

13. See Van Houtte (1977), Huizinga (1968), Wilson (1968), Kossman (1970), Aymard (1982). Also see discussion in Schama (1988, chap. 5), where he summarizes the opinions of a number of writers during the sixteenth and seventeenth centuries on these subjects. He devotes special attention to Melchior Fokkens' book, which appeared in 1662 and attributed the flourishing of the new republic to the fact that other cities exhausted themselves in wars, whereas the Dutch opened the gates to provide shelter to the persecuted and the oppressed of neighboring states. Also see North and Thomas (1973, chap. 11).

14. Outsiders may thus have observed, for a while, a modest lifestyle.

15. See Trevor-Roper (1961), Barbour (1966, 57), Brenner (1983, chap. 1 and chap. 5). There is something unsettling in the observation that those who have been trading people for a very long time—be they the Dutch, the Italians, the English, or now the Americans—have been the most tolerant. It may take a long time to learn this cultural skill. See discussion in chapter 5 about the difficulty in establishing institutions necessary for trade in societies that have not practiced it.

16. See Kindleberger (1978) on Hamburg and other European trading centers and Gibney (1992) on the Asian ones.

17. See Gibney (1992, 274–75).

18. See Brenner (1983, chap. 1 and chap. 5), Origo (1992), Kotkin (1992). Gibney (1992, 236) notes that the Chinese Taiwanese, for example, were initially restricted to trade, not unlike Jews in Europe.

19. Hong Kong was also helped by its low taxes, lack of exchange controls, few regulations on incorporations, overseas profits, and capital remittances.

20. See Zumthor (1959), Dudley (1991, chap. 5). After 1586, Netherlands' government also paid for a number of secondary schools. See Zumthor (1959,

122–32). In addition, municipalities had a welfare system and helped finance hospitals.

21. See Appleby (1978, 77), and Viner (1978, 161–63). Viner also notes that none of these writers attribute the success to any religious influence.

22. See Appleby (1978, 77).

23. See Schama (1988, 223), who also adds that "The perennial commentary of foreigners that the intricacies of Dutch federalism were a 'chaos' of government spoke to their incomprehension, not to the historical truth" (224).

24. See Schama (1988, chap. 4), about the choice of advisers to English monarchs during these times.

25. See McNeill (1974, 14; and discussion, 14–21).

26. See Barbour (1966, 17, 34). She also notes that both merchants and ship owners rejected attempts to regulate the insurance market. The chamber succeeded in regulating itself, establishing a reputation for honesty, and attracting European maritime insurance business until the eighteenth century. Also see Aymard (1982), Kossman (1970), Van Houtte (1977), and Ehrenberg (1928) on the development of trade and finance.

27. The Exchange Bank was the first and, for a long time, the greatest public bank in northern Europe. It was administered and supervised by the city, and there was confidence in its stability. Initially it had monopoly power, but that power was relaxed. See Barbour (1966, 43).

28. See Barbour (1966, 20).

29. See Barbour (1966, 28–29, 80). The Dutch, like those living in Singapore or Hong Kong today, could invest and speculate less in land, which was expensive and heavily taxed.

30. See Schama (1988, chap. 5), and Barbour (1966, 141).

31. See Schama (1988, 349). He also adds, "This was sailing very close to the wind—indeed it became known as trading in the wind . . . and it aroused the indignation of the magistracy as well as the church, which condemned it as a form of fraud" (349). But Schama points out with good reason that, moralizing aside, the practice was not different from that of governments spending money by "anticipating" revenues for coming years (350).

32. See Barbour (1966, 78).

33. See Barbour (1966, 79). Until then, a share was an investment in a trading venture, recoverable only when the enterprise completed it.

34. Barbour (1966, 75), quoting from John Carry's *An Essay on the State of England in Relation to Its Trade* (Bristol, 1695).

35. Maybe they had such access in Venice, though that city was not so open to foreigners as Amsterdam. See McNeill (1974, chap. 1, 12–20 in particular). As for innovative financial arrangements elsewhere in Italy, see Origo (1992).

36. The same was true of Venice during earlier centuries. See McNeill (1974, chap. 1, 19–20).

37. See Barbour (1966, 54).

38. All this happened in spite of the fact that Amsterdam's regulations and guilds also hampered "experimentation, enterprise and organization, and that flexibility of

adjustment to the market which is the life of competitive industry" (Barbour 1966, 71).

39. See Barbour (1966, 119–20).

40. See historical discussion on these three distinct functions in Vance (1970, chap. 7 in particular). Also see Kindleberger (1978, chap. 3).

41. The lack of visibility explains, in part, the persistent condemnation of outsiders and the regulations imposed on them, especially when they became "too rich." Not until the sixteenth century did mercantilism legitimize traders, arguing that nations could gain wealth through trade, rather than through agriculture and mining special metals. See Vance (1970, 61–79, 147). The value of such skills becomes evident when for one reason or another there is a significant change in the flow of information. Vance notes that "the correspondence in time of the eclipse of the American merchant marine and the growth of domestic manufacturing caused several of the classic trading towns to shift from foreign venturing to factory manufacturing. Providence, Salem, and New Bedford each followed this course and the subsequent role each played shifted the city away from wholesale. In seeking to explain why, we may begin to discern the variable factors within the system. The collapse of foreign trade quickly shut off the supply of information about potential markets. No longer was there a class of Yankee skippers who could quote for you the more recent prices for ginseng in Canton or the best sources of cocoa in Spanish America. And with that loss went the awareness of what goods would best buy those staples. Only the American market, protected by laws of cabotage, remained both open and known to the New England merchant, and that domestic commerce became attached to the cities that had forged interior ties by canal and railroad in the system of metropolitan mercantilism effected through wholesaling" (156).

42. See Needham (1961, vol. 1, table 8, p. 242).

43. The Italian, the Dutch, the English traders later (as well as other tribes before them) exported this skill I call the "commercialization of knowledge." See Kotkin (1992).

44. See Brenner (1983, 1985, 1987).

45. When and where this did not happen, people settled into routines. The evidence suggests that knowledge fails to advance if one interacts with people who have the same "human capital." Their capital must be different. See chapter 5.

46. Melloan (1993), quoting Andrew Brick.

47. See McKay (1970).

48. Protected hierarchies oppose changes since they expect to lose; in this sense the transition toward trade and the "democratization of capital" is no free lunch. (The term in quotation marks is the subtitle of Spurge's [1991] book, also discussed by Yago [1991], who examines how the high-yield securities were used to restructure American corporations.) Societies with established though not legally protected hierarchies will choose, from the variety of ideas that intellectuals offer, the ones that justify both imposing constraints on the democratization of capital and at the same time giving themselves new roles that maintain their power. The opposition prevents the "democratization of capital," which also means giving the young and poor—those without a history of credit rating—access to unlock their potential.

49. It is no accident that seventeenth-century English public discourse on catching up with the Dutch used nationalistic terms—England competing with the Dutch. In contrast, firms in Holland just competed one with the other, trying to establish better and closer relations with customers, whatever their nationality. There is nothing new about the ideas of "global competitiveness," quality of service, competing by innovation, or crossing national frontiers. Amsterdam's traders—many of foreign origin, as emphasized—practiced them during the seventeenth century. Also see Rosecrance (1986), who deals with the rise of the trading states, though from different angles.

50. See Homer (1963, chap. 11).

51. See Lane (1966).

52. Holland's population stayed unchanged at 2 million between 1650 and 1800. See Kindleberger (1978, 140–45), McEvedy and Jones (1980, 64), Dudley (1991, chap. 5). Adam Smith (1976, 444–45) was right when he noted that a "merchant . . . is not necessarily the citizen of any particular country," and that "the ordinary revolutions of war and government easily dry up the sources of that wealth which arises from commerce only."

53. This includes, not surprisingly, Adam Smith's appropriately titled *Wealth of Nations.* After all, the book was written in 1776. Its opening sentence is, "The annual labour of every *nation* is the fund which originally supplies it with all the necessaries and conveniences of life which it annually consumes, and which consist always either in the immediate produce of that labour, or in what is purchased with that produce from other nations" (1; italics added). However, notice how this departure point would mislead if one wanted to understand Sweden's development, for example, without taking Amsterdam's role into account. Also see discussion in Jacobs (1985).

54. See data in Grobar et al. (1989 a, b).

55. As they were: consider France, the major arms exporter after the United States, having a large government sector and also a high standard of living. Not to mention that the numbers about defense are not readily available, as noted in chapter 2, and that we do not know exactly where they appear in the national accounting. White and Wildavsky (1989, 35) also note that "A guide to the politics of defense spending requires a guide to defense numbers; that is not easy to assemble. Edwin Dale, associate director of OMB for Public Affairs in the Reagan administration, comments that at one point the New York Times ran four stories in ten days, each with different figures—and all were correct!" Also notice that during such times "nationalism" becomes a profitable ideology to pursue, at least for a while, and not only for some interest groups. By diverting trade, the whole "nation" can benefit.

56. Although, of course, the fact that Communist China's leaders allowed opportunities to be exploited plays a central role. The Canadian evidence especially illuminates the fact that national governments' spending does not lead to development, no matter what they measure about incomes and "job creation" in a region. Ottawa's continuing support of the Atlantic Provinces succeeded in creating a situation where there soon will be more fishermen than fish.

57. Also note that from 1974 to 1989, when the total number of Americans working in the private sector rose by 56 percent to 91 million, virtually all of the new jobs were created by what is called, "noninvestment-grade" companies. They raised

$360 billion during these years through capital markets, using a wide variety of financial instruments rather than loans from established banks. The Fortune 500 companies' employment diminished during that same time by 2.3 million. See Spurge (1991, 12) and Yago (1991).

58. See Jacobs (1985) and Lane (1966, chap. 30).

59. See Brenner, Dagenais, and Montmarquette (1991): the essence of the work is summarized in appendix 3.

60. The latter is not guaranteed when governments manipulate their accounting, or when public property is used.

61. Some writers viewed savings in even broader contexts. Theories of imperialism argued at times that "oversaving," i.e., an excess of capital, was a great cause of economic distress and social tension. Charles A. Conant, for example, thought that imperialism brings about a glut of unsold goods and requires an outlet for the surplus savings. The doubt that domestic demand cannot be sufficiently increased led to the idea of investing such capital in the development of Asia and Africa. Others (J. A. Hobson, for example), argued for an alternative solution: expansion of domestic demand through the redistribution of wealth. See discussion on their viewpoints in Schlesinger (1986, 121). These are just two examples of the general tendency of vague ideas getting more and more obscure. See Brenner (1991c) and Colander and Brenner (1992, chap. 1) on these general trends.

62. See detailed discussion on these points in Brenner (1985, chap. 5).

63. See *Oxford Dictionary,* Oxford: Clarendon Press (1933), and discussion in Spielman (1971, 62). But also see Brenner (1989, chap. 3) on the negative connotation being given to the term *enthusiasm.*

64. See page 185 in the 1988 edition of his *Fable of the Bees.* Viner (1978, 162) notes that Sir William Temple, in an essay written in 1673, links the Dutch success to "poverty in natural resources and density of population." See discussion in the last chapter.

65. See Mandeville (1986, 186).

66. See Schama (1988, 223). He adds that "to this day, public life in the Netherlands retains a pleasure in ceremony. Conventionally mistaken for royalism dressed down, it is in fact republicanism dressed up."

67. See Schama (1988, 295), Appleby (1978), and Schumpeter (1972, 325).

68. As quoted in Bauer (1984, 176). For detailed discussion on others see Jacobs (1985), Bairoch (1988).

69. There is extensive literature on the subject by historians, anthropologists, and economists. See Gibbon (1990), Cipolla (1970), Olson (1982), Brenner (1983), Kennedy (1987), and Tainter (1988).

70. Unless population is diminishing, a case that is never discussed.

71. It seems to me that the theorists of economic development are falling for the same type of sterile exercises today as they did in the sixties and seventies, when the large majority of the practitioners of this field wrote models upon models about the pervasiveness of vicious circles. Although those who criticized the models mentioned Hong Kong, Taiwan, South Korea, and a few other countries as counter-examples, they were dismissed with the statement that generalizations cannot be dismissed with counter examples, and the appropriate method of testing is validity in a statistical

sense. See discussion in Bauer (1984, chap. 9). If the models are discarded, Barro's empirical analyses lose all meaning.

72. In Barro's first study in the sequence, used only to examine the historical pattern of growth in the United States, he viewed each state as a small, closed economy, producing identical goods. The government appears as just one of the nine standard sectors in each state. It has no special effect on incentives. This may not be a very restrictive assumption when Barro compares the fifty states, since they had similar laws, regulations, and institutions, and thus people living within their borders had similar incentives. However, in studies where he examines the international evidence, the variables explaining variations in growth rates are, among others, government consumption (he excludes education and defense—but does not explain why defense should be excluded; my guess is that he excludes education in order not to double-count it, since there is a schooling variable in the model); tariff rates; black-market premium; frequency of revolution; and others. This means that variations in national growth rates depend not only on capital-labor ratios but on what one intuitively would think of as "incentives."

73. Before discussing a few straightforward and a few complicated problems with Barro's analyses, I want to clarify that I have no doubt that societies with *similar* institutions and incentive structure eventually converge, though, as explained below, not through the process Barro emphasizes but because of innovations. Already Baumol (1986) found such convergence for sixteen advanced countries but not for the less-developed countries. See discussion in Brenner (1993).

74. See Huff (1954, 134).

75. See Kuznets (1942), Usher (1968), and Bauer (1984, chap. 9) for references, calculations, and discussion. Usher shows how biases, which do not remain constant over time, amount for less-developed countries to several hundred percent.

76. I do not want to imply that, correctly calculated, average income per capita in the United States regions were the same every year, and that the convergence is just a statistical artifact, though I suspect that frequently this is the case when regions under one political system are being compared over longer periods of time, so that the effects of state-specific innovations are eliminated.

77. Obviously, growth must refer to length of time of more than five or ten years, and some economic historians claim that it must be thirty to be meaningful. See Lane (1966) and Usher (1969).

78. See North and Weingast (1989).

79. See Berman (1983), Hill (1992), and Brenner (1983, 1990). Consider the extreme stability of "primitive" societies, which did not grow at all. See Brenner (1983, chap. 2), for discussion of the evidence. Also see Tawney (1963).

80. The importance of this rather than other features can be seen by comparing the communist countries' performance with that of other dictatorial countries that did not prohibit trade.

81. See discussion on the meaning of statistics in the communist bloc in Brenner (1990, 1991a, b).

82. See Lucas (1988) and Romer (1990).

83. See discussion in Brenner (1993).

84. The only sector whose subsidy was not yet justified on similar general grounds is the capital market, though as Jack Carr (1993) points out, models to justify intervention in the banking sector on such grounds abound. It can even be done on general grounds, though it would be wrong to start writing such models. North and Weingast (1989) show how, once political stability was achieved, there was a rapid development of capital markets, of a wide range of securities, and of negotiable instruments, which were all important in England's subsequent growth. McNeill (1974, chap. 1), shows how one of the main aspects of the Italian city-states' spectacular rise was due to the creation of ad hoc corporations. The previous sections showed the importance of finance in Amsterdam. All this evidence, however, does not imply that financial markets should be subsidized.

85. The nature of the incentive structure is implicit in the model of human behavior presented in Brenner and Brenner (1990, appendix 1). It explains the meaning of leapfrogging for individuals.

86. This is the way I interpret Adam Smith's statement on the "division of labor being limited by the extent of the market." Coase (1988) calls this process "contracting out," which in his view also leads to specialization. Others view it as being linked to increasing returns. I prefer to view it as being linked to innovations. When people think about innovations, "increasing returns" are not observable: they are the entrepreneurs' expectations. See discussion on this point in Brenner (1987).

87. See Brenner (1993). Here are some additional numbers about urbanization, covering the international sample for the period of 1960 to 1990. In the industrialized world, 61 percent of the population lived in cities in 1960, and 73 in 1990. For the poorest countries, the numbers were, respectively, 16 and 28; for those with "medium human development," 25 and 42; and for the more developed Asian and South-American countries, 52 and 75. For the industrialized world, the annual rate of increase in urban population was 1.4 percent, which is very close to Barro's convergence number. For the relatively developed Asian and South American countries, it was about 3.6 percent—and Barro's estimated rate of convergence for Japan is 3 percent per year. Briefly: one simple number leads approximately to the same prediction that Barro's analyses do. The difference is that he gets his results by complex manipulations of incomprehensible numbers and by relying on an approach—the "neoclassical growth model"—which, as Ronald Coase (1988, 2–3), put it, is detached from his subject matter—human beings.

88. See Brenner and Brenner (1990).

89. See Panati (1987, 159–60).

90. See Blanchard (1991).

91. See Young (1928), Coase (1988), Schultz (1990), and Colander and Brenner (1992) making this point in various contexts.

92. After all, firms—unless one considers those having monopoly on some resource that cannot be transferred—are little more than a complex set of contracts. If these contracts are taxed because of political uncertainty (as shown in chap. 5), inflation (as shown in chap. 4), or otherwise, they will be rewritten in those places where these taxes are smaller.

93. Within U.S. regions and cities are pockets of growth and pockets of decline. More can be learned by examining them than by looking at any aggregates. Maybe

within a few years research will be able to show how much of the United States's prosperity after the Second World War can be attributed to the European immigrants who came in massive numbers to its shores. Parker (1959) held the view that government boundaries are less important in determining growth patterns than "resources." Also see Brenner (1992) and Wriston (1992).

Chapter 4

1. As quoted in Gavin and Stockman (1993).

2. In Canada, since 1986, tax brackets have only been adjusted for inflation over 3 percent, pushing many into higher brackets without real increases in gross income. Estimates put the windfall at CA$1 billion. The federal banking regulator in Canada, Mr. Michael Mackenzie, also revealed that faulty inflation assumptions were behind many bad loans made by financial institutions. See Beauchesne (1993).

3. If at that point foreigners happen to hold a large fraction of this debt, they will pay the tax, and citizens of the country who issued the debt, benefit.

4. The possibility that there is a stable, inverse relationship between inflation and unemployment—the so-called Phillips curve—which can be used to guide policy, has no foundations, although such a relationship will exist in some circumstances. See chapter 2, later discussion in the text, and also Brenner (1985, chap. 5).

5. This happened frequently in Israel. People received bonuses that could be spent in a few stores on items ranging from carpets to kitchen appliances.

6. Such demands are rarely linked with inflation and its fiscal consequences, though a look at the sequence of events in countries with inflationary history shows that they are. A simple numerical example shows why. Let us say that one is in the 50 percent marginal tax bracket. He is then better off making efforts to get $1,100 untaxed benefit in kind from the government than $2,000 additional monetary income from the government or from any other source.

7. See discussion later in the text.

8. See discussion later in the text.

9. See Beauchesne (1993) for reference on the faulty decisions made by Canada's financial institutions.

10. See Spurge (1991).

11. People also invested in gold, paintings, and so forth.

12. Economists do not take into account the costs of hyperinflation, in wiping out savings in particular, and the destabilizing effect it has on society, probably because they cannot be assigned a numerical value.

13. As quoted in De Long and Summers (1992).

14. What this means is that if the government obtained the same revenues by raising other taxes, these additional transaction costs could have been avoided.

15. The same thing can be said about the effects of taxes and regulations.

16. The recent crash of real estate in the United States should have been expected. Inflationary expectations were lowered, and lower marginal tax rates diminished the attractiveness of this form of investment.

17. Suppose aggregates had only this and no other flaws. Then, if one compared countries with similar institutions, the only difference being that central banks pursued

a policy of fluctuating inflation in one and not in others, one could expect that the country with fluctuating inflation would show slower improvements in well-being.

18. See Brenner and Patinkin (1977, 388). All this reflects the fact that, even though in both cases the lender receives a negative interest rate of roughly 2 percent per year, instead of the roughly 6 percent that he expected, the short-term lender will suffer the loss for only three months, after which he is able to make a new loan the return on which will reflect the new inflationary anticipations. This same argument holds true for contracts negotiated in labor markets. But it should be noticed that on occasion indexed contracts had shorter duration. See data on labor markets in Brenner (1985, chap. 5). The reason was the inaccuracy of price indices, as will be shown below.

19. See Brenner (1977).

20. See Brenner (1985) for detailed discussion and data.

21. Until some innovations are done that restore wealth. See Brenner (1985, 1987).

22. Higher unemployment may lead to increased pressures on governments to pursue an expansionary monetary policy or subsidize some sectors. If governments respond to such pressures, additional sectors may try their luck too, and if they are successful, a process popularly labeled "wage catch-up" or "spillovers" may result among sectors. However, this is a process that can occur whether there is indexation or not, and it can lead to inflation (with the central bank's cooperation). In this sense, therefore, the argument that "indexation" of wages causes inflation is still inaccurate.

23. Contracts were linked to the wholesale price index, which at that time included 92 products. Coffee, which was subsidized, accounted for 17 percent of the index, for example. See Ellis (1969), Fishlow (1974), Brenner (1977). De Long and Summers (1992) do not mention the manipulation of price indices either, though Brazil, Israel, and France, countries where the index was manipulated, are part of their sample.

24. See Brenner (1977) and Page and Trollope (1974).

25. The positive correlation between higher inflation and more strikes is known. See "Zero Inflation," *Economist,* November 7, 1992, 23–26, replicating the international data published by the U.K. Department of Employment.

26. While there were slight differences between indexed and non-indexed wages in the annual rates of change between 1970 and 1977, the averages for the whole period were identical: 11.8 percent. The fact that, when the CPI rose by an average of 7 percent per year, "real" wages (as measured by this index) grew by an average of 4.8 percent, implies that the contract had many other clauses determining changes in wages. If COLAs were the sole factor and had even provided 100 percent protection against rises in the CPI, the purchasing power of wages would have been unchanged instead of increasing. There were several reasons for the partial protection. In 36 percent of the agreements with COLA clauses, the clauses were "capped," that is, limited to a certain amount. If the realized change in the CPI was 12 percent, but it was agreed that a maximum compensation of 10 percent would be awarded, then only the 10 percent was automatically paid. In 27 percent of the agreements, the COLA clauses were triggered only after some minimum inflation rate. This meant that for a 5 percent rise in the CPI, no compensation was given, but if the rise was 10 percent, then a 5 percent automatic compensation was given. In 60 percent of the agreements, the COLA

clauses did not cover the entire contract period. (The fact that the percentages of labor contracts with the various clauses add up to more than 100 percent means that in some of the contracts more than one constraint was imposed on the COLA formula.) David Wilton derived these data from 1405 major collective agreements signed between 1968 and 1975. He also found that the degree of protection afforded by all the COLA clauses against changes in the CPI was only 47 percent. Thus, the COLA clauses guaranteed that, on average, for a 10 percent rise in the CPI, wages would rise by only 4.7 percent, and implied a 5.3 percent erosion in purchasing power. Productivity (as measured by output per man-hour) increased at an average annual rate of 4.4 percent for the years 1966–71 and 1.8 percent during the period 1971–75. (See *Canada Year Book, 1976–77,* 998–99.) These increases in productivity, combined with the 5.3 percent decrease in the purchasing power of wages (for every 10 percent increase in inflation) due to the less-than-full indexing, meant that wage increases due to indexation did not exceed productivity gains. The fact that the wage increases were of the same magnitude whether wages were indexed or not, and that productivity gains even at their worst averaged 1.8 percent during this period, when indexation clauses provided only a 47 percent protection, suggests that wage indexation per se was not inflationary. This conclusion does not imply either that the total increase in negotiated wages did not contribute to inflationary pressures, or that full indexation of government bonds, as shown later in the text, might not have contributed to such pressures.

27. In Brazil, however, in spite of "official" indexation, the real wages of unskilled workers declined more than 30 percent between 1964 and 1967, in spite of the fact that output per capita increased during this same period. See Baer and Beckerman (1974), Ellis (1969), and Fishlow (1974).

28. See Cousineau and Lacroix (1981), and discussion in Brenner (1985). This finding does not imply that the overall increase in labor costs, resulting from the negotiated settlements that exceeded productivity growth, might not have contributed to inflationary pressures.

29. In Israel, the Histadruth represents most workers.

30. This practice means that indexation was implicitly used for redistributing wealth, rather than keeping the distribution independent of inflation, which is frequently argued—in theory—to be its goal.

31. Yet, such arrangements meant that, as in Canada, the indexation clauses turned out to be just one component of the compensation package, since, as in Canada, real wages were increasing in Israel during this time. Partial indexation also meant that the difference in practice between indexed and non-indexed wage contracts were not as sharp as assumed theoretically.

32. The Family Allowance Act, 1973, which came into effect on January 1, 1974, provided for Family Allowances and Special Allowances to be increased at the beginning of each year by the expected increase in the CPI (although in 1976 full indexation was suspended for a year as a result of the federal government's expenditure-restraint program.) See *Canada Year Book, 1976–77,* 250. Recently, the Canadian Tax Foundation estimated that, because of the miscalculation of the index in Canada, the federal and provincial governments lost $5 to $12 billion in tax revenues since 1974. See *The Gazette,* July 16, 1991: B14.

33. Although one finds much discussion about indexation of financial assets in France in the 1950s, a closer examination reveals that what was done there was not "indexation" the way this term is being interpreted today, but something else. The so-called government "index" bonds were linked either to the price of the Napoleon, a gold coin; to some index of stock and bond prices; or to an index of industrial production. There was such "indexation" to the prices of specific products in Israel too. See Brenner and Patinkin (1977). The CPI was never used because the courts on several occasions declared such contracts to be illegal. Other "indexed" bonds were linked to the price of various products: electricity, coal, cement, steel, or railway tickets. However, in 1958 the indexation of any new assets in the financial market was declared illegal. See sources in Brenner (1977).

34. There was some indexation in Finland, again offered only by the government and never by the private sector. See Puumanen (1967) and Ahtiala (1967). In 1968, after the 24 percent devaluation, the government ended all indexation.

35. In 1973, the Brazilian government suspended the sale of indexed bonds. The Brazilian variable inflation rates continue, with devastating impacts. A recent article in the *Financial Times* (December 5, 1991) notes that "the mystery of why Brazilian shops sell a pound of best filet mignon for the same price as a packet of butter, or a hairbrush for the same as a small sofa is at least resolved. A survey by KPMG Peat Marwick Dreyfus has finally revealed the secret of how Brazilian manufacturers decide on their prices. It seems that the most important factor for 80 percent of companies is government measures. The actual cost of production comes way down the list with little more than a quarter of companies surveyed considering this to have any relevance to their calculations. The Brazilian Banking Association has a simple explanation for this apparently irrational behavior. Its latest report shows that in the past decade Brazil has suffered eight stabilization policies, 15 wage policies, 54 attempts at imposing price controls, 18 exchange rate policies and 11 changes in the way the government measures inflation."

36. In addition, there was a 9 percent interest rate ceiling in Israel. See Brenner (1977) and Brenner and Patinkin (1977).

37. This section draws on Brenner and Patinkin (1977).

38. As we saw, this is why labor contracts have been renegotiated.

39. It may be interesting to note that it also issued an "option bond" that gave its purchaser the right of choosing at the time of its redemption—five years after the issue—either the nominal option (which yielded a nominal return of 10.76 percent per year) or the indexed option (which yielded a "real" return of 4.84 percent). The Israeli government, however, no longer indexed the loans it gave out—which turned out to be a major blunder. See Brenner and Patinkin (1977).

40. In fact, indexed bonds became a substitute for money in the portfolios of individuals. See Bronfeld and Brenner (1977).

41. There was no logic either in the government's policy of not lowering the real rate of interest on the indexed bonds and taking advantage of the greatly increased demand for them. Only in 1974 was the rate lowered. See Brenner and Patinkin (1977, 405). Keeping the real interest rates artificially high meant not only that less savings were channeled to the private sector but also that, eventually, more had to be paid to

service the debt. But the former may have the more significant effect. The latter has an effect on the distribution of wealth.

42. It should be noted that the private sector never issued bonds indexed to the CPI or any other general index. Such bonds were issued by governments only—a sign that one should be cautious with these instruments to start with.

43. But after 1966, borrowers were required to pay a 3 to 4 percent insurance "against linkage," which turned out to be an insignificant amount when the inflation rates increased significantly.

44. It is sometimes thought that the indexation of government debt reduces the government's incentive to pursue inflationary policies. If giving such a signal is indeed an important consideration for governments, it would have been even more important for the Israeli one. For, as noticed above, it was borrowing indexed and lending non-indexed. This meant that, by 1973, for example, the nominal debt to the private sector (money plus short-term debt) became less than the nominal debt of the private sector to it (because of loans the government gave out at low interest rates). See Kleiman (1974). But the argument that indexed bonds may dissuade governments from undertaking inflationary policies and convince the public of its intentions, has no good theoretical foundations. Some macro-economists argue that, if the private sector takes full account of the future taxes that will be levied upon it in order to service the government debt which it holds, it does not matter how the government pays the debt, since the debt does not represent net wealth. See Patinkin (1965, 288, ff.), and more recently Barro (1989) more formally. Even if some would come up with such "foundations," the facts presented above would contradict them anyway. Neither the existence of indexed bonds nor of indexed contracts in the labor market prevented increases in inflation in Brazil, Israel, or the other countries surveyed here. Alfred Marshall thought that indexed bonds might be useful in deflationary and not just inflationary times, since interest rates would automatically drop with the declines in price indices. This would have the beneficial effect that people would end up paying only the anticipated real rate, rather than an agreed upon nominal rate that would turn out to be a high real one. Marshall wrote this in 1887, and the article was reprinted in 1925. But he does not explain why people would not hold on to cash, which during deflation gives a higher return than indexed bonds.

45. Their conclusion is based on the view that inflation can be beneficial, based on some Keynesian views of the world. See DeLong and Summers (1992, 26). In contrast, I argue in this chapter that "too much pursuit of price stability" can be harmful because central banks pursue it mistakenly, relying on badly measured price indices, though recognizing that inflation is harmful at all times. The discussion on "reflation" in the previous chapter is not a contradiction: that is exactly why I used the term "reflation" there.

46. See *The Consumer Price Index Reference Paper* (Catalogue 62–553), occasional, February 1985, 50.

47. See *The Consumer Price Index Reference Paper*, 19.

48. See Segal (1977).

49. Not until 1988, when the report on the CPI was written. When such a long time elapses between two surveys, a number of serious problems might arise, not only for domestic comparisons but for international ones too. Segal (1977, 51), for example,

notes that in 1974, 83.4 percent of all retail sales in Canada were made through Combination Stores and only 5.4 percent through Grocery Stores. Segal thus recommended that the smaller stores not be included in the sample. Casual observation, however, suggests that the importance of both superstores (Loblaws in Toronto, Super Carnaval in Quebec—neither is in the sample of outlets on page 23 in the Evaluation Report) and smaller stores has increased significantly, in part because of the massive increase in the participation of women in the labor force and the fact that the smaller stores were opened on Sundays. For this same reason there has been a large increase in enterprises specializing in "home delivery"—one wonders about the way they were included in the sample.

50. By 1982, housing accounted for 38.1 percent and food 20 percent (see *Statistics Canada Catalogue,* no. 62001, January 1988, 37). Similar lags exist in the United States. In a recent article, Irving Kristol (1991) made the following comment: "The price level may well be an adequate proxy for inflation over very long periods of time. To look at the CPI or the PPI every month, as we now do, and to try to draw conclusions about the value of 30-year Treasury Bonds, is ridiculous. Nevertheless, our economists—most of them, anyhow—are busily engaged in this exercise. . . . For the central bank to jiggle short-term interest rates in the light of these monthly numbers is equally ridiculous. We are fortunate that Alan Greenspan thinks so too. What makes the whole business even more absurd, in fact as well as in theory, is that the consumer price index is revised, and its 'representative' basket of goods made current, only intermittently over the decade. It is common for years to pass before the Bureau of Labor Statistics can get around to bringing us up to date on how we are distributing our purchasing power. . . . The price level the CPI reports always lags well behind reality. This would not be so important were it not for the fact that the CPI is reported in tenths of one percent, and these small variations in an anachronistic set of monthly statistics, are seized upon by commentators and analysts as possibly signifying a trend."

51. Many may also decide to save less, rather than instantly diminish their consumption.

52. See Stevens (1981, 5).

53. See Stevens (1981, 5–6) and Blinder (1980). Though the PCE-deflator also has its problems, it is a better one for indexation purposes since weights are adjusted.

54. See the *Geneva Report.*

55. See Ip (1991).

56. See Hadekel (1992). When demand diminishes, regulated prices are not lowered, and neither is the quantity supplied (of transportation, let us say). Thus other prices will be lowered more in response to monetary pressures, and so will quantities. But when and how these changes will be captured, we do not know. Regulated prices in Canada account for 25 percent of the CPI, much more than in the United States.

57. See *Statistics Canada Catalogue* 62001, 1989, 37, table 1. The Statistics Canada report notices that "Tobacco products and alcoholic beverages have also been consistent driving forces in maintaining a higher price movement for the regulated basket since 1982." See Ip (1991, 48).

58. In the case of alcohol, because of provincial monopoly power. When the government raises taxes and thus prices for these two items, the increase leads to an overestimation of the CPI for additional reasons. Recent reports suggest that since the

cigarettes started to cost about CA$43, and only about US$15 south of the border, the quantity bought in Quebec plunged, but exports of Canadian companies to the United States surged. (Every U.S. farm south of the border now advertises the selling of milk, eggs, and cigarettes.) It is probably not a wild guess that, at such a price differential, many otherwise honest Canadians became less so as far as their buying habits of cigarettes were concerned. (Indeed Montreal has a number of well-known streets where they sell cheap cigarettes. Advertising cigarettes on television is disallowed, but some news programs announce where they can be bought cheaply and illegally). The government succeeded in diminishing its receipts, making Canadians less honest, and also contributing to overestimating the change in the CPI. After all, Canadians are now buying cheap, smuggled cigarettes. Another example: in October 1992, an 8.4 percent increase in property taxes over 1991 pushed the annual rate to 1.6 percent. Without the increased tax, the inflation rate would have been 1.3 percent. Several observers added that there is actual deflation in consumer-product prices, and only "public services" drive the price index up. See Rinehart (1992).

59. See Gordon (1990, 38–39), who tries to deal with it, though without examining the CPI and admitting that even the revisions he makes cannot deal with a wide variety of problems.

60. See Gordon (1990), in particular the introduction and chapter 1, for numerous additions to this list.

61. In order to correct, in part, for such distortion, one should use the so-called chained price index. When used, it gives 0.5 percent less real growth than the alternative, fixed-weight index. Other U.S. studies suggested that deregulation of many American industries in the 1970s and 1980s obliterated the reporting of reams of information to regulatory agencies, and that import figures are harder to come by as well. See Brenner (1992).

62. The Geneva participants also discussed the issues of officially fixed prices, leading to quality deterioration—the case of postal services in the United States and Canada (and of medical services in Canada) fit into this category. The decision was that the hidden changes should be taken into account. See detailed discussion on some of these points in Gordon (1990, chap. 1).

63. This is true for all durable assets. That is why they pose the greatest problem in the calculation of price indices. In fact Gordon's (1990) study concerns aspects of the measurement of durable goods prices (though without even referring to speculation).

64. Although it was noted that the same reasons for which housing is excluded would also lead to the exclusion of education and health care.

65. Although there are substantial problems with such a methodology, since tax treatments are significantly different in the two countries.

66. See DeVries and Baldwin (1985, ix).

67. And which index should be used in academic research for calculating real interest rates?

68. This would imply taking into account foregone interest on owners' equity and capital gains.

69. From 1987 to 1989, when the population of Toronto was rapidly rising, the yearly "inflation" rate was more than 1 percent higher there than elsewhere in Canada:

about 4 percent in Canada, and more than 5 percent in Toronto. The difference was due to housing, which increased by about 4 percent in Canada but between 6 and 8 percent in Toronto. See *Statistics Canada Catalogue* no. 62010 (1987, 1989) and 62001 (1988, 1989). Before moving toward large-scale supply of indexed government bonds, Statistics Canada should be asked to review its practice concerning the measurement of homeownership, paying special attention to the argument that the weight of mortgages should be significantly diminished, in particular when there are good reasons to believe that more investment and more speculation are going on.

70. But Switzerland does. A recent article in the *Economist* (February 15, 1992, 77) attributes the recent increases in the CPI there to this fact and to the peculiar indexation practice. It remarks that "housing rents are, in effect, indexed to mortgage interest rates. When the government raises interest rates in order to squeeze inflation, rents—and hence the consumer price index—automatically increase." With two thirds of the population living in rented accommodation, and rents accounting for almost a fifth of the CPI, this increases measured inflation. Also, Switzerland's traditional practice is to index wages to the previous year's inflation, "and it is easy to see why inflation has been slow to respond to a tighter monetary policy."

71. See Blinder (1980).

72. See Blinder (1980, 564).

73. From 1974 to 1991, countries with low inflation had the lowest jobless rate: Switzerland, West Germany, Austria, Holland, Belgium, and Japan. Those with the highest inflation rate also had the highest measured unemployment: Spain, Italy, Ireland. See table 6 in "Zero Inflation," *Economist,* November 7, 1992. Taking into account what was said in chapter 1, these data may also reflect two things. First, in Spain and Italy unemployment rates have been systematically overestimated. Second, since the administration in Italy is known to be corrupt, and people avoid paying taxes, it is possible that the government resorted to inflation to impose a tax.

74. See Weiner (1992).

75. See Clark and Malabre (1993).

76. See summary in Becketti and Morris (1992), Gavin and Stockman (1993). Friedman (1992) suggests the adoption of long-range targets for M2.

77. M1, which is used by Canadian banks as an indicator, dropped by more than 5 percent during 1990. See Royal Bank of Canada data reprinted in Ip (1992).

78. The fact that there might be an increase in unemployment when inflationary expectations are eliminated after decades does not imply that there is any trade-off. It only implies that, as explained in the first section of this chapter, there were many markets, financial as well as real estate, whose sole raison d'être was that they emerged and persisted because of the volatile inflation. This means that, once inflation is eliminated these markets will collapse, and it takes time until people are retrained.

79. As mentioned in the text, such a scenario did take place in Canada. When one subtracts the effect of increased taxation (due to the introduction of the GST) and of increases in regulated prices from the CPI, one gets a negative number. (See, for example, *Consumer Price Index, Statistics Canada Catalogue* 62001, February 1992, 16–19.) Yet the CPI increased, and John Crow, the governor of the Bank of Canada, did not cease talking about fighting inflation, and set monetary aggregates accordingly.

80. See Volcker (1990).

81. Recall that, even though budget deficits grew in seven of President Reagan's eight years, long-term interest rates fell, and whatever measure one looks at—creation of new businesses and expansion of what are called non-Fortune 500 companies—showed prosperity. See Spurge (1991, 12).

82. See Spurge (1991, 17).

83. See discussion in chapter 1.

84. The disappointment means that the productive part of Germany now has higher "overhead" costs, which diminish its ability to compete.

85. The information on the distribution of wealth is not relevant, as explained in the previous chapters. What matters is the movement within the distribution. There is no evidence that the mobility diminished. See Brenner (1987, 1990) discussing why mobility within the distribution matters.

86. One of the worst things central banks could do is get into the currency speculation business. It involves the taxpayers in speculation whose outcome depends on many foreign governments' and central banks' policies. (Anyway, who gave central bankers the right to do that?) Experience suggests that financiers are much better at speculation than central bankers, as events of 1992 showed. The European Central Banks are estimated to have lost $6 billion defending various currencies.

Chapter 5

1. A group of seventeen Soviet economists visiting Washington in April 1990 suggested that even the CIA's picture was too rosy. (See Auerbach, 1990). They described an economy about half the size the CIA had estimated for years (and thus with a military budget of not 20 percent but 40 percent of the GNP), and poorer living standards than Brazil's. The surprise is the CIA's significant overestimation. (Though maybe it should not be. After all, their budget depended, in part, on these numbers.) Other figures for the USSR came from a series published jointly by the Bank for International Settlements and the Organization for Economic Cooperation and Development (OECD). They suggest, for example, that foreign debt increased from $1.8 billion in 1971 to $48 billion in 1989, although in a recent speech Prime Minister Ryzhkov gave a higher figure for 1989. However, Bush (1990) argues that he might have done it for political reasons to counter a lobby that has argued for massive imports of consumer goods to diminish discontent. We just do not know. Also see Rowen and Wolf (1990).

2. Infant mortality increased from about 24 deaths in first year per 1,000 live births in the early 1970s to 28 in the late 1970s, and life expectancy for males, for example, diminished from 64 in the 1970s to 62 in the 1980s. See The United Nation's *Demographic Yearbooks*.

3. See tables at the end of Brzezinski (1990).

4. Neither was it accidental that many of the so-called dissident Russian paintings by Chemiakin, Tselkov, Jarki, and others have this feature in common: people wearing masks, upon masks, upon masks.

5. Alexis de Tocqueville captured the difference when he wrote that "men are not corrupted by the exercise of power, or debased by the habit of obedience; but by the

exercise of power which they believe to be illegitimate, and by obedience to a rule they consider to be usurped and oppressive." As quoted in Malia (1989, 315–16).

6. See Clines (1990a, b).

7. Another incident shows how everything in Russia still follows this principle. On January 6, 1990, a chauffeur-driven black Volga sedan, used only by elite party functionaries, was involved in accident. When the trunk snapped open, it revealed to the ordinary citizens a sight that they were not used to: plenty of high quality food, from smoked meat to bottles of expensive liquor. The crowd dragged the car five kilometers to the center of Chernigov, a city of 280,000, where a huge demonstration followed, during which the local party leadership was asked to resign. As a compromise, the party replaced the regional first secretary, the official responsible for ideology and the head of the party organizing committee, whose Volga had caused the scandal. See "How a Ukrainian Fender-Bender Set Off Earthquake," *Los Angeles Times,* as reprinted in *The Gazette,* March 3, 1990. See also Bohlen (1990).

8. See Feldbrugge (1989, 301). As shown later in the text, such activities were all carried out under, what will seem unusual names and arrangements to those living in the West. Article 154 somehow assumes that people can be motivated to carry out normal, everyday transactions without the goal of personal interest in mind. But even that article was inconsistently applied: while not allowed to pursue profits, enterprises were encouraged to make them; this was called the "khozraschet" principle. (See Feldbrugge 1989, 323.) What was not allowed was making a living from constant buying or selling. What is common between all the codes is not only that they cover a range of normal, everyday activities that people since time immemorial have been engaged in, unless they were prevented from doing so, but that they prevented competition with the state's monopoly in every facet of life.

9. See E. de Jong (1976) and Feldbrugge (1989, 311–12).

10. According to Grossman (1977, 35), the CIA estimated that in 1968, 10 percent of the GNP came from the legal private sector (76 percent of that in agriculture, 22 percent in housing). In building, regular gangs of builders (called "shabashniki") were said to complete one-third more houses than the state-owned ones. Although, as can be seen in this chapter, these figures should not be taken too seriously since the boundaries between what was legally and illegally produced in the Eastern bloc countries cannot be sharply drawn.

11. See Feldbrugge (1989, 311).

12. See Feldbrugge (1989, 323–25). Theater and opera tickets were frequently unavailable at the box office but available from "speculators" on the streets. Traveling abroad was a privilege, not because of seeing sights but for bringing back valuable commodities—textiles, watches, books, small appliances, foreign currency, etc.— which could then be sold to those with connections in the black markets. Liquor turned out to be used as a widespread means of exchange in the illegal economy: its value derived probably from the fact that the Russians had very little else in which to bury their sorrow or, to put it more positively, with which to entertain themselves. See similar reactions of poor people in England during the eighteenth and nineteenth centuries in Brenner and Brenner (1990, chap. 3).

13. See Feldbrugge (1989, 308, 319) and O'Hearn (1980, 221).

14. It is clear why the bureaucracy closes its eyes to such practices: their benefits are supplied by the sector that the law considers illegal. The powerful bureaucracy sticks together not from ideological commitment, but, ironically, from the material interest provided to large extent by the illegal activities. No wonder that the harshest punishments were given to those daring to conduct their activities outside the customary sphere, avoiding the customary bribes. Even when the links between those operating in the black market and high officials was proven, the first was shot and the second merely transferred to another, less conspicuous bureaucratic position. The reason that this could be done was again due to the vagueness of the legal system, of the criminal laws in particular. More on these points later, and also see Feldbrugge (1989, 334–35).

15. See Feldbrugge (1989, 313).

16. But Feldbrugge (1989, 322) quotes *Izvestia,* which reported that instructors charged twenty-five rubles for a passing grade in correcting examination papers. The reasons for getting bribes were endless: the head of a welfare agency in Baku, in charge of allocating cars to disabled drivers, sold permits to others. When he was arrested, he owned two apartments, a dacha with a swimming pool, old paintings, antiques, and thirty-four kilograms of gold. This episode may remind one of the recent welfare department scandal in Washington. Doctors could get richer by giving certificates for proving that one was disabled (so one could get a car) or charging fees for certificates for those who wanted to stay away from work for a few days. Although Grossman (1977) makes a distinction between bribes and the custom of *prinoshenie* (which means "bringing to"), and which he says is "a general and regular way of ingratiating oneself with authority," there is no real distinction between the two. Money simply meant far less for some people in these societies than getting the goods since they may not have known the "right" people from whom to get the goods themselves.

17. See Acton (1985, 6–7).

18. Peculiar as this proposal may sound to Western ears, the fact is that the practice may not raise too many eyebrows in Eastern bloc countries, since they adopted it in the past, although inconsistently. When federal ministers like Ishkov (USSR Minister of Fisheries) in 1980; Furtseva (USSR Minister of Culture) in 1974; republican party First Secretaries Akhundov (Azerbaidzhan, 1974) and Mzhavanadze (Georgia, 1972); Kurbanov, the Prime Minister of Uzbekistan; and Nasridinnova, the Supreme Soviet Presidium Chairman of Uzbekistan, were all involved with black marketeers and bribery, all were quietly removed but not put in jail. See Feldbrugge (1989). Those at the bottom, however, were.

19. Although in the West, the privileged classes' standard of living in the communist countries has been known for a while.

20. Recall that already in 1972 Roy Medvedev wrote that, if privileges are taken into account, bureaucrats were earning twenty times more than a worker. See Zinoviev (1984), Medvedev (1972, 268), and Todd (1976, 43–47).

21. Whether or not the Soviet workers now know how opulently their leaders are living is not clear. Apparently not: see Klose (1984, 182).

22. Though when Gorbachev in his misguided policy increased the price of alcoholic beverages to prohibitive levels, the black market adjusted very quickly. All sugar disappeared from stores for the two years during which this experiment lasted. This by itself is a sign that entrepreneurship is alive and well among the Russians.

23. See Smith (1990a, b).

24. See Brenner (1983, chap. 2) summarizing evidence that literacy does not necessarily lead to prosperity: after all, the communist countries were indeed literate. Also notice that Tetris, one of Nintendo's best-selling games, was written by a Russian in Russia; Russians sold biomedicine technology like intraocular lenses, surgical staples, and ultrasonic surgical scalpels; in metallurgy they sold electroslag remelting, pipe welding, etc. See Lourie (1991, 3).

25. See Rieber (1982), Brenner (1991a).

26. Though nobody knows the extent of the crimes. Neither can one trust declarations by officers of the Interior Ministry since they have every reason to exaggerate, so as to keep their jobs. Grigory Sheludko, a major general at the interior ministry, which combines functions of local police and the FBI, states, "We are . . . reaching the high levels of crime witnessed in the United States during the 1920s and 1930s. We have the same disease America had in the decades of Al Capone and the other mob families." (Shanker, 1991a). This should not be taken too seriously. Moreover, if this is the magnitude of the problem, it might not be so severe. Also, if this is the right analogy, then we also know the remedy: cancel prohibitions, and do not outlaw things that most people want to indulge in.

27. Investigators at the Soviet Interior Ministry say some protection rackets demand payment of up to 50 percent of profits. In this cooperative's case, the gross was 50,000 rubles for the four owners. Even after expenses and pay to the "guards" the amount each could earn was far above the 300 rubles average salary. See Shanker (1991a, b).

28. See Shanker (1991a, b).

29. See Brenner (1983, chap. 2) on trust and oral contracts.

30. See Grossman (1989, 85). On black markets in general, also see Los (1990), where one can find descriptions of how black markets in Angola, Tanzania, etc., were tolerated, got unofficial support, and helped maintain the system. Also see Grossman (1977).

31. See Grossman (1989, 85); italics in original.

32. See Grossman (1989, 82).

33. See Grossman (1989, 89).

34. These were some of the questions raised, according to Grossman (1989).

35. See Grossman (1989, 89–90).

36. The plan seems to have been ignored by independently elected governments of some republics and cities. A signed letter in the *Komsomolskaya Pravda* said that the writers organized armed lynch mobs to patrol stores and food distribution centers, and apparently were unafraid that such acts would result in criminal accusations against them. Nobody was alarmed by the letter, and many expressed solidarity with the writers. On the first of December, large-scale food-rationing was introduced for the first time in Leningrad since its siege during the Second World War. The ration coupons gave one the right to buy: one kilogram of salami or cold cuts, 1.5 kilogram of meat, 0.5 kilogram of butter, ten eggs, 0.2 kilogram of oil, 0.5 kilogram of flour, and 1 kilogram of cereal or pasta for *a month*. See "Vigilantes to Monitor Soviet Stores," *New York Times*, as reprinted in *The Gazette*, December 2, 1990: B6.

37. See Asman (1990). At the same conference, Gavriil Popov charged that the nomenklatura tried to turn private property over to themselves.

38. Edward Lazear from the Hoover Institute told me how impressed he was that during his one-week visit to Romania, some of the ideas he suggested found their way within a week into some bills. One should be not impressed but skeptical of what such ease means—nothing more than things written on paper.

39. See Aganbegyan (1989, 169–71); italics added. But the damage was done: a number of cooperatives closed down, and others diminished production significantly. Also see Kiselev (1990).

40. See Shane (1991).

41. See Brzezinski (1993).

42. See Gibney (1992, 241).

43. See Clines (1991).

44. In the planned April 1993 referendum, Boris Yeltsin intended to do the right thing and ask Russians whether they favor private ownership of land. The parliament (whose members were still elected in 1990 and represent the old guards) opposed the referendum.

45. See detailed discussion in Brenner (1990) and sources quoted there.

46. How much of what was counted as "investment" just maintained an oppressive regime? Not just the direct expenditures should be taken into account. The costly dispersion of population was carried out to break down resistance. The dispersion of cities and keeping them down to size was intended to diminish the chances of revolts. No wonder that one can have much statistical investment and no growth.

47. There were 181 abortions per 1,000 women aged 15 to 44 in the USSR, 91 in Romania (but there were times when abortions were illegal), 61 in China, but only between 6 and 30 in Western countries. See "The Globalization of the Abortion Debate," *Time,* August 1989, 52.

48. The production of the latter during the few years that Gorbachev experimented with prohibitive prices came entirely from the illegal sector. During the experiment sugar all but disappeared from the stores.

49. However, those living on fixed pensions, having time to stay in line, may oppose such a jump.

50. Estimates for the "overhang" vary between 160 to 500 billion rubles. See Desai (1989) and Bush (1990).

51. Desai (1990, 5) notes that "in a rare display of *glasnost* . . . [official sources admitted] that the price index of produce in collective farm markets . . . rose at 2.6 percent from 1981 to 1985 but much more rapidly at 9.4 percent in 1986." The report by Goskomstat, the state committee for statistics, claimed a 3 percent nominal increase in GNP for 1989. The report mentioned a 2 percent inflation rate only, but admitted that "taking into account the increase in unsatisfied demand, the scale of inflation in the consumer sector reached 7.5 percent" (as quoted in Bush 1990). What the latter number means, or how it was calculated, is anybody's guess. Other estimates put the inflation rate for 1989 well into the double digits, suggesting a severe decline in output. It must also be noted that the decline may not be "real." After all, stopping the production of much that was unwanted, was warranted.

52. See Birman (1981), Wiles (1962), and Shelton (1990) about reasons for misleading numbers and magnitudes.

53. Due in part to the bad idea of the temporary prohibition of alcoholic beverages. Prohibition, or very high prices on drinking and gambling, have always had bad consequences, and not only on the governments' budgets. In a country where entertainment alternatives are few, where did Gorbachev expect his people to bury their sorrow and forget for a while their present misery? His arguments sounded exactly like those of the English moralists of the eighteenth and nineteenth centuries, who also misunderstood the reasons for people's frequent visits to pubs and thought that drinking and gambling were the main reasons for the English workers' lower productivity and, eventually, England's decline. See Brenner and Brenner (1990, chap. 3). Soviet citizens and their government would be far better off, if instead of taxing drinking so heavily, they would let gambling and betting, drinking and entertainment business flourish (in fact, betting on sports has been legal and popular in the communist countries, and the premium paid on winning tickets was a sign of the widespread existence of black markets).

54. See Desai (1989, 4).

55. State enterprises were freed from some controls, but the prices of their outputs often remained controlled. As a result, the enterprises were sheltered from competition through cheap credits and tax breaks. Unsurprisingly, workers asked for higher wages and got them, knowing the government would prevent bankruptcy, which in turn fueled inflationary expectations. Worse still: the enterprises asked for foreign loans and got them. In the USSR promises were made to end subsidies to 7,500 state enterprises. It was not carried out: see Desai (1989, 16). Also see "Eastern Europe's Economies," *Economist,* January 13, 1990, 22.

56. See Kornai (1980, 1982, 1983).

57. The Hungarians and the Poles have broken up their old banking system, and their central banks have the same roles as in the West. Commercial banks are now in the business of borrowing and lending and may compete (up to a point). See Survey of Eastern Europe, *Economist,* August 12, 1989. Thus, transferring lending functions to banks, based on commercial principles, would be the solution. Also note that according to some estimates half of the Russian 1991 budget went for the military (including the 4 million–man army). Fifteen percent of the annual Soviet budget was regularly spent on subsidizing meat, dairy products, and vegetables (Dobbs 1990), and subsidies to unprofitable enterprises consumed about 30 to 40 percent of both the Soviets' and the other post-communist countries' budgets.

58. See Brenner (1990).

59. Or for diminished productions in a wide range of sectors whose prices may be decontrolled, but whose outputs are used as inputs in the sectors whose prices are still controlled. These are the two possible scenarios when, let us say, the prices of cattle or tractors are decontrolled, but those of milk and of wheat products are not. Add to these revised plans the flip-flop policies concerning the Law on Cooperatives and their taxation, as well as the uncertain implications of the land-leasing law and the establishment of a new bureaucracy—the "farm committees"—to supervise it, and one should not be surprised that outputs did not increase.

60. See Desai (1990, 4).

61. See Desai (1989).

62. And per capita even lower, the USSR's population being 280 million (and if the figures are even vaguely reliable).

63. Some may still argue that letting foreign banks help manage the Russian economy may be politically unfeasible (though it is unclear why: if Russians now want to cooperate with NATO, why not with foreign banks?). Anyway, what is the alternative? Aftalion (1987) shows what happens when governments continue to print money, the "assignats" and then the "mandats" failing to raise tax revenues to finance the necessary roles of government of maintaining law and order. The effects were not dissimilar to those already taking place now in Russia: hoarding, famine, riots, and, eventually, significantly increased mortality rates, which only ended when Napoleon came to power.

64. Yet it may not be as far-fetched as it seems at first sight. The Russians invited foreigners to help manage their country in the past, not only under Peter the Great and not only their monetary policy. Also, in 862, a Normand chief, Rurik, was invited to rule the Slavs. According to *Nestor's Chronicles,* the invitation, which he accepted, said the following: "Our land is great and fertile, but there is disorder in our land: come, be our prince and govern us!" Though, one must admit that Rurik's story may be another myth. It is quite possible that the Vikings had already invaded Russia and established control, and then invented the tale to justify their actions. See Lourie (1991, 9).

65. This is how commerce started. See Thirsk (1978, 8), for example, who notes that "In broader terms these industrial by-employments heralded the development of a consumer society that embraced not only the nobility and gentry and the substantial English yeomen, but included humble peasants, labourers, and servants as well. It gave them cash and something to spend the cash on, whether it was a brass pot for the kitchen shelf, a colourful pair of striped stockings, or a knitted . . . cap." Today this may be a radio, record player, or computer, but the process is the same.

66. By completely wiping out people's savings, and without giving assets, restoring a level of savings, or legalizing black markets, one is left either with the option of relying on foreign investors or on government loans and investments. But in the latter case one would be back in the system from which one wanted to escape. How the Japanese dealt with their bureaucracy at the end of the nineteenth century is discussed in Brenner (1990). Even if trade starts in Russia, the road to prosperity will be longer than elsewhere. In Germany after the war and the inflation, weich wiped out people's savings, trade resumed when each family and each enterprise was givea financial assistance. The Germans had access to financial markets and familiarity with trade, whereas most of the Russians have neither. Also, the Dutch did not have any established hierarchy that tried by all means to maintain power, and Germany after the war, like many other societies after war, had weakened hierarchies. In Russia, the nomenklatura was not substantially weakened. It only changed its mask.

67. See Smith (1990a, 71).

68. See Smith (1990a, 71) and Shmelev (1988, 1989).

69. See Hosking (1990, 29–30).

70. On envy and ambition, in general, see Brenner (1983, 1985, 1987) and Brenner and Brenner (1990).

71. See Brenner (1983, 1985, 1987, 1990) for discussion and evidence.

72. See Jacoby (1983, 313). Also see Johnson (1983, 681–82).

73. See Hosking (1990, 43).

74. One of the Russians interviewed in Klose's (1984, 259–60) book gives an additional, although related, reason for the prevailing mediocrity: "There is another reason why party people no longer believe in the ideology, if they ever did. You can't really move ahead anywhere *without* the party. If you look at the middle management of this country, you will see that 99 percent of it is party while the party only accounts for about 6 percent of the total population. Were we so smart as to chose right in each and every case, finding only the most brilliant managers and bureaucrats to run our country [among party members]? Not at all! Membership in the Communist party of the Soviet Union is far more important than talent or brains. To move ahead, it helps to be talented, of course. But whenever there is advancement, the first question is: 'Is he a party member?' If the answer is, 'No,' the chance for promotion is practically zero. . . . Complete mediocrity rules this country at most levels" (italics in original).

75. See detailed discussion in Brenner (1990), Gomulka (1989), and Jones and Moskoff (1989).

76. See Brenner (1983, 1985). Tolstoy says that we only call our ignorance "chance."

77. See McNeill (1979, 1982) and Lourie (1991).

78. See Berman (1983, 2).

79. See Massie (1980, 793).

80. See Massie (1980, 794). This background also helps one to understand why in some societies it was easier to turn dogma into obedience. The adherence to party lines was made inseparable from nationhood and thus patriotism. Disloyalty toward the party came to be interpreted as disloyalty toward the motherland and could thus be severely punished. The Russian experience is not the only discomforting one where the lack of separation between state and church, or state and ideology, and the absence of some countervailing power to authority, had long-term, destructive consequences. See Brenner (1990).

81. This idea too had a history. Ivan III declared Russia's sovereignty in 1480, and Moscow then became the only great and independent Orthodox state. The Russian clergy soon came up with the idea that Moscow was the Third Rome, succeeding Rome and Constantinople, and, as McNeill (1979, 251–52) pointed out, "Ever since then the notion that Russia was uniquely chosen for the special mission of guarding the true faith on earth has never ceased to play part in Russian public life, not least since the Communist revolution of 1917."

82. After Peter the Great and under Catherine the Great, the policy took other forms, as she herself expressed. "My dear Prince," she once said, "do not distress yourself because the Russians have no desire for knowledge: if I institute schools it is not for ourselves, but for Europe, in whose estimation we must maintain our standing; but if our peasants should really wish to become enlightened, neither you nor I could continue in our places." Marquis de Custine (1989, 450–51), who quotes this conversation in his book about his journey through Russia, adds, "A government which wields power by maintaining ignorance, is more terrible than stable: a feeling of uneasiness in the nation—a degraded brutality in the army—a terror around the administration, a

terror shared by those who govern . . . and Siberia for them all." He wrote these lines in 1839. He also added that "tranquility is maintained among this people by the length and difficulties of communication, and by the secrecy of the government, which perpetuates the evil under the fear of disclosing it . . . By the time a crime is made public, it has already become ancient, weakening its impact" (548), which reminds one of the point made earlier when the question was raised, what prevented the system from collapsing earlier? Also see McClelland (1979).

83. Only 25 million lived in cities, most people maintaining strong ties with the family in the villages. The number of peasants grew from 56 million in 1867. To put this number in the right perspective, recall that in pre–First World War Russia there were less than 3.5 million factory workers, and even the broadest definition of "proletariat" could come up with only 15 million. See Johnson (1983), McNeill (1979), and Mironov (1985).

84. In spite of the Tsarist regime's cruel reputation, the number of people executed was on the decline: in the eighty years leading up to 1917, seventeen a year were executed, most in the midst of the nineteenth century. Compare that to the tens of millions starved and executed under communism (see Johnson 1983, 66). By 1918 through 1919, the Cheka was executing 1,000 a month for "political" offenses alone.

85. Though only two years, after which he turned to privatisation with as much fervor as Margaret Thatcher.

86. Such obedience has precedents in Russian history. As McNeill (1979, 328–32) points out, as long as the Grand Duke of Moscow had to appease the distant but terrible rulers in Kazan in the sixteenth century, the Russian people saw the necessity of obedience and submission to the Grand Duke tax collectors. But once this danger was gone—the consequence of innovations in weapons as infantry became equipped with guns, and the supremacy of the cavalry archers of the nomads were thus lost—emigration into new lands started along the Volga and Ukraine.

87. See Malia (1990, 321), and similar points in Hosking (1990, chap. 1), and Todd (1976, 191). Thus although the nomenklatura as a "caste" flourished under Stalin, it became rigid only later. The nomenklatura had the privileges of better housing, superior medical care, and special stores with cheap, good food supplies. Higher in the hierarchy they had their dacha, the best doctors and apartments, a holiday abroad, etc. They also had better access to higher education at a time when, as Hosking (1990, 4) notes, "the chances of getting into university, a prerequisite of moving up in the Russian hierarchy, [became] half of what they were." Thus privileges were not measured in monetary terms, but their perfect equivalents. In other words, the typical thing happened: the increased monopoly power led to stagnation, the increased security bred increased timidity, a common phenomenon across countries, time, and all human activity.

88. It is no accident that bureaucrats were in favor of relatively small cities, USSR favoring those at or below the 2 million mark in order to avoid the danger of crowds, something that Marx was quite aware of. Moscow has about 8 million inhabitants, which is small compared to other countries whose population is 280 million. Leningrad has only about 5 million. The Russian bureaucrats preferred cities of between 500, 000 and 2 million. They could control the size of cities since people's mobility and the location of enterprises were under their control.

89. Not only could the West spend much more on the military during the 1980s, but it also thrived otherwise. And yet the fact became evident that democracies were not intending military actions unless provoked.

90. See Shelton (1989), Goldman (1990).

91. It might possibly have been prevented if more significant institutional changes were made, the type discussed in the final section of the next chapter. The contrast with China is understandable when looked upon from this angle. Privatization and land reforms there do not threaten its territorial integrity as much (with the exception of Tibet). There are no nationalist groups annexed there by force.

92. Looked upon from this perspective, the debate about gradual versus abrupt reforms (Jeffrey Sachs' sound-byte of "shock therapy") seems an entirely academic exercise. Some reforms can be done abruptly. To others, at best, one can make commitments. See also Joseph (1990).

Chapter 6

1. Eisner (1988, 1616).

2. Milton Friedman (1988) brought to my attention that about twenty years ago, when he met with Hong Kong's financial secretary, the latter confessed that he refused to permit the construction of GNP statistics for Hong Kong. He argued that if they were available, they would inevitably tend to promote central planning, to which he was strongly opposed.

3. Though once it is known that policymakers use them in a predictable way to shape policies, traders on the stock markets must pay attention to them, no matter if they are wrong.

4. Which rose with our largely increased numbers, an issue whose other facets are discussed in the first part of this chapter. Also see Brenner (1983, 1985).

5. See Goldstein (1988) and Eklund (1980).

6. That is why the much-discussed result of the "prisoner's dilemma" is of marginal interest. It assumes that the game is played only once. Yet, except for "flight-by-night" operators, which confirm the game's prediction, plenty of signals have been invented to suggest that the "game" between buyers and sellers will be played more than once. These are the roles played by warranties, advertising, brand names, insurances, etc. See Brenner (1983, chap. 2) on trust.

7. See Brenner (1983, chap. 2 and chap. 3).

8. Evidence to support these conclusions is presented in Brenner (1983, 1985).

9. See Yoshikawa and Ohtake (1988, 29). Hayashi (1986, 177) reports a higher figure of 67 percent of persons 65 and older living with their children in Japan in 1983, whereas over 80 percent did in 1960. For persons 80 years and over, the proportion was 90 percent in 1983. This blurs the meaning of savings and may make meaningless comparisons among countries with wildly disparate housing arrangements. Both Hayashi, and Yoshikawa and Ohtake note that land and housing are the major vehicles of bequest. But if families lived together in the same house the notions of "personal savings," of "personal wealth," are blurred. Also see Ando's (1986) comments on this point in Hayashi's article.

10. Eventually, economists will discover that the divergence in performance among the previous communist countries can be linked to the length of time their people traded, rather than to any macroeconomic therapy. If Poland and Hungary succeed more than some of their neighbors, it will be because its traders have been allowed to travel for a longer time, their farms did not become collectives, and they practiced trade, though on small scales. Hungarians practiced small trade after 1956, and during the 1980s Polish small traders could be found not only in other neighboring communist countries but also in Greece and Turkey. These traders' skills, combined with openness to foreign entrepreneurs, sow the seeds for prosperity. See discussion in chapter 3.

11. Easier divorce, for example.

12. See Brenner (1983, chap. 1 and chap. 2) for theory and evidence.

13. This implies that the aforementioned demographic changes diminish wealth per capita.

14. See Brenner (1993) on nationalism and the state, recall the arguments in chapter 3, and see appendix 4.

15. See Brenner (1983, chap. 2).

16. In 1989 the estimated number was 750,000. See Koretz (1989, 64).

17. One can think of many other examples: in one country, donating blood is a custom; in another, there is a market for it. In one country, grandparents still live with their children and grandchildren, providing a wide range of services; in another, services are purchased from maids and babysitters or provided by dishwashers and television or VCR. In one place, grandparents are still the source of myths and fairy tales; in another, books are bought and read. Which countries are richer? As measured by the GNP, the richer countries are those in which money is exchanged for services. But this may be misleading. (See Crosette 1990). In a 1977 survey of 300 households in England, Ferman and Berndt (1981) found that 60 percent of the services that households reported using were secured through the "social economy." They were produced within the household itself, or provided by friends, relatives, and neighbors without monetary payment. Of the services, 10 percent were purchased through the black economy, 30 percent through regular supplies. The fact that the ratio of tort costs per capita is between 3 to 5 times higher in the United States than in the other Western countries does not imply that consumers and workers are far better protected against injuries and malpractice, but that the tort laws may be bad, in which case the expenditures on lawyers diminish income and wealth and do not merely redistribute them from one group to another. According to Koretz (1989), some people defend the tort system in the United States on the grounds that the tort litigation substitutes for the lack of the government's social programs. If that is the case, the meaning of the numbers is further blurred.

18. See Laband (1988). By 1989 there were an estimated 750,000 in the United States and according to Koretz (1989) the ratio of tort costs to gross domestic product increased from 1.3 percent between 1965 and 1975 to 2.6 percent in 1989. This in contrast to Canada, France, West Germany, Britain, and Japan, where these costs are stable and hover around 0.5 percent.

19. Japan's legal professionals also consists of many licensed non-lawyer legal specialists. These include tax agents (*zerishi*), patent agents (*benrishi*), judicial

scriveners (*shisho shoshi*), and administrative scriveners (*gyosei shoshi*). They perform work done in the United States by lawyers. Based on figures published by the Supreme Court in Japan in 1984, Japan's legal professionals would have numbered 93 per 100,000 if these categories were included. The scarcity of lawyers (*bengoshi*) is, apparently, due to regulation. But for resolving many disputes, paralegals are used. See Levin (1991).

20. This should be kept in mind, in addition to all those factors mentioned in chapter 3, in particular by those who claim to have discovered statistical "regularities" in history—called Kondratieff cycles.

21. "Unexpectedly" according to demographers. See Preston (1984a, 44).

22. Between 1960 and 1982. See Preston (1988a, 44).

23. See Preston (1988a, b). Voting patterns can explain the divergence.

24. See Preston (1988a, 45).

25. The corresponding gain at age 15 was less than a year, growing steadily to three years at the age of 45. See Preston (1988a, 47).

26. Although Hayashi (1986) does not raise this particular problem at all, he notes many of the significant differences between the ways accounting is done in the United States and in Japan. Romer (1986, 223), in his comments on Hayashi's article, remarks, "In the case of capital accumulation by the government, skepticism about the data overwhelms any conceptual issue."

27. Remedies to the problem of a suddenly aging population can be to increase the age of retirement (why should society be stuck with a regulation dating back to Bismarck?), lower Social Security benefits, encourage immigration of younger people, etc. See Brenner (1991a) discussing these and other options.

28. See Brenner (1991a) on the options.

29. Adopted only on May 29, 1874.

30. See Tiebout (1956). The European community's arrangements are on the way to changing that. But it should be emphasized that, elsewhere in the world, the mobility of labor is disallowed, talks about "free trade" notwithstanding (differential social legislation among countries being a major obstacle).

31. The competition among provinces within federations incurs some costs because each province may try to impose the harms (environmental ones, for example) on the other provinces, trying at the same time to internalize benefits. Such competition between states carves a role for the federal government too (or for a supranational institution): to overcome the harmful external effects fostered by competition between states (preventing lax pollution standards in one state, which imposes a cost on another, for example). In the absence of such government (or the supranational institution), finding solutions to this problem between politically independent states is costlier and takes longer.

32. See Frey (1992).

33. On July 7, 1891, the amendment on "Initiative" was added to the constitution, stating that the right can be exercised when 50,000 Swiss demand it.

34. Known in France in the past as *plebiscites,* which had a negative connotation—with good reason. There they have been used at moments of national excitement by unscrupulous politicians. In contrast, referenda should act through regular channels, established by constitutional law. See McCracken (1892).

35. Moreover, in the city of Montreal, for example, the option of initiative could be and was abolished during the eighties by local politicians.

36. The advantage of the Swiss system is particularly striking when one sees how it solves linguistic tensions. The mobility of people is viewed as beneficial in North America since it imposes a check on any state's power; for nationalists and those wanting to maintain a language, such mobility is viewed as a high price to pay for achieving this goal. Thus they favor a unitary state, which, to prevent abuses of power, must divide it. But unitary states are at a disadvantage relative to federal ones in establishing and maintaining credibility about keeping their governments in check. The Swiss found federalist principles that enabled groups with different religions and languages not just to coexist but to be united. They became united without speaking the same language and without adhering to the principle of the melting pot. Keeping distinct cultural identities without linking them to political framework based on ethnicity is thus feasible. It is not a theory nor a utopia. See detailed discussion and reference in Brenner (1991a).

37. See Kendall and Louw (1989) and Louw and Kendall (1986).

38. See Pommerehne (1978, 1990), Frey (1992), and sources quoted in the latter.

39. The two features, referenda on separate issues and the "legal" mobility, solve another problem that causes many troubles in other parts of the world. They remove issues from national politics and fragment them, crossing linguistic and religious groups, and thus unite people with different languages and religions. But by giving the right to create new cantons, decisions on language and education are determined to a large extent on local levels. Still, the federal government subsidizes radio, television, and textbooks for the smallest minorities. The Italian schools receive seven times the normal subsidy, whereas the Romansch (there are just about 60,000 of them) receive ten. See detailed discussion and reference in Brenner (1991a).

40. Initially, a similar arrangement was introduced in 1831 in the Canton of St. Gallen.

41. But the Jesuits were discriminated against, and Article 51 of the 1874 Federal Constitution explicitly stated that "The order of Jesuits, and the societies affiliated with them, shall not be received into any part of Switzerland; and all action in church and school is forbidden to its members. This prohibition may be extended also, by federal ordinance, to other religious orders, the action of which is dangerous to the state or disturbs the peace between sects" (as reprinted in McCracken 1892, 378).

42. Just as one cannot expect lawyers to advocate the adoption of the English rule, since it significantly diminishes incentives to sue. Matsusaka and Palda (1993, 10) note that those who believe that interest groups will get stronger when there are such institutions, are wrong. "California's experience suggests that militant special interests have not captured the referendum process and that the broad majority of voters have found referendums a useful way of expressing their views." They also note that only 33 percent of initiatives pass, and that there is evidence that, if the electorate cannot understand what a measure proposes to do, they will vote it down.

43. See the *Economist,* "People Power," December 26, 1992–January 8, 1993, 13.

44. Governor Pete Wilson announced in 1992 that his welfare reform package

would also be on a ballot in the form of an initiative. The required number of signatures shows how politicians may tinker with the initiative process: increasing the number of signatures required to put an initiative on the ballot. A constitutional amendment can prevent that and fix the number at a percentage of the voting population.

45. See discussion in Brenner (1991b).

46. See Brenner (1987).

47. See Brenner (1987).

48. There might be a price paid for it. Though the Swiss made the aforementioned significant innovations in law, they are not known for many other innovations, except in watches, cuckoo clocks, and secret bank accounts. Indeed, they are known for having a relatively uneventful past. But remember: happy people might not have a history. See Brenner (1983, 1985, 1991b). But these are really implications for the *very* long run.

49. One reason Japan and Germany could outperform other Western countries was that they did not have to spend on the military, though they got the benefits of the West's military umbrella. As for the other rising countries in Far East, Latin and South America: once these countries have changed their political regimes and moved toward a Western model, some of the West's advantages, like attracting investments and talented people, will diminish. These changes also diminished the Western governments' ability to tax. This means that for a while these countries will grow faster than the West—unless Western countries successfully compensate through legal-political changes, where they have a relative advantage because of their longer experience.

50. See North (1990), who also tries to explain why a similar sequence of events did not happen in Spain.

51. See Barbour (1966, 80).

52. See Schama (1989, 65).

53. See Schama (1989, 83).

54. See Homer (1963, chap. 16).

55. See Gibney (1992, chap. 3).

56. And more: they can provide a solution to national, ethnic, and linguistic strifes too. See Brenner (1991a, b). For the latter, however, a Karl Renner–type solution would be better. See discussion in Brenner (1992).

57. The institutions of referendum and initiative also diminish the role of the press and the media in general. The "common" men and women will vote and will not need the media to represent them. The role of the media has increased exactly because the electoral process became less relevant in the current federal system, characterized by the interaction between lobbying groups and the growing empires of government bureaucracies. The media substitute, imperfectly, for the voters' diminished power.

58. Such a system would approximate Karl Popper's idea of an "open society," which he defined as one where people are confronted with personal decisions. By letting everyone have a stake in what a business society is doing, many societies have already been opened. The referendum and initiative would open it further by allowing more people—rather than those belonging to well-organized interest groups as today—to have a stake in what governments are doing too.

Appendix 1

1. Some try to make a distinction between "underground" economy and the criminal activities of the underworld. This distinction is not always sharp: prohibitions of gambling, drinking, and prostitution lead many otherwise law-abiding citizens to violate laws and regulations. Some may view this as just a defiance of political authority. Others, however, may view people's gambling, drinking, and patronizing prostitutes as inflicting "wrongs on society." Sennholz (1986, 5–6) tries to make this distinction when writing that: "The underground economy must be distinguished clearly and unmistakably from the criminal activities of the underworld. Government officials and agents are ever eager to lump both together, the criminals and their organization with the procedures in the underground. Both groups are knowingly violating laws and regulations and defying political authority. But they differ radically in the role they play in society. The underworld comprises criminals who are committing acts of bribery, fraud, and racketeering, and willfully inflicting wrongs on society. The underground economy involves otherwise law-abiding citizens who are seeking refuge from the wrongs inflicted on them by the government." Such distinction is simplistic; see Brenner and Brenner (1990) on attitudes toward gambling and speculation.

2. Boskin (1988, 10), for example, notes that one reason for the underestimation of wealth may be "the household sector in which substantial saving occurs—no profits, trusts, pensions, and other vehicles which may be either excluded from household surveys or where individual responses may be subject to considerable error (e.g. accrued net saving in life insurance)."

3. Of course, people's reluctance in this case is still understandable. Suppose they told the truth, which would reveal significant underreporting of income. The results of the "scientific" inquiry are published and brought to the attention of the respective tax authorities, who then may ask for funds for greater enforcement. Would people risk that in the name of "science"?

4. See Hessing et al. (1988, 405).

5. Gutman (1979a) put it more bluntly: "plenty of respondents (for the U.S. Current Population Survey) lie; they lie consistently, and they lie with good reason" (as quoted in Smith 1986, 77), since they want to disguise their undeclared income, be its source in the legal or illegal sector. Another possible response to a voluntary survey is simply not to reply at all. Most official surveys have a considerable percentage of nonrespondents (in the United Kingdom's Family Expenditure Survey, for example, it is about 30 percent). See Smith (1986, 77), on the United Kingdom and Boskin's (1988) summary of similar problems and magnitudes in the United States. These problems were examined by Curtin et al. (1988) in the United States when they found wide discrepancies in answers to questions about people's wealth. They attributed it not only to unwillingness to tell the truth, either by not replying or by understating the value of some assets, but also to the facts that the questions might have been posed to the wrong person in the household, and that people had "an image" they wanted to project to the interviewer. For this and other reasons, it has been documented for a long time that people do not tell the truth about their expenditures on drink, gambling, and alcohol (and no survey has ever raised questions on prostitution or vacations in Switzerland or

the Bahamas, when the suspicion could arise that they were paid for with holdings in these countries' secret bank accounts). See Brenner and Brenner (1990). In recent years, declared expenditures on gambling in Canada equaled, at most, 60 percent of the true expenditures. In the United Kingdom, the Family Expenditure Survey (FES) understates consumers' expenditures on alcohol and tobacco considerably (about two-thirds being reported), either because respondents underreport their drinking or smoking, or because alcoholics and heavy smokers do not even bother to fill in questionnaires. On this last point see Smith (1986, 116, 121).

6. See Smith (1986, 78), Brown et al.(1984), and Gutman (1979a, b).

7. As already noted, there are strong incentives not to reply truthfully even in this case, when the issue is taxation. The observation on the inaccuracy of surveys is not new: McKibbin (1979, 151) notes that "The scanty yield from the private budget analyses is . . . not surprising. As Hilton [in a study written in 1944] pointed out, interrogators were unlikely to ask awkward questions and respondents were unlikely to give truthful answers."

8. Sennholz (1984, 10) notes that since 1965 in the United States the marginal tax rate for a family of four earning the median income has risen from 17 to 24 percent. This means that the incentives to make false declarations in order to evade taxes have changed too. How much of a measured recession is "real," and how much due to undeclared incomes?

9. See MacAfee (1980, 81) and Smith (1986, 116).

10. In the United Kingdom, it is also known that the FES are not representative of the population as a whole: a lower proportion of high income earners and residents of the south of the country (a richer area) reply to the survey. Also, the FES does *not* sample any of the population living in institutions, the elderly in particular. See Smith (1986, 120), O'Higgins (1981).

11. See Smith (1986, 112).

12. See Smith (1986, 113).

13. As noted, one discrepancy is due to the tax evasion of the self-employed. Smith (1986, 55) notes that a random compliance study, based on investigation of a random sample of taxpayers, would be the best way of assessing how much tax evasion went undetected. While the Inland Revenue in the United Kingdom does not have the power to undertake investigations at random, a pilot study undertaken in 1981 makes it possible to assess what proportion of suspect cases are not investigated due to lack of resources: "A random sample of 5,500 . . . tax returns by the self-employed was drawn, and District Inspectors were asked to categorize them, on the basis of their experience, as to whether they thought that an investigation, if started, would reveal an understatement of profit" (Smith 1986, 55–56). In 20 percent of accounts involved, the inspectors said that there was a "probable" understatement of income. In an additional 40 percent, they said that there was a "possible" understatement. In 80 percent of the "probable" understatement category, the inspectors judged that sufficient grounds for starting an investigation actually existed. Also, whereas the United States Internal Revenue Service has the power to carry out a random compliance study, the United Kingdom's Inland Revenue Service, as noted, does not. Such a difference may also blur the meaning of comparisons made between countries.

Appendix 2

1. This is different from the problem Sargent (1989, 252) examines. He notes that "The idea is that an economic theory determines a stationary stochastic process for some true variables of interest to an economist. The economist (though not an agent within the model) is dependent for data on a reporting agency that observes only error-ridden versions of the data. . . . Provided that the economic model is tightly enough restricted, say by cross-equation restrictions of the rational expectations variety, and provided that the measurement error process is sufficiently restricted, this model can be estimated econometrically." As shown here, the problem is different: the economists do the exercise *because* "agents within the model" use them.

2. However, linking it not with measurement problems but only with the uncertain relationship between income and full-employment policies, Friedman (1953) raised similar issues, and in his model too the effectiveness of policy depended, in part, on the correlation coefficient between income and the variable reflecting the counter-cyclical policy.

3. See chapter 1.

4. Although even in this case the measurement of output may encounter many difficulties because of hoarding and barter. See discussion in chapter 5.

5. See Brenner (1990 a, c).

6. In Lucas's model, as noted, firms always adjust, although the adjustments depend on the relative variance and general price changes.

7. One can expect declined outputs in these circumstances since the continuous high inflation is a signal of political uncertainty. See Brenner (1985, chap. 5).

8. Schwartz (1987, 52–53) concluded that "the most convincing evidence supporting the idea that money plays an important independent part is . . . that garnered from study of the historical circumstances underlying the changes that occurred in the stock of money. This evidence is much more clear cut for major movements than for minor." The arguments presented here explain why.

9. Still, the covariance term stays as before and gives meaning to "discretionary" policy in the sense of reacting to new information "impinging on the system as a whole," as Sargent and Wallace put it; however, this type of reaction is not Keynesian, and they decided not to deal with it. But, as noted, the relationships postulated in Sargent and Wallace (1975) does not: monetary surprise is not necessary to get Lucas's results, when one assumes that the price indices mismeasure things.

10. This is discussed by Blinder (1980), Brenner and Patinkin (1977), and Brenner (1985, chap. 6); we shall return to it in chapter 4.

11. When there are mismeasurements, one cannot recommend rules of "full indexation," for example. Discretion is necessary. Of course, indexation would not be needed if a constant monetary growth rule was pursued to start with.

12. See Keynes (1973, 502).

13. "Normal" being defined as when the rate of growth in the money supply and in real output are thought to be of the same magnitude as the standard deviations of the measurement errors.

Appendix 3

1. See summaries of the debate on savings in Kotlikoff (1989), Boskin (1988), and Bosworth (1990), none of which examines the links between savings and the demographic changes resulting from women's increased participation in the labor force.

2. This view does not exclude the possibility that the last recession unexpectedly led to diminished savings since people saved less expecting better times, and suddenly were disappointed.

3. Or foregone sums, in the case of accepting lower wages during training. Investments in education and training are justly called "human capital." See Becker (1975).

4. Or, in some developing countries, investing in female children in order to get more brideprices, or in males if they are of help in agricultural work and are expected to provide social security. See Brenner (1983, chap. 2) and sources quoted there. Also see Shipton (1990).

5. On durable goods see Blum and Gaudry (1989) and Dagenais (1989).

6. Boskin (1988) summarizes the critical literature on the subject. Obstfeld (1986, 82) notes not only the problems summarized by Boskin but also that "since national product figures represent the nominal value of goods and services produced by a country's factors, as measured by realized financial flows, exchange-rate induced redistribution of wealth between nations do not enter into the NIPA definition of national income or saving. Also ignored are the changes in the real value of net external debts due to inflation." Bradford (1990) argues that more attention should be paid to measures of national wealth at asset market values. But he does not enter into the more fundamental problems linked with the measurement of savings and wealth. See Brenner (1983, chap. 2) on the relationship between demographic changes and what we may be measuring in particular, to which we shall also return in the last chapter.

7. Additional issues linked with the mismeasurement of savings are discussed in Hayashi (1986, 1989), Ando (1986), and Bosworth (1990).

8. The change in women's behavior is no free lunch. Women, children, and men might suffer when the probability of divorce rises, and women's productivity at home might diminish (neither they, nor the men have the time to perform household chores). Evidence on this point can be found not only in frequent newspaper articles today about how children's education at home, cleaning, etc., are often not well provided for, but also in articles published during and after the Industrial Revolution in England. See Brenner and Brenner (1990, chap. 3). These changes might not be captured by the conventional measures or might even be perversely measured.

9. In contrast the husbands experienced a 42 percent increase in their standard of living. See Weitzman (1985, chap. 10). Weitzman also notes that fathers fail to pay an estimated $4 billion in child support, and that more than half of divorced women who are due child support (53 percent) do not receive the court-ordered support. See Weitzman (1985, chap. 9, 262). Johnson and Skinner (1986, 458) also document the drop: they note that, for the recently divorced woman, income apart from her earnings

dropped from $9,938 one year before the split to $3,032 during the year of the separation, and they add, "While consumption requirements may be less for single-headed households, it seems clear that the substantial loss in income provides an important incentive for increasing work-hours."

10. See Weitzman (1985, 215).

11. See Vickery (1979).

12. Johnson and Skinner found that the rise in the frequency of divorce may account for one-third of the unexplained increase in women's postwar labor force participation.

13. See Jacob (1988, 19) and *Yearbook of Labor Statistics,* BIT.

14. See Jacob (1988, 30).

15. Wisconsin passed a no-fault statute in 1977, and Illinois in 1978. See Jacob (1988, 96–101).

16. See Glendon (1989, 188).

17. See United Nations *Demographic Yearbooks* for 1968, 1972, 1980, and 1986. In contrast, the respective 1985 rates for England and Wales were 3.20; France 1.95; West Germany, 2.10; and Sweden, 2.37. Horioka (1986) also examined what might explain the differences between the OECD countries' and the United States' savings rate and that of Japan, but did not introduce as an explanatory variable the significant differences in marital arrangements. Yet in this respect the data leaves no doubt: Japan remains the most traditional of the thirteen developed nations, with low (though slowly increasing) rates of divorce and low rates of out-of-wedlock births. It also has the largest share of married couples. These findings are quoted in "Traditional Households Are Fading World-Wide," *Wall Street Journal,* May 4, 1990: B1, based on a U.S. Bureau of Labor Statistics study, summarized by the staff of *American Demographics* magazine.

18. See also Barro and Becker (1987, 1988), Kodde (1986).

19. There are economic models that try to explain the causes of marital instability. But none of them has linked the issue with possible macroeconomic impacts and measurements. See Becker (1981), Landes (1978), Michael (1985), and Peters (1976).

20. A plus sign over the variable indicates an expected positive effect, while a negative sign indicates an expected negative effect and a question mark indicates that although the corresponding variable is expected to influence the dependent variable, there is no definite expectation on the direction of this influence.

21. See Weitzman (1985).

22. This dummy was assumed to take the value 0 until 1967 and to take the value 1 from 1977 on. For the years in between, the values of the variable were set by linear interpolation.

23. See Johnson and Skinner (1986, 459–60); italics in original.

24. However, it should be noted that the reference to "risk-averse" elderly is debatable. The facts are that the elderly spend more on gambling than younger people, *ceteris paribus.* See chapter 2 in Brenner and Brenner (1990). Also see Jenkins (1989) and Noguchi (1986) on models about the relationship between demography and savings.

25. But it is well known that many empirical works on Social Security did not find this relationship. See discussion later in the text.

26. To compensate for the increased volatility.

27. This regularity has been identified in a number of studies. See discussion later in the text.

28. This raises the issue of the bequest motive and the degree of risk aversion of the elderly. In Brenner, Brenner, and Montmarquette (1990), we found that the elderly gamble more than the rest of the population, *ceteris paribus.*

29. It should be noted that any analyses of savings today should include many additional variables; the pressures for private savings have been significantly diminished during the last decades because of the expansion of the welfare system, of Medicaid, and of unemployment benefits. The pressures to save have also been significantly diminished by the provision of Social Security (if people believe in its solvency, which depends on changes in the proportion between the elderly and the young). The fact of governments subsidizing education diminished incentives to save for the children's education too. (To what extent such government expenditures have diminished the incentives to save depends on whether or not people believed that the subsidized, public education was a proper substitute for a private one.) It is thus important to realize that, in computing such aggregates as national income and savings, we are making assumptions that are not reached by scientific analysis but are conventional. This may be fine as long as changes are gradual, but not when they are drastic, be it about demography or the quality of services offered by governments.

30. Modigliani concluded that his explanatory variables appeared to account for two-thirds to four-fifths of the intercountry variance in the saving ratio. Although the objection about taking into account the changing structure of households thus cannot be made when examining this research, other questions can be raised, namely, about including in the same cross-country statistical analyses countries like Congo, Trinidad, where the notion of "savings" is significantly different than in the developed countries (see Brenner 1983, chap. 2, and Shipton 1990), and other countries like Italy and Peru, where black markets are supposed to add anywhere between 25 and 50 percent to the official figures, the extent of these markets varying from year to year. Also, Horioka (1986) found that the discrepancy in saving rates among countries is to a large extent explained by significant differences in their age structure, but found the rate of growth in income per capita relatively less important. In contrast, Modigliani and Sterling (1983) found that this factor, rather than the demographic one, is dominant. Horioka explains the different results by the fact that, for the period of time his research covered, there were no significant differences between Japan's and the other countries' growth rate. Modigliani and Sterling covered a period of time when the differences became larger.

31. See Barro and MacDonald (1979), Koskela and Viren (1983, 1989), and Graham (1987).

32. He also presents a brief model in which each "representative" individual is assumed to live for three periods of equal length, though the relationship between this model and the statistical tests are not clear. Longer life expectancy is not a feature of his model but is implicit in his statistical analyses. The period covered by the statistical examination, 1970 to 1980, was one where the nature of the "representative" individual changed significantly, both because the last life-cycle span was significantly lengthened and because the "traditional" individual faded, as shown in our text. Koskela and Viren (1989) also question the accuracy of Graham's data.

33. But see Koskela's and Viren's (1989) criticism on Graham's research, although not on this point. Graham finds the significant negative effect upon saving rates of the increased labor force participation of women in his revisions. See Graham (1989, 1504–6). Also see Yoshikawa and Ohtake (1988), examining the relationship between female labor supply and saving rates in Japan.

34. In a more recent paper, Auerbach and Kotlikoff (1989) take into account the aging of the population but not the demographic changes we discuss. They still conclude that what happened to U.S. saving in the 1980s remains an "intriguing puzzle" (28). Also see Haurin (1989), Hurd (1990).

35. This model is related to that discussed in Brenner and Kiefer (1981) on the effect of a probability of confiscation on investment in human capital.

36. See Becker (1975).

37. In this calibration, we implicitly assume that at the margin the disutility of one hour of work is equal to the disutility of one hour of acquiring human capital.

38. A complete set of results, along with the computer program, are available upon request.

Appendix 4

1. See McNeill (1976), Brenner (1983, 1985), and Heclo (1974). Consider the diagram in Heclo (1974, 20).

2. For a while, the United States, Canada, Brazil, Argentina, and Australia fit this category.

3. This, however, meant keeping the population in place. At this stage again, in principle there are two options: keep them in place voluntarily or by force, by law and its physical enforcement. Russia chose the latter. For a while the United States chose the middle road: on one side there was the slavery of the New World; on the other the egalitarian and libertarian origins were not wiped out as population grew. Maybe it is useful to recall that serfdom was abolished in 1861 in Russia, in 1863 in the United States. The legal change started with Great Britain in 1833, and was finally outlawed in Brazil in 1888.

4. On the notion of innovations, leapfrogging, and wars, see Brenner (1983, 1985, 1987), and McNeill (1982).

5. "Natural" resources are less important: consider Japan, Hong Kong, Switzerland, not only transforming rocks into opportunities, but producing good chocolate, while cocoa is imported, etc. On the contrary, the presence of natural resources, and sudden, unexpected increase in their value diminish entrepreneurship: see Brenner (1983, 1987). The lack of such resources forces reliance on wits and thus trade, under some circumstances.

6. See Brenner (1983, 1985).

References

Chapter 1

Ashenfelter, O., and G. Solon. "Longitudinal Labor Market Data: Sources, Uses, and Limitations." In *What's Happening to American Labor Force and Productivity Measurements?* Washington, D.C.: National Council on Employment Policy, 1982.

Beauchesne, E. "Statscan Cuts Keeping Us in Dark about Health, Economy." *The Gazette,* June 20, 1990, B1.

Bhagwati, J. N., ed. *Illegal Transactions in International Trade: Theory and Measurement.* Amsterdam: North-Holland, 1974.

Blinder, Alan S. "The Consumer Price Index and the Measurement of Recent Inflation." *Brookings Papers on Economic Activity* 2 (1980): 539–65.

Boskin, M. J. "Issues in the Measurement and Interpretation of Savings and Wealth." Working Paper No. 2633, NBER, June 1988.

Boskin, M. J., M. S. Robinson, and A. M. Huber. "New Estimates of States and Local Government Tangible Capital and Net Investment." Working Paper No. 2131, NBER, 1987a.

Boskin, M. J., M. S. Robinson, and A. M. Huber. "Government Saving, Capital Formation and Wealth in the United States, 1947–1985." Working Paper No. 2352, NBER, 1987b.

Bradford, D. F. "What Is National Saving?: Alternative Measures in Historical and International Context." Working Paper No. 3341, NBER, April 1990.

Brenner, R. *History—The Human Gamble.* Chicago: University of Chicago Press, 1983.

Brenner, R. *Betting on Ideas: Wars, Invention, Inflation.* Chicago: University of Chicago Press, 1985.

Brenner, R. *Rivalry: in Business, Science, among Nations.* Cambridge: Cambridge University Press, 1987.

Brenner, R. "The Long Road from Serfdom and How to Shorten It." *Canadian Business Law Review* 17 (1990a): 195–225.

Brenner, R. "Numbers and Policies." Presentation before the House of Commons Finance Committee, May 30, 1990b.

Brenner, R. "Legal Reforms Before Monetary and Macroeconomic Policies." In *Exchange Rate Policies in Developing and Post-Socialist Countries,* edited by E. M. Claassen, 151–75. San Francisco: International Center for Economic Growth, ICS Press, 1991. (French translation appeared as "Pays de l'Est: d'abord les réformes légales, ensuite les politiques monétaires et macroéconomiques." *Journal des Économistes et des Études Humaines* 1 (1990c): 253–77.

Brenner, R. "Extracting Sunbeams Out of Cucumbers: or What Is Bad Social Science, and Why Is It Practised?" *Queen's Quarterly* 99 (1991): 519–53.

Brenner, R., and G. A. Brenner. *Gambling and Speculation: A Theory, a History and a Future of Some Human Decisions.* Cambridge: Cambridge University Press, 1990.

Brenner, R., and D. Patinkin. "Indexation in Israel." In *Inflation Theory and Anti-inflation Policy,* edited by E. Lundberg, 387–416. London: Macmillan, 1977.

Brookes, W. T. "Hiding a Boom in a Statistical Bust." *Wall Street Journal,* August 6, 1987.

Brown, C. V., E. J. Levin, P. J. Rosa, and D. T. Ulph. "Tax Evasion and Avoidance on Earned Income: Some Survey Evidence." *Fiscal Studies* 5 (1984): 1–22.

Bruno, M. "Econometrics and the Design of Economic Reform." Working Paper No. 2718, NBER, September 1988.

Bruno, M. "Economic Analysis and the Political Economy of Policy Formation." Working Paper No. 3183, NBER, November 1989.

Colander, D. C., and A. Klamer. "The Making of an Economist." *Journal of Economic Perspectives* 1 (1987): 95–112.

Crutsinger, M. "The Flaw in the Statistics." *Globe and Mail,* July 2, 1990.

Curtin, R. T., F. T. Juster, and J. N. Morgan. "Survey Estimates of Wealth: an Assessment of Quality." Working Paper, Survey Research Center, Institute for Social Research, University of Michigan, Ann Arbor, 1988.

DeVries, P., and A. Baldwin. "Impact of Different Homeownership Methodologies on Consumer Price Index Behaviour Between Canada and the United States." *Canadian Statistical Review* 1985: vi-xiv.

Duncan, G., and D. Hill. "An Investigation of the Extent and Consequences of Measurement Error in Labor-Economic Survey Data." *Journal of Labor Economics* 3 (1985): 508–32.

Duncan J. W., and W. C. Shelton. *Revolution in United States Government Statistics.* Washington, D.C.: U.S. Department of Commerce, Office of Federal Statistical Policy and Standards, October 1978.

Ethier, M. "L'économie souterraine." In *La répartition du revenu et la sécurité économique au Canada,* F. Vaillancourt (research coordinator), 87–124. Ottawa: Ministère des Approvisionnements et Services, Canada, 1986.

Feige, E. L. "A New Perspective on Macroeconomic Phenomena—the Theory and Measurement of the Unobserved Sector of the United States Economy: Causes, Consequences and Implications." Paper presented at the Ninety-Third Annual Meeting of the American Economic Association, September 1980.

Feige, E. L., ed. *The Underground Economy.* Cambridge: Cambridge University Press, 1989.

Ferman, L. A., and L. E. Berndt. "The Irregular Economy." In *Can I Have it in Cash?* edited by S. Henry, 26–42, London: Astragal Books, 1981.

Friedman, M. "Statistics and Its Methods." *American Economic Review* 30 (1940): 657–60.

Friedman, M. "The Effects of a Full-Employment Policy on Economic Stability." In *Essays in Positive Economics,* 117–33. Chicago: University of Chicago Press, 1953.

Friedman, M. *A Program of Monetary Stability.* New York: Fordham Foundation, 1960.

Friedman, M. *The Optimum Quantity of Money and Other Essays.* Chicago: University of Chicago Press, 1969.

Friedman, M. Letter to the author, August 30, 1988.

Friedman, M., and A. J. Schwartz. *A Monetary History of the United States.* Princeton: Princeton University Press, 1971.

Giavazzi, F., and L. Spaventa, eds. *High Public Debt: the Italian Experience.* Cambridge: Cambridge University Press, 1988

Griliches, Z. "Errors in Variables and Other Unobservables." *Econometrica* 42 (1974): 971–98.

Griliches, Z. "Data Problems in Econometrics." In *Handbook of Econometrics,* edited by M. Intriligator and Z. Griliches. Vol. 3. Amsterdam: North-Holland, 1985.

Gutman, P. M. "The Grand Unemployment Illusion." *Journal of the Institute for Socioeconomic Studies* 4 (1979a): 20–29.

Gutman, P. M. "Statistical Illusions, Mistaken Policies." *Challenge* 22 (1979b): 14–27.

Heckman, J. J. "Murky Numbers on the Black Economic Progress." *Wall Street Journal,* August 22, 1989, A14.

Hessing, D. J., H. Elffers, and R. H. Weigel. "Exploring the Limits of Self-Reports and Reasoned Action: An Investigation of the Psychology of Tax Evasion Behavior." *Journal of Personality and Social* Psychology 54 (1988): 405–13.

Holloway, Th. M. "The Present NIPA Saving Measures: Their Characteristics and Limitations." Paper presented at the Conference on the Measurement of Saving, Maryland, March 1987.

Keenan, A., and P. N. Dean. "Moral Evaluations of Tax Evasion." *Social Policy and Administration* 14 (1980): 209–20.

Keynes, J. M. *The General Theory of Employment, Interest and Money.* London: Macmillan, 1936.

Keynes, J. M. *The General Theory and After, Part I: Preparation.* Vol. 13 of *Collected Writings,* edited by Donald Moggridge. London: Macmillan, 1973.

Klein, L. R., and A. S. Goldberger. *An Econometric Model of the United States, 1929–1952.* Amsterdam: North-Holland, 1955.

Koretz, G. "Are Computer Sales Distorting GNP Growth Estimates?" *Business Week,* October 24, 1988.

Kuznets, S. *National Income and Its Composition.* National Bureau of Economic Research, Vol. 2, 1942.

Kydland, F., and E. Prescott. "Rules rather than Discretion: The Inconsistency of Optimal Plans." *Journal of Political Economy* 85 (1977): 473–91.

Lucas, R. E., Jr. "Some International Evidence on Output-Inflation Tradeoffs." *American Economic Review* 63 (1973): 326–34.

Lucas, R. E., Jr. *Studies in Business Cycle Theory.* Cambridge, Mass.: MIT Press, 1989.

MacAfee, K. "A Glimpse of the Hidden Economy in the National Accounts." *Economic Trends* 316 (1980): 81–87.

Malabre, A. L., Jr., and L. H. Clark, Jr. "Productivity Statistics for the Service Sector may Understate Gains." *Wall Street Journal,* August 12, 1992, A1.

Mankiw, G. N. "A Quick Refresher Course in Macroeconomics." Working Paper No. 3256, NBER, February 1990.

Mankiw, G. N., and M. Shapiro. "News or Noise: An Analysis of GNP Revisions." *Survey of Current Business* 66 (1986): 20–25.

Maurice, R. *National Accounts Statistics: Sources and Methods.* London: Her Majesty's Stationery Office, 1968.

McKibbin, R. "Working-class Gambling in Britain, 1880–1939." *Past and Present* 82 (1979): 147–78.

McMillion, Ch. W. "Facing the Economy's Grim Reality." *New York Times,* February 23, 1992, F13.

Mills, J. *The Underground Empire: Where Crime and Governments Embrace.* Garden City: Doubleday, 1986.

Moffett, M. "Off-the Books Growth Is Fueling Mexico, but Underground Is a Two-Edged Sword." *Wall Street Journal,* October 4, 1989, A2.

Morgenstern, O. *On the Accuracy of Economic Observations.* Princeton: Princeton University Press, 1963.

Murray, A. "Revised U.S. Statistics Apt to Show Bigger, More Productive Economy." *Wall Street Journal,* November 11, 1985, 27.

Obstfeld, M. "Capital Mobility in the World Economy: Theory and Measurement." *Carnegie-Rochester Conference Series on Public Policy* 24 (1986): 55–104.

O'Higgins, M. "Aggregate Measures of Tax Evasion: An Assessment." *British Tax Review* 5 (1981): 286–302.

Park, T. "Reconciliation Between Personal Income and Taxable Income, 1947–78." *Survey of Current Business* 61 (1981): 24–8, 46.

Report of the Seminar on the CPI. Mimeo, Economic Commission of Europe, Geneva, 1986.

Sargent, Th. J. *Rational Expectations and Inflation.* New York: Harper & Row, 1986.

Sargent, Th. J. "Two Models of Measurements and the Investment Accelerator." *Journal of Political Economy* 97 (1989): 251–87.

Sargent, Th. J., and N. Wallace. "Rational Expectations and the Theory of Economic Policy." *Federal Reserve Bank of Minneapolis,* June 1975.

Sayers, R. S. *The Bank of England, 1891–1944.* Cambridge: Cambridge University Press, 1976.

Schwartz, A. J. *Money in Historical Perspective.* Chicago: University of Chicago Press, 1987.

Segal, H. *A Study of the Quantity and Sources of Price Quotations for the Consumer Price Index.* Mimeo, Statistics Canada, November 1977.

Sennholz, H. *The Underground Economy.* Auburn: The Ludwig von Mises Institute, 1984.

Singer, M. "The Vitality of Mythical Numbers." *Public Interest* 23 (1971): 3–9.

Smith, S. *Britain's Shadow Economy.* Oxford: Clarendon Press, 1986.

Solomou, S., and M. Weale. "British Economic Growth, 1870–1913: Facts and Artifacts." Working Paper No. 886, Department of Applied Economics, University of Cambridge, 1988.

Solon, G. "The Value of Panel Data in Economic Research." In *Panel Surveys,* edited by G. Kalton, D. Kasprzyk, and J. Duncan. New York: Wiley, 1987.

Soto, de H. *The Other Path.* New York: Harper & Row, 1989.

Spaventa, L. "Introduction: Is There a Public Debt Problem in Italy?" In *High Public Debt: The Italian Experience,* edited by F. Giavazzi, and L. Spaventa, 1–24. Cambridge: Cambridge University Press, 1988.

Statistics Canada. *Evaluation of Issues Relating to the Price Index.* Mimeo, March 1988.

Stournaras, Y. A. "Public Sector Debt and Deficits in Greece: The Experience of the 1980s." Paper presented at the Conference on Fiscal Policy, McGill University, December 6–8, 1989.

Stout, H. "Shaky Numbers: U.S. Statistics Mills Grind Out More Data That Are then Revised." *Wall Street Journal,* August 31, 1989, A1.

Stout, H. "Eagerly Awaited GNP Is a Product of Calls, Number Crunching," *Wall Street Journal,* January 20, 1990, A2.

Tinbergen, J. *Economic Policy: Principles and Design.* Amsterdam: North-Holland, 1956.

United Nations. *A System of National Accounts and Supporting Tables.* Studies in Methods, no. 2, Department of Economic Affairs, Statistical Office: New York, 1953.

U.S. Internal Revenue Service, Estimates of Income Unreported on Individual Income Tax Returns. Publication No. 1104, Washington, D.C.: Government Printing Office, 1979.

Waring, M. *If Women Counted.* San Francisco: Harper & Row, 1988.

Wilcox, D. "What Do We Know About Consumption." Working paper presented at the NBER Program on Economic Fluctuations Research Meeting, Cambridge, Mass., July 22, 1988.

Winiecki, J. *The Distorted World of Soviet-Type Economies.* Pittsburgh: University of Pittsburgh Press, 1988.

White, J. B. *When Words Lose Their Meaning.* Chicago: University of Chicago Press, 1984.

White, J., and A. Wildavsky. *The Deficit and the Public Interest: The Search for Responsible Budgeting in the 1980s.* Berkeley: University of California Press, and New York: Russell Sage Foundation, 1989.

Wriston, W. "On Track with the Deficit." *Wall Street Journal,* January 6, 1989.

Chapter 2

Aganbegyan, A. *Inside Perestroika.* New York: Harper & Row, 1989.

Appleby, J. O. *Economic Thought and Ideology in Seventeenth Century England.* Princeton: Princeton University Press, 1978.

Arthur Anderson & Co. *Sound Financial Reporting in the US Government: a Prerequisite to Fiscal Responsibility.* 1986.

Auerbach, A. J., and L. J. Kotlikoff. *Dynamic Fiscal Policy.* Cambridge: Cambridge University Press, 1987.

Ayres, C. E. *The Theory of Economic Progress.* Chapel Hill: University of North Carolina Press, 1944.

Barro, R. J. "The Ricardian Approach to Budget Deficits." *Journal of Economic Perspectives* 3 (1989): 37–54.

Bernheim, D. "A Neoclassical Perspective on Budget Deficits." *Journal of Economic Perspectives* 3 (1989): 55–72.

Blaug, M. "Kuhn versus Lakatos, or Paradigms versus Research Programmes in the History of Economics." In *Method and Appraisal in Economics,* edited by S. J. Latsis. Cambridge: Cambridge University Press, 1976.

Bloch, M. *The Historian's Craft.* New York: Alfred A. Knopf, 1953.

Boskin, M. J. "Federal Government Deficits: Myths and Realities." *American Economic Review* 72 (1982): 296–303.

Boskin, M. J., M. S. Robinson, and A. M. Huber. "New Estimates of States and Local Government Tangible Capital and Net Investment." Working Paper No. 2131, NBER, 1987a.

Boskin, M. J., M. S. Robinson, and A. M. Huber. "Government Saving, Capital Formation and Wealth in the United States, 1947–1985." Working Paper No. 2352, NBER, 1987b.

Botero, G. *The Reason of State.* Extracts reprinted in *The Renaissance: Readings in Western Civilization,* edited by E. Cochrane and J. Kirshner, 230–51. Chicago: University of Chicago Press, 1986.

Brenner, R. "Unemployment, Justice, and Keynes's 'General Theory.'" *Journal of Political Economy* 87 (1979): 837–50.

Brenner, R. "The Role of Nominal Wage Contracts in Keynes's General Theory." *History of Political Economy* 12 (1980): 582–87.

Brenner, R. *History—The Human Gamble.* Chicago: University of Chicago Press, 1983.

Brenner, R. *Betting on Ideas: Wars, Invention, Inflation.* Chicago: University of Chicago Press, 1985.

Brenner, R. *Rivalry: In Business, Science, among Nations.* Cambridge: Cambridge University Press, 1987.

Brenner, R. "Extracting Sunbeams Out of Cucumbers: What is Bad Social Science and Why Is It Practised?" *Queen's Quarterly* 99 (1991): 519–53.

Brenner, R., and G. A. Brenner. *Gambling and Speculation: A Theory, a History and a Future of Some Human Decisions.* Cambridge: Cambridge University Press, 1990.

Bridenbaugh, C. *Vexed and Troubled Englishmen, 1590–1642.* New York: Oxford University Press, 1968.

Brittan, S. "Learn from Keynes but Don't Be a Parrot." *Financial Times,* November 12, 1992.

Brooks, G. "Half a Loaf: Lavish U.S. Food Aid to Egypt Has Bought Peace, but Little Else." *Wall Street Journal,* April 3, 1989, A1.

Colander, D., and R. Brenner, eds. *Educating Economists.* Ann Arbor: University of Michigan Press, 1992.

Craig, A. *Germany 1866–1945.* Oxford: Clarendon Press, 1978.

De Custine, Marquis. *Empire of the Czar.* 1839. New York: Doubleday, 1989.

Di Guardi, J. "GAAP's Budget Gaps Will Surprise." *Wall Street Journal,* November 6, 1987.

Dobbs, M. "Gorbachev to Speed Up Economic Reform." *Washington Post,* as reprinted in *The Gazette,* April 11, 1990, A9.

Eberstadt, N. "Foreign Aid's Industrialized Poverty." *Wall Street Journal,* November 8, 1989.

Eisner, R. *How Real is the Federal Deficit?* New York: Free Press, 1986.

Eisner, R. "Extended Accounts for National Income and Product." *Journal of Economic Literature* 26 (1988): 1611–84.

Eisner, R., and P. J. Pieper. "A New View of the Federal Debt and Budget Deficits." *American Economic Review* 74 (1984): 11–29.

Eisner, R., and J. Pieper. "How to Make Sense of the Deficit." *Public Interest* 78 (1985): 101–18.

Fialka, J. J. "Unsettling Specter of Peace Has Caused War Among Analysts Over the Possible Consequences." *Wall Street Journal,* August 31, 1989, A16.

Fisher, I. "The Debt Deflation Theory of Great Depressions." *Econometrica* 1 (1933).

Fisher, I. *Mastering the Crisis.* London: George Allen, 1934.

Fitzgerald, E. A. *The High Priests of Waste.* New York: W. W. Norton, 1972.

Freeman, Ch. *The Economics of Industrial Innovation.* Cambridge, Mass.: MIT Press, 1983.

Frenkel, J. A., and A. Razin. "Spending, Taxes, and Deficits: International-Intertemporal Approach." Working Paper No. 63, Princeton Studies in International Finance, December 1988.

Friedman, M., and R. Friedman. "The Facts: Government Spending, Taxes, and Deficits." In *A Nation in Debt: Economists Debate the Federal Budget Deficit,* edited by R. H. Fink and J. C. High, 119–35. Frederick: University Publications of America, 1987.

Geld, E. "Brazil's Illiterates Not Helped by Central Planning." *Wall Street Journal,* February 2, 1990, A15.

Gramlich, E. M. "Budget Deficits and National Saving: Are Politicians Exogenous?" *Economic Perspectives* 3 (1989): 23–35.

Goldstein, J. S. *Long Cycles.* New Haven: Yale University Press, 1988.

Hill, C. P. *British Economic and Social History 1700–1982.* 1957. 5th ed. London: Edward Arnold, 1986.

Homer, S. *A History of Interest Rates.* New Brunswick: Rutgers University Press, 1963.

Hutt, W. H. *The Keynesian Episode.* Indianapolis: Liberty Fund, 1979.

Johnson, P. *History of the Modern World.* London: Weidenfeld and Nicholson, 1983.

Jordan, W. K. *Philanthropy in England 1480–1660: A Study of the Changing Pattern of English Social Aspirations.* London: George Allen & Unwin, 1959.

Kennedy, G. *The Economics of Defense.* London: Faber and Faber, 1975.

Keynes, J. M. *The General Theory of Employment, Interest and Money.* London: Macmillan, 1936.

Kotlikoff, L. J. "Deficit Delusion." *Public Interest* 84 (1986): 53–65.

Lane, F. C. *Venice and History.* Baltimore: Johns Hopkins University Press, 1966.

Leijonhufvud, A. *On Keynesian Economics and the Economics of Keynes: a Study in Monetary History.* Oxford: Oxford University Press, 1968.

McEvedy, C., and R. Jones. *Atlas of the World Population History.* Middlesex: Penguin, 1978.

McClelland, J. C. *Autocrats and Academics.* Chicago: University of Chicago Press, 1979.

McNeill, W. H. *Venice: the Hinge of Europe 1081–1797.* Chicago: University of Chicago Press, 1974.

Modigliani, F. "Long-run Implications of Alternative Fiscal Policies and the Burden of the National Debt." *Economic Journal* 71 (1961): 730–55.

Mommsen, W. J., ed. *The Emergence of the Welfare State in Britain and Germany, 1850–1950.* London: Croom Helm, 1981.

Morgenstern, O. *On the Accuracy of Economic Observations.* Princeton: Princeton University Press, 1963.

Morris, C. R. "Deficit Figuring Does Not Add Up." *New York Times Magazine,* February 12, 1989, 36–40.

Musgrave, J. C. "Government-Owned Fixed Capital in the United States, 1925–79." *Survey of Current Business,* 60 (1980): 33–43.

Nettler, G. *Exploring Crime.* 2d ed. New York: McGraw-Hill, 1978.

Pinson, K. S. *Modern Germany.* New York: Macmillan, 1954.

Rimlinger, G. V. "The Historical Analysis of National Welfare Systems." In *Explorations in New Economic History: Essays in Honor of Douglass C. North,* edited by R. L. Ransom, R. Sutch, and G. M. Walton. New York: New York Academic Press, 1982.

Robbins, L. *An Essay on the Nature and Significance of Economic Science.* 1932. 2d ed. London: Macmillan, 1952.

Robinson, J. *Economic Philosophy.* London: Penguin Books, 1962.

Savage, J. D. *Balanced Budgets & American Politics.* Ithaca: Cornell University Press, 1988.

Schumpeter, J. A. *History of Economic Analysis.* London: George Allen & Unwin, 1972.

Smith, A. *An Inquiry into the Nature and Causes of the Wealth of Nations.* 1776. Chicago: University of Chicago Press, 1976.

Stern, F. *Gold and Iron: Bismarck, Bleichroder, and the Building of the German Empire.* London: George Allen & Unwin, 1977.

Stulz, R. M. "Capital Mobility in the World Economy: Theory and Measurement—a Comment." *Carnegie-Rochester Conference Series on Public Policy* 24 (1986): 105–113.

Teitelbaum, M. S., and J. M. Winter. *The Fear of Population Decline.* New York: New York Academic Press, 1985.

Vogel, H. L. *Entertainment Industry Economics.* Cambridge: Cambridge University Press, 1988.

Watson, W. "The Sweet Mysteries of Canadian Infrastructure." *Financial Post,* November 26, 1992.

Winiecki, J. *Gorbachev's Way Out?* London: The Center for Research into Communist Economies, 1988.

Wright, K. N. *The Great American Crime Myth.* New York: Praeger, 1985.

Wriston, W. "On Track with the Deficit." *Wall Street Journal,* January 6, 1989.

Yellen, J. L. "Symposium on the Budget Deficit." *Journal of Economic Perspectives* 3 (1989): 17–21.
Young, M. *The Rise of Meritocracy.* 1958. Middlesex: Penguin, 1973.

Chapter 3

Ando, A. "Comment," on F. Hayashi's "Why Is Japan's Saving Rate So Apparently High?" In *NBER Macroeconomics Annual,* edited by S. Fischer, 211–20. Cambridge, Mass.: MIT Press, 1986.
Appleby, J. O. *Economic Thought and Ideology in Seventeenth Century England.* Princeton: Princeton University Press, 1978.
Auerbach, A. J., and L. J. Kotlikoff. "Demographics, Fiscal Policy, and U.S. Saving in the 1980s and Beyond." Working Paper No. 3150, NBER, October 1989.
Aymard, M., ed. *Dutch Capitalism and World Capitalism.* Cambridge: Cambridge University Press, 1982.
Bairoch, P. *Cities in Economic Development.* Chicago: University of Chicago Press, 1988.
Barbour, V. *Capitalism in Amsterdam in the 17th Century.* Ann Arbor: University of Michigan Press, 1966.
Barro, R. J. "Economic Growth in a Cross Section of Countries." *Quarterly Journal of Economics* 106 (1991): 407–43.
Barro, R. J. "Economic Growth, Convergence, and Government Policies." In *Economic Policy, Financial Markets and Economic Growth,* edited by L. Solmon and B. Zycher. Los Angeles: MICJF, 1993.
Barro, R., and G. Becker. "Fertility Choice in a Model of Economic Growth." Working Paper, Department of Economics, Harvard University, 1987.
Barro, R., and G. Becker. "A Reformulation of the Economic Theory of Fertility." *Quarterly Journal of Economics* 53 (1988): 1–26.
Barro, R., and G. MacDonald. "Social Security and Consumer Spending in an International Cross Section." *Journal of Public Economics* 11 (1979): 275–90.
Barro, R. J., and X. Sala-i-Martin. "Convergence Across States and Regions." *Brookings Papers on Economic Activity* 1 (1991): 107–58.
Bauer, P. T. *Reality and Rhetoric: Studies in the Economics of Development.* Cambridge, Mass.: Harvard University Press, 1984.
Baumol, W. J. "Productivity Growth, Convergence, and Welfare: What the Long Run Data Show." *American Economic Review* 76 (1986): 1072–85.
Becker, G. S. *Human Capital.* New York: Columbia University Press, 1975.
Becker, G. S. *A Treatise on the Family.* Cambridge, Mass.: Harvard University Press, 1981.
Berman, H. *Law and Revolution.* Cambridge, Mass.: Harvard University Press, 1983.
Blades, D., and P. Sturm. "The Concept and Measurement of Savings: the United States and Other Industrialized Countries." *Federal Reserve Bank of Boston Conference Series* 25, 1982.
Blum, C. H. U., and M. J. I. Gaudry. "Are Car Purchases Savings? An Analysis of

German Households." Working Paper No. 8934, Department of Economics, Université de Montréal, September 1989.

Blanchard, O. J. "Comments and Discussion." *Brookings Papers on Economic Activity* 1 (1991): 159–77.

Boskin, M. J. "Issues in the Measurement and Interpretation of Saving and Wealth." Working Paper No. 2633, NBER, June 1988.

Bosworth, B. P. "International Differences in Saving." *American Economic Review* 80 (1990): 377–381.

Bradford, D. F. "What Is National Saving?: Alternative Measures in Historical and International Context." Working Paper No. 3341, NBER, April 1990.

Brenner, R. *History—the Human Gamble.* Chicago: University of Chicago Press, 1983.

Brenner, R. *Betting on Ideas: Wars, Invention, Inflation.* 1985, Chicago: University of Chicago Press, 1989.

Brenner, R. *Rivalry.* Cambridge: Cambridge University Press, 1987.

Brenner, R. "The Long Road from Serfdom and How to Shorten It." *Canadian Business Law Journal* 17 (1990): 195–226.

Brenner, R. "From Envy and Distrust to Trust and Ambition." *Rivista di Politica Economica* 81 (1991a): 31–59 (in English and Italian).

Brenner, R. "Legal Reforms in the Eastern Bloc: a Precondition to Monetary and Fiscal Policies." In *Exchange Rate Policies of the Less Developed Market and Socialist Economies,* edited by E. M. Claassen , 151–74. San Francisco: International Center for Economic Growth, 1991b.

Brenner, R. "Extracting Sunbeams Out of Cucumbers: or, What Is Bad Social Science, and Why Is It Practiced?" *Queen's Quarterly* 99 (1991c): 519–54.

Brenner, R. "An Alternative View of Growth: Comments on Barro and Carr." In *Economic Policy, Financial Markets and Economic Growth,* edited by L. Solmon and B. Zycher. Los Angeles: MICJF, 1993.

Brenner, R. "Nationalism and the State." *Queen's Quarterly,* forthcoming 1993.

Brenner, R., and G. A. Brenner. *Gambling and Speculation: A Theory, a History and a Future of Some Human Decisions.* Cambridge: Cambridge University Press, 1990.

Brenner, R., G. A. Brenner, and C. Montmarquette. "A Statistical Profile of Gamblers." In *Gambling and Speculation.* Cambridge, Mass.: Cambridge University Press, 1990.

Brenner, R., and N. M. Kiefer. "The Economics of the Diaspora: Discrimination and Occupational Structure." *Economic Development and Cultural Change* 29 (1981): 517–34.

Carr, J. L. "Deposit Insurance, Savings and Economic Growth." In *Economic Policy, Financial Markets and Economic Growth,* edited by L. Solmon and B. Zycher. Los Angeles: MICJF, 1993.

Cipolla, C., ed. *The Economic Decline of Empires.* London: Methuen, 1970.

Coase, R. *The Firm, the Market and the Law.* Chicago: University of Chicago Press, 1988.

Colander, D., and R. Brenner, eds. *Educating Economists.* Ann Arbor: University of Michigan Press, 1992.

Dagenais, M. "Measuring Personal Savings, Consumption and Disposable Income, in

Canada, Since 1962." Working Paper, Department of Economics, Université de Montréal, November 1990.

De Long, B. J., and L. H. Summers. "Macroeconomic Policy and Long-Run Growth." Federal Reserve Bank of Kansas City, *Economic Review* 77 (1992): 5–31.

Dudley, L. M. *The Word and the Sword.* Cambridge, Mass.: Blackwell, 1991.

Ehrenberg, R. *Capital and Finance in the Age of Renaissance.* Jonathan Cape, 1928.

Eisner, R. *How Real is the Federal Deficit?* New York: Free Press, 1986.

Feige, E. L. *The Underground Economy.* Cambridge: Cambridge University Press, 1989.

Feldstein, M. "Social Security and Private Savings: International Evidence in an Extended Life-Cycle Model." In *The Economics of Public Services,* edited by M. Feldstein, 174–205. New York: Macmillan, 1977.

Feldstein, M. "International Differences in Social Security and Saving." *Journal of Public Economics* 12 (1980): 225–44.

Friedman, M., and A. J. Schwartz. *A Monetary History of the United States, 1867–1960.* Princeton: Princeton University Press, 1963.

Gibbon, E. *Decline and Fall of the Roman Empire.* New York: Fawcett Premier, 1990.

Gibney, F. *The Pacific Century.* New York: Charles Scribner's Sons, 1992.

Glendon, M. A. *The Transformation of Family Law.* Chicago: University of Chicago Press, 1989.

Graham, J. W. "International Differences in Saving Rates and the Life Cycle Hypothesis." *European Economic Review* 31 (1987): 1509–29.

Graham, J. W. "International Differences in Saving Rates and the Life Cycle Hypothesis: Reply and Further Evidence." *European Economic Review* 33 (1989): 1499–1507.

Grobar, L. M., and R. M. Stern. "A Data Set on International Trade in Armaments for the Major Western Industrialized and Developing Countries for 1980: Sources and Methodological Issues." Seminar Discussion Paper No. 236, July 20, 1989a.

Grobar, L. M., R. M. Stern, and A. V. Deardorff. "The Economic Effects of International Trade in Armaments in the Major Western Industrialized and Developing Countries." Seminar Discussion Paper No. 237, June 16, 1989b.

Haurin, D. R. "Women's Labour Reactions to Family Disruptions." *Review of Economics and Statistics* 71 (1989): 54–61.

Hayashi, F. "Why Is Japan's Saving Rate So Apparently High?" In *NBER Macroeconomics Annual* edited by S. Fischer, 147–210. Cambridge, Mass.: MIT Press, 1986.

Hayashi, F. "Japan's Saving Rate: New Data and Reflections." Working Paper No. 3205, NBER, December 1989.

Hill, Ch. "The Integration of the Middle East into the World Economy." Paper presented at the Mont Pélerin Society Meetings, Vancouver, August 1992.

Horioka, Ch. Y. "Pourquoi le taux d'épargne privée est-il si élevé au Japon?" *Finance et développement* 23 (1986): 22–25.

Holloway, Th. M. "Present NIPA Saving Measures: Their Characteristics and Limitations." In *The Measurement of Saving, Investment and Wealth,* edited by R. E. Lipsey and H. S. Tice, 21–93. Chicago: University of Chicago Press, 1989.

Homer, S. *A History of Interest Rates.* New Brunswick: Rutgers University Press, 1963.

Huff, D. *How to Lie with Statistics.* New York: W. W. Norton, 1954.

Huizinga, J. H. *Dutch Civilization in the Seventeenth Century.* New York: Collins, 1968.

Hurd, M. D. "Research on the Elderly: Economic Status, Retirement, and Consumption and Saving." *Journal of Economic Literature* 28 (1990): 565–637.

Jacob, H. *Silent Revolution: The Transformation of Divorce Law in the United States.* Chicago: University of Chicago Press, 1988.

Jacobs, J. *Cities and the Wealth of Nations.* New York: Vintage Books, 1985.

Jenkins, G. P. "Effects of Changing Age Structure on Consumption and Saving." Working Paper No. 89–05, Department of Finance, Fiscal Policy and Economic Analysis Branch, 1989.

Johnson, W. R., and J. Skinner. "Labor Supply and Marital Separation." *American Economic Review* 76 (1986): 455–69.

Jump, G. V. "Interest Rates, Inflation Expectations, and Spurious Elements in Measured Real Income and Saving." *American Economic Review* 70 (1980): 990–1004.

Kennedy, P. *The Rise and Fall of the Great Powers.* New York: Random House, 1987.

Keynes, J. M. *The General Theory of Employment, Interest and Money.* London: Macmillan, 1936.

Kindleberger, Ch. *Economic Responses.* Cambridge, Mass.: Harvard University Press, 1978.

Kodde, D. A. "Uncertainty and the Demand for Education." *Review of Economics and Statistics* 68 (1986): 460–67.

Kotkin, J. *Tribes.* New York: Random House, 1993.

Koskela, E., and M. Viren. "A Note on Long-Term Determinants of the Private Savings Ratio." *Economic Letters* 11 (1983): 107–13.

Koskela, E., and M. Viren. "International Differences in Saving Rates and the Life Cycle Hypothesis." *European Economic Review* 33 (1989): 1489–98.

Kossman, E. H. "The Low Countries." In *New Cambridge Modern History.* Vol. 4, edited by J. P. Cooper, 359–84. Cambridge: Cambridge University Press, 1970.

Kotlikoff, L. J. *What Determines Savings?* Cambridge, Mass.: MIT Press, 1989.

Krugman, P. *The Age of Diminished Expectations.* Cambridge, Mass.: MIT Press, 1990.

Kuznets, S. *National Income and Its Composition.* National Bureau of Economic Research. Vol. 2, 1942.

Landes, E. "Economics of Alimony." *Journal of Legal Studies* 7 (1978): 35–63.

Lane, F. C. *Venice and History.* Baltimore: Johns Hopkins University Press, 1966.

Lucas, R. E., Jr. "On the Mechanics of Economic Development." *Journal of Monetary Economics* 22 (1988): 3–42.

de Mandeville, B. *The Fable of the Bees.* 1714. New York: Capricorn Books, 1962.

McEvedy, C., and R. Jones. *Atlas of the World Population History.* Middlesex: Penguin, 1980.

McKay, J. P. *Pioneers for Profit.* Chicago: University of Chicago Press, 1970.

McKibbin, R. "Working-class Gambling in Britain, 1880–1939." *Past & Present* 82 (1979): 147–78.

McNeill, W. H. *Venice: the Hinge of Europe 1081–1797.* Chicago: University of Chicago Press, 1974.

McNeill, W. H. *Mythistory and Other Essays.* Chicago: University of Chicago Press, 1986.

Melloan, G. "China's Miracle Workers Mostly Live Elsewhere." *Wall Street Journal,* March 8, 1993, A13.

Michael, R. "Consequences of the Rise in Female Labor Force Participation Rates: Questions and Probes." *Journal of Labor Economics* 3 (1985): S117–46.

Modigliani, F. "The Life Cycle Hypothesis of Saving and Inter-Country Differences in the Saving Ratio." In *Induction, Growth and Trade: Essays in Honor of Sir Roy Harrod,* edited by W. A. Eltis, et al., 197–225. London: Clarendon Press, 1970.

Modigliani, F., and A. Sterling. "Determinants of Private Saving with Special Reference to the Role of Social Security—Cross-Country Tests." In *The Determinants of National Saving and Wealth,* edited by F. Modigliani and R. Hemming, 24–55. New York: St. Martins, 1983.

Nations Unies. *Rapport Mondial sur le Développement Humain.* Paris: Economica, 1991.

Needham, J. *Science and Civilisation in China.* 1954. Vol. 1, Cambridge: Cambridge University Press, 1961.

Noguchi, Y. "Demographic Conditions, Social Security, and Capital Accumulation: a Simulation Analysis." Working Paper, NBER, 1986.

North, D. C. *Institutions, Institutional Change and Economic Performance.* Cambridge: Cambridge University Press, 1990.

North, D. C., and R. P. Thomas. *The Rise of the Western World: a New Economic History.* Cambridge: Cambridge University Press, 1973.

North, D. C., and B. W. Weingast. "The Evolution of Institutions Governing Public Choice in 17th Century England." *Journal of Economic History* 49 (1989): 803–32.

Obstfeld, M. "Capital Mobility in the World Economy: Theory and Measurement." *Carnegie-Rochester Conference Series on Public Policy* 24 (1986): 55–104.

Olson, M. *The Rise and Decline of Nations.* New Haven: Yale University Press, 1982.

Origo, I. *The Merchant of Prato.* 1957. New York: Penguin Books, 1992.

Panati, Ch. *Extraordinary Origins of Everyday Things.* New York: Harper & Row, 1987.

Parker, W. N. "National States and National Development: French and German Ore Mining in the Late Nineteenth Century." In *The State of Economic Growth,* edited by H. G. Aitken, 201–12. New York: Social Science Research Council, 195 .

Peters, H. E. "Marriage and Divorce: Informational Constraints and Private Contracting." *American Economic Review* 76 (1986): 437–54.

Romer, P. M. "Comment," on F. Hayashi's "Why Is Japan's Saving Rate So Apparently High?" In *NBER Macroeconomics Annual,* edited by S. Fischer, 220–33. Cambridge, Mass.: MIT Press, 1986.

Romer, P. M. "Endogenous Technological Change." *Journal of Political Economy* 98 (1990, supplement): S71–S102.

Rosecrance, R. *The Rise of the Trading State.* New York: Basic Books, 1986.

Savage, J. D. *Balanced Budgets & American Politics.* Ithaca: Cornell University Press, 1988

Schama, S. *The Embarrassment of Riches.* Berkeley: University of California Press, 1988.

Schlesinger, A. M., Jr. *The Cycles of American History.* Boston: Houghton Mifflin Co., 1986

Schultz, T. W. *Restoring Economic Equilibrium.* Oxford: Basil Blackwell, 1990.

Schumpeter, J. A. *History of Economic Analysis.* 1954. London: George Allen & Unwin, 1972.

Shipton, P. "How Gambians Save—and What Their Strategies Imply for International Aid." Working paper, Agriculture and Rural Development Department, The World Bank, April 1990.

Smith, A. *The Wealth of Nations.* 1776. Chicago: University of Chicago Press, 1976.

Solow, R. M. "A Contribution to the Economic Theory of Growth." *Quarterly Journal of Economics* 70 (1956): 65–94.

Spielman, P. M. "Envy and Jealousy: an Attempt at Clarification." *Psychoanalytic Quarterly* 40 (1971): 59–82.

Spurge, L. *An American Renaissance.* Beverly Hills: Knowledge Exchange Inc., 1991.

Tainter, J. A. *The Collapse of Complex Societies.* Cambridge: Cambridge University Press, 1988.

Tawney, R. H. *Religion and the Rise of Capitalism.* 1926. New York: Mentor Book, 1963.

Thirsk, J. *Economic Policy and Projects.* Oxford: Clarendon Press, 1978.

Trevor-Hoper, H. R. "Religion, the Reformation and Social Change." *Historical Studies* 4 (1961): 19–29.

Usher, D. *The Price Mechanism and the Meaning of Income Statistics.* Oxford: Oxford University Press, 1968.

Usher, P. A. "The Significance of Modern Empiricism for History and Economics." *Journal of Economic History* 9 (1949).

Vance, J. E. *The Merchant's World: the Geography of Wholesaling.* Englewood Cliffs, N.J.: Prentice-Hall, 1970.

Van Houtte, J. A. *An Economic History of the Low Countries, 800–1800.* London: Weidenfeld and Nicholson, 1977.

Vickery, C. "Women's Economic Contribution to the Family." In *The Subtle Revolution,* edited by R. E. Smith. Washington, D.C.: The Urban Institute, 1979.

Viner J. *Religious Thought and Economic Society.* Durham: Duke University Press, 1978.

Weitzman, L. J. *The Divorce Revolution.* New York: Free Press, 1985.

Wilcox, D. "What Do We Know About Consumption." Paper presented at the NBER Program on Economic Fluctuations Research Meeting, Cambridge, Mass., 1988.

White, J., and A. Wildavsky. *The Deficit and the Public Interest: The Search for Responsible Budgeting in the 1980s.* Berkeley: University of California Press and New York: Russell Sage Foundation, 1989

Wilson, Ch. *The Dutch Republic and the Civilization of the Seventeenth Century.* New York: McGraw-Hill, 1968.

Wriston, W. B. *The Twilight of Sovereignty.* New York: Charles Scribner's Sons, 1992.

Yago, G. *Junk Bonds.* Oxford: Oxford University Press, 1991.

Yoshikawa, H., and F. Ohtake. "An Analysis of Female Labor Supply, Housing Demand and the Saving Rate in Japan." Discussion Paper No. 171, The Institute of Social and Economic Research, Osaka University, July 1988.

Young, A. A. "Increasing Returns and Economic Progress." *Economic Journal* 38 (1928): 527–42.

Zumthor, P. *La Vie quotidienne en Hollande au temps de Rembrandt.* Paris: Hachette, 1959.

Chapter 4

Ahtiala, P. *Indexed Linked Debts.* Tampere: Acta Universitatis Tampereuris, 1967.

Alesina, A., and L. H. Summers. "Central Bank Independence and Macroeconomic Performance: Some Comparative Evidence." Working paper, Harvard University, 1991.

Baer, W., and P. Beckerman. "Indexing in Brazil." *World Development* 2 (1974): 35–47.

Barro, R. J. "The Ricardian Approach to Budget Deficits." *Journal of Economic Perspectives* 3 (1989): 37–54.

Beauchesne, E. "Despite High Cost of Battle, We're Better Off with Low Inflation, Experts Say." *The Gazette,* January 23, 1993, C2.

Becketti, S., and Ch. Morris. "Does Money Still Forecast Economic Activity?" Federal Reserve Bank of Kansas City, *Economic Review* 77 (1992): 65–79.

Blinder, A. "The Consumer Price Index and the Measurement of Recent Inflation." *Brookings Papers on Economic Activity* 2 (1980): 539–73.

Brenner, R. *Micro- and Macro-economic Aspects of Indexation.* Ph.D. thesis, Department of Economics, Hebrew University, 1977.

Brenner, R. "What Insurance Can Indexation Provide?" In *Betting on Ideas: Wars, Invention, Inflation,* 166–85. Chicago: University of Chicago Press, 1985.

Brenner, R. *Rivalry: in Business, Science, among Nations.* Cambridge: Cambridge University Press, 1987.

Brenner, R., and D. Patinkin. "Indexation in Israel." In *Inflation Theory and Anti-Inflation Policy,* edited by E. Lundberg, 387–416. London: Macmillan, 1977.

Bronfeld, S., and R. Brenner. "Index Bonds—a Liquid Asset?" *Bank of Israel Economic Review* 44 (1977): 1–28.

Canada Year Book. Special edition. Ottawa: Statistics Canada, 1977.

Clark, L. H., Jr., and A. L. Malabre, Jr. "Belying Forecasts, U.S. Prints More Cash." In *Readings for the Economics of Money, Banking, and Financial Institutions,* edited by J. W. Eaton and F. S. Mishkin, 267–70. New York: Harper Collins, 1993.

The Consumer Price Index Reference Paper. Catalogue 62–553. Occasional, Ottawa: Statistics Canada, February 1985.

Cousineau, J. M., and R. Lacroix . *L'indexation des salaires.* Manuscript, Department of Economics, Université de Montréal, 1981.

De Long, B. J., and L. H. Summers. "Macroeconomic Policy and Long-Run Growth." Federal Reserve Bank of Kansas City, *Economic Review* 77 (1992): 5–31.

DeVries, P., and A. Baldwin. "Impact of Different Homeownership Methodologies on Consumer Price Index Behaviour Between Canada and the United States." *Canadian Statistical Review* (1985): vi-xiv.

The Economist. "Switzerland's Slippery Slope." February 15, 1992, 77.

Ellis, M. S. "Corrective Inflation in Brazil, 1964–1966." In *The Economy of Brazil,* edited by H. S. Ellis, 177–212. Berkeley: University of California Press, 1969.

Fishlow, A. "Indexing Brazilian Style: Inflation Without Tears?" *Brookings Papers on Economic Activity* 1 (1974): 261–82.

Foss, M. F., ed. *The U.S. National Income and Product Accounts.* Chicago: University of Chicago Press/NBER, 1983.

Friedman, M. *The Optimum Quantity of Money.* Chicago: Aldine Publishing Co., 1969.

Friedman, M. "Too Tight for a Strong Recovery." *Wall Street Journal,* October 23, 1992.

Gavin, W. T., and A. C. Stockman. "A Price Objective for Monetary Policy." In *Readings for the Economics of Money, Banking, and Financial Institutions,* edited by J. W. Eaton and F. S. Mishkin, 309–16. New York: Harper Collins, 1993.

The Gazette. "$12 Billion in Tax Revenue Lost by Overestimating Inflation, Economists Say." July 16, 1991, B14.

Gordon. R. J. *The Measurement of Durable Good Prices.* Chicago: University of Chicago Press/NBER, 1990.

Hadekel, P. "Price Hikes by Governments Sabotage Central Bank's Effort to Fight Inflation." *The Gazette,* January 4, 1992.

Ip, G. "Government Cited as Main Inflation Source." *Financial Post,* October 25, 1991, 47.

Ip, G. "C$ 'Crisis' May Pay Off." *Financial Post,* December 12, 1992.

Kleiman, E. "Inflation and the Distribution of Public Capital." *Quarterly Economic Review* 83 (1974) (in Hebrew).

Kristol, I. "Inflation: Almost Never What It Seems." *Wall Street Journal,* May 16, 1991.

Krugman, P. *The Age of Diminished Expectations.* Cambridge, Mass.: MIT Press, 1990.

Marshall, A. "Remedies for Fluctuations in General Prices." 1887. As reprinted in *Memorials of Alfred Marshall,* edited by A. C. Pigou, London: MacMillan and Co., 1925: 188–211.

Page, S. A., and S. Trollope. "An International Survey of Indexing and Its Effects." *National Institute Economic Review* 70 (1974): 46–60.

Patinkin, D. *Money, Interest and Prices.* 2d ed. New York: Harper & Row, 1965.

Puumanen, K. "Some Aspects of the Finnish Experience in Index-Tied Deposits." *Bank of Finland Monthly Bulletin* 41 (1967).

Report of the Seminar on the CPI. Mimeo, conference organized by the Economic Commission of Europe and the International Labour Organisation, Geneva, 1988.

Rinehart, D. "Property-tax Increases Push Up Inflation." *The Gazette,* November 20, 1992, C3.

Segal, H. *A Study of the Quantity and Sources of Price Quotations for the Consumer Price Index With Detailed Proposals for Revamping the Outlet Sample.* Mimeo, November 1977.

Spurge, L. *An American Renaissance.* Beverly Hills: Knowledge Exchange Inc., 1991.

Statistics Canada. *The Evaluation of Issues Relating to the Price Index.* Internal document, March 1988.

Stevens, N. A. "Indexation of Social Security Benefits—a Reform in Need of Reform." *Federal Reserve Bank of St. Louis* 63 (1981): 3–11.

Volcker, P. "Reflections of a Central Banker." (Adapted from a lecture delivered in Washington, September 1991). *Wall Street Journal,* October 16, 1990.

Weiner, S. E. "The Changing Role of Reserve Requirements in Monetary Policy." Federal Reserve Bank of Kansas City, *Economic Review* 77 (1992): 45–65.

Wilton, D. "An Analysis of Canadian Wage Contracts with Cost-of-Living Allowance Clauses." Document No. 165, Ottawa: Economic Council of Canada, 1980.

Chapter 5

Acton, Lord J. E. E. *Essays in the History of Liberty.* Indianapolis: Liberty Press, 1985.

Aftalion, F. *L'économie de la Révolution Française.* Paris: Hachette, 1987.

Aganbegyan, A. *Inside Perestroika.* New York: Harper & Row, 1989.

Asman, D. "Moscow Prepares for Its Own Boston Tea Party." *Wall Street Journal,* September 18, 1990, A30

Auerbach, S. "Soviets Say CIA Picture of Economy Was Too Rosy." *Washington Press,* as reprinted in *The Gazette,* April 24, 1990.

Berman, H. J. *Law and Revolution.* Cambridge, Mass.: Harvard University Press, 1983.

Birman, I. *Secret Incomes of the Soviet State Budget.* The Hague: Martinus Nijhoff Publishers, 1981.

Bohlen, C. "Police Spying Dies Hard in Hungary." *New York Times,* January 14, 1990, A14.

Brenner, R. *History—the Human Gamble.* Chicago: University of Chicago Press, 1983.

Brenner, R. *Betting on Ideas: Wars, Inventions, Inflation.* Chicago: University of Chicago Press, 1985.

Brenner, R. *Rivalry: In Business, Science, among Nations.* Cambridge: Cambridge University Press, 1987.

Brenner, R. "Don't Frighten the East Bloc Bureaucrats." *Wall Street Journal,* December 26, 1989, A6.

Brenner, R. "Numbers Out of a Hat." Mimeo, 1990c.

Brenner, R. "The Long Road from Serfdom and How to Shorten It." *Canadian Business Law Journal* 17 (1990): 195–226.

Brenner, R. "From Envy and Distrust to Trust and Ambition." *Rivista di Politica Economica* 81 (1991a): 31–59 (in English and Italian).

Brenner, R. "Legal Reforms in the Eastern Bloc: A Precondition to Monetary and Fiscal Policies." In *Exchange Rate Policies of the Less Developed Market and Socialist Economies,* edited by E. M. Claassen, 151–75. San Francisco: International Center for Economic Growth, 1991b. (French translation in *Journal des Économistes et des Études Humaines: Bilingual Journal of Interdisciplinary Studies* 3 (1990): 253–77).

Brenner, R. "Entrepreneurship in the New Commonwealth." Executive Forum, *Journal of Business Venturing* 7 (1992): 431–40.

Brenner, R., and G. A. Brenner. *Gambling and Speculation: A Theory, a History, and a Future of Some Human Decisions.* Cambridge: Cambridge University Press, 1990.

Brzezinski, M. "When Crossing the Border Can Take Up to Six Days." *The Gazette,* January 19, 1993, B3.

Brzezinski, Z. *The Grand Failure.* New York: Collier, 1990.

Bush, K. "Soviets' Credit Rating Slips." *Wall Street Journal,* March 12, 1990.

Central Intelligence Agency. *USSR: Estimates of Personal Income and Savings.* Directorate of Intelligence, SOV 89–10035, U.S. Government, April 1989.

Clines, F. X. "Amid Shortages, Gorbachev Vows Fruitful New Year." *New York Times,* as reprinted in *The Gazette,* January 2, 1990, A6.

Clines, F. X. "From Moscow, a Plan to Junk Communism in 500 Days." *New York Times,* September 9, 1990, sec. 4, p. 1.

Clines, F. X. "Yeltsin Signs Law on Land Reform as Part of Wider Economic Plan." *New York Times,* December 29, 1991, 10.

De Custine, Marquis. *Empire of the Czar.* 1839. New York: Doubleday, 1989.

Desai, P. "Perestroika, Prices, and the Rubble Problem." *Harriman Institute Forum* 2 (1989).

Desai, P. "Perestroika: Is It on Track?" Mimeo, Department of Economics, Columbia University, 1990.

Dobbs, M. "Gorbachev to Speed up Economic Reform." *Washington Press,* as reprinted in *The Gazette,* April 11, 1990, A9.

Feldbrugge, F. J. M. "The Soviet Second Economy in a Political and Legal Perspective." *The Underground Economy,* edited by E. L. Feige, 297–339. Cambridge: Cambridge University Press, 1989.

Gibney, F. *The Pacific Century.* New York: Charles Scribner's Sons, 1992.

Goldman, M. I. "Gorbachev's Other Crisis." *New York Times,* April 22, 1990.

Gomulka, S. "Gorbachev's Economic Reforms in the Context of the Soviet Political System." In *Economic Reforms in the Socialist World,* edited by S. Gomulka, Yong-Chool Ha, and Cae-One Kim, 59–78. Armonk, N.Y.: M. E. Sharpe, 1989.

Grossman, G. "The 'Second Economy' of the USSR." *Problems of Communism* 5 (1977): 25–40.

Grossman, G. "The Second Economy: Boon or Bane for the Reform of the First Economy?" In *Economic Reforms in the Socialist World,* edited by S. Gomulka, Yong-Chool Ha, and Cae-One Kim, 79–96. Armonk, N.Y.: M. E. Sharpe, 1989.

Hosking, G. *The Awakening of the Soviet Union.* London: Heinemann, 1990.

Jacoby, S. *Wild Justice.* New York: Harper & Row, 1983.

Johnson, P. *A History of the Modern World.* London: Weidenfeld and Nicholson, 1983.

Jones, A., and W. Moskoff, eds. *Perestroika and the Economy.* Armonk, N.Y.: M. E. Sharpe, 1989.

de Jong, E. "Statute on Handicraft-Artisan Trade." *Review of Socialist Law* 4 (1976): 266–67.

Joseph, L. E. "Prague's Spring into Capitalism." *New York Times Magazine, Part 2: The Business World,* December 2, 1990.

Kiselev, D. "New Forms of Entrepreneurship in the USSR." *Journal of Small Business Management* 28 (1990): 76–80.

Klose, K. *Russia and the Russians.* New York: W. W. Norton, 1984.

Kornai, J. *Economics of Shortage.* Vols. 1 and 2. The Hague: North-Holland, 1980.

Kornai, J. *Growth, Shortage and Efficiency.* Oxford: Basil-Blackwell, 1982.

Kornai, J. *Contradictions and Dilemmas: Studies on the Socialist Economy and Society.* 1983, Cambridge, Mass.: MIT Press, 1986.

Los, M. *The Second Economy in Marxist States.* New York: St. Martin's, 1990.

Lourie, R. *Russia's Future.* New York: Whittle Direct Books, 1991.

Malia, M. (signed under 'Z'). "To the Stalin Mausoleum." *Daedalus* 1989: 295–344.

Malia, M. "The Soviet Union Is Dead: Thus Spoke 'Z'." *Herald Tribune,* September 1–2, 1990, 4.

de Mandeville, B. *The Fable of the Bees.* 1714. New York: Capricorn Books, 1962.

Massie, R. K. *Peter the Great.* New York: Ballantine Books, 1980.

McClelland, J. C. *Autocrats and Academics.* Chicago: University of Chicago Press, 1979.

McKay, J. P. *Pioneers for Profit: Foreign Entrepreneurship and Russian Industrialization.* Chicago: University of Chicago Press, 1970.

McNeill, W. H. *A World History.* Oxford: Oxford University Press, 1979.

McNeill, W. H. *The Pursuit of Power.* Chicago: University of Chicago Press, 1982.

Medvedev, R. *De la démocratie socialiste.* Paris: Grasset, 1972.

Mironov, B. "The Russian Peasant Commune After the Reforms of the 1860s." *Slavic Review* 44 (1985): 438–67.

Morgenstern, O. *On the Accuracy of Economic Observations.* Princeton: Princeton University Press, 1965.

O'Hearn, D. "The Consumer Second Economy: Size and Effects." *Soviet Studies* 2 (1980): 218–34.

Rieber, A. J. *Merchants and Entrepreneurs in Imperial Russia.* Chapel Hill: University of North Carolina Press, 1982.

Rowen, H. S., and Ch. Wolf, Jr., eds. *The Impoverished Superpower.* San Francisco: Institute for Contemporary Studies, 1990

Schwartz, A. J. *Money in Historical Perspective.* Chicago: University of Chicago Press, 1987.

Shane, S. "Arrest of Businessman Shows KGB Still Doesn't Understand Art of the Deal." *Baltimore Sun,* as reprinted in *The Gazette,* January 13, 1991, D10.

Shanker, T. "Free-market Economy Is a Bonanza for the Mob." *The Gazette,* October 26, 1991a, B8.

Shanker, T. "Crime and Punishment." *The Gazette,* October 26, 1991b, B1.

Shelton, J. *The Coming Soviet Crash.* New York: Free Press, 1989.

Shelton, J. "Only Gold Can Save the Soviets." *Wall Street Journal,* February 27, 1990.

Shmelev, N. "Supporters and Opponents of Perestroika: the Second Joint Soviet Economy Roundtable." *Soviet Economy* 4 (1988).

Shmelev, N. "Economics and Common Sense. " In *Perestroika and the Economy,* edited by Jones, A., and W. Moskoff, 267–77. Armonk, N.Y.: M. E. Sharpe, 1989.

Smith, H. "The Russian Character." *New York Times Magazine*, October 28, 1990a, 31.

Smith, H. *The New Russians.* New York: Random House, 1990b.

Thirsk, J. *Economic Policy and Projects.* Oxford: Clarendon Press, 1978.

Todd, E. *La chute finale.* Paris: Robert Laffont, 1976.

Wiles, P. *The Political Economy of Communism.* Oxford: Blackwell, 1962.

Winiecki, J. *Gorbachev's Way Out?* London: The Centre for Research into Communist Economies: 1988.

Zinoviev, A. *The Reality of Communism.* London: Victor Gollanz, 1984.

Chapter 6

Ando, A. "Comment." In *NBER Macroeconomics Annual,* edited by S. Fischer, 211–20. Cambridge, Mass.: MIT Press, 1986.

Barbour, V. *Capitalism in Amsterdam in the 17th Century.* Ann Arbor: University of Michigan Press, 1966.

Brenner, R. *History—The Human Gamble.* Chicago: University of Chicago Press, 1983.

Brenner, R. *Betting on Ideas: Wars, Invention, Inflation.* Chicago: University of Chicago Press, 1985.

Brenner, R. "Les choix du Québec." In *Les avis des spécialistes invités à répondre aux huit questions posées par la Commission,* 119–56. Assemblée Nationale, Québec: Documents Parlementaires, 1991a.

Brenner, R. "Canadian Choices." In *Economic Dimensions of Constitutional Change,* edited by R. Boadway, T. Courchene, and D. Purvis, 117–48. Kingston: John Deutsch Institute, 1991b.

Brenner, R. "Extracting Sunbeams Out of Cucumbers: or, What Is Bad Social Science and Why Is It Practiced." *Queen's Quarterly* 99 (1991c): 519–53.

Brenner, R. "Nationalism and the State." Proceedings of the Mont Pélerin Society, Vancouver, 1992.

Brenner, R., and G. A. Brenner. *Gambling and Speculation: A Theory, a History and a Future of Some Human Decisions.* Cambridge: Cambridge University Press, 1990

Cohen, L. R., R. G. Noll, et al. *The Technology Pork Barrel.* Washington, D.C.: Brookings, 1991.

Crosette, B. "Higher Incomes Don't Assure a Better Life, UN Report Finds," *New York Times,* as reprinted in *The Gazette,* June 5, 1990.

The Economist. "Adieu, Napoleon." March 28, 1992, 46.

Eisner, R. "Extended Accounts for National Income and Product." *Journal of Economic Literature* 26 (1988): 1611–84.

Eklund, K. "Long Waves in the Development of Capitalism." *Kyklos* 33 (1980): 383–419.

Ferman, L. A., and L. E. Berndt. "The Irregular Economy." In *Can I Have It in Cash?* edited by S. Henry, 26–47. London: Astragal Books, 1981.

Frey, B. S. "The Relationship Between Efficiency and Political Organisation." Paper presented at Mont Pélerin Society Meeting, Vancouver, 1992.

Friedman, M. Letter to the author, 1988.

Gibney, F. *The Pacific Century.* New York: Charles Scribner's Sons, 1992.

Goldstein, J. S. *Long Cycles: Prosperity and War in Modern Age.* New Haven: Yale University Press, 1988.

Hayashi, F. "Why Is Japan's Saving Rate So Apparently High?" In *NBER Macroeconomics Annual,* edited by S. Fischer, 147–210. Cambridge, Mass.: MIT Press, 1986.

Heclo, H. *Modern Social Politics in Britain and Sweden.* New Haven: Yale University Press, 1974.

Homer, S. *A History of Interest Rates.* New Brunswick: Rutgers University Press, 1963.

Kendall, F., and L. Louw. *Let the People Govern.* Norwood: Amagi Publications, 1989.

Koretz, G. "Litigation's Cost Is Rocketing—its Efficiency Isn't." *Business Week,* November 6, 1989, 64

Kuznets, S. *Growth, Population and Income Distribution.* New York: W. W. Norton, 1979.

Laband, N. "Nothing Could Be Finer: Lawyers Shun Carolina." *Wall Street Journal,* November 28, 1988.

Levin, M. A. "What Statistics on Japan's Lawyers Mean." *New York Times,* August 23, 1991, A20.

Louw, L., and F. Kendall. *South Africa: The Solution.* Norwood: Amagi Publications, 1986.

Matsusaka, J. G., and F. Palda. "Referendum: Has Their Time Come?" In *Fraser Forum,* 5–11. Vancouver: The Fraser Institute, February 1993.

McCracken, W. D. *The Rise of the Swiss Republic.* Boston, Mass.: Arena Publishing Co., 1892.

McNeill, W. H. *Plagues and People.* New York: Anchor Books, 1976.

McNeill, W. H. *The Pursuit of Power.* Chicago: University of Chicago Press, 1982.

National Advisory Board on Science and Technology. *Science and Technology, Innovation and National Prosperity: the Need for Canada to Change Course.* April 1991.

North, D. C. *Institutions, Institutional Change and Economic Performance.* Cambridge: Cambridge University Press, 1990.

Pommerehne, W. W. "Institutional Approaches to Public Expenditure: Empirical Evidence from Swiss Municipalities." *Journal of Public Economics* 9 (1978): 255–80.

Pommehrene, W. W. "The Empirical Relevance of Comparative Institutional Analysis." *European Economic Review* 34 (1990): 458–69.

Popper, K. *The Open Society and Its Enemies.* London: Routledge, 1945.

Preston, S. H. "Children and the Elderly in the U.S." *Scientific American* 251 (1984a): 44–49.

Preston, S. H. "Children and the Elderly: Divergent Paths for America's Dependents." *Demography* 21 (1984b): 435–57.

Report of the Royal Commission on the Economic Union and Development Prospects for Canada. Vol. 3. Ottawa: Minister of Supply and Services, 1985.

Romer, P. M. "Comment." In *NBER Macroeconomics Annual,* edited by S. Fischer, 220–33. Cambridge, Mass.: MIT Press, 1986.

Schama, S. *Citizens.* New York: Knopf, 1989.

Schumach, M. *Diamond People.* New York: W. W. Norton, 1981.

Schumpeter, J. A. *The Economics and Sociology of Capitalism.* Edited by R. Swedberg. Princeton: Princeton University Press, 1991

Switzerland, Département Fédéral de l'Intérieur. *Le Quadrilinguisme en Suisse— présent et futur.* August 1989.

Tiebout, Ch.M. "A Pure Theory of Local Expenditure." *Journal of Political Economy* 64 (1956): 416–24.

Yoshikowa, H., and F. Ohtake. "An Analysis of Female Labor Supply, Housing Demand and the Saving Rate in Japan." Working Paper No. 171. The Institute of Social and Economic Research, Osaka University, July 1988.

Name Index

Subject Index

prosperity, 14, 51, 55–56, 64, 77, 145, 212n. 3, 217n. 71
statistics, 73, 204n. 64, 237n. 2
taxes in, 213n. 18, 214n. 29
Hope, of poor, xi, 32, 72
See also Ambition; Aspiration; Credit; Envy; Leapfrogging; Public works
Huguenots, 53, 55–56, 136, 213n. 10

Idleness
of poor, 31–32, 210n. 67
of soldiers, 210n. 67
See also Public works; Welfare
Illegal activity, 1, 11, 35, 113–29, 169–70, 197n. 4, 198nn. 10, 11, 225n. 58, 229nn. 10, 12, 230n. 14, 232n. 48
Immigrants, 18, 20, 34
and foreign aid, 38, 42
and prosperity, 52, 55–56, 60–62, 154, 213n. 9, 220n. 93, 239n. 27
Incentives
to accuracy, 45–48
to invest, 32, 55, 58, 66–67, 75, 152–53, 218nn. 72–73, 80, 82
and taxes, 1–2, 11, 35, 152–53, 203n. 62, 209n. 54
See also Cost-of-living adjustments (COLA)
Inequality, 21, 206n. 16
mismeasured, 1–2
See also Wealth: redistribution, of; Unemployment
Infant mortality, 48, 112
Inflation, ix, xvii–xviii, 54, 219n. 92
anticipated (expected), 86, 204n. 2, 220n. 16, 221n. 18, 224n. 44
in Canada, 8–10, 90–101, 202n. 46, 220nn. 2, 9, 224nn. 46–49, 225nn. 50, 56–58, 226nn. 62, 69
costs of, 86–89
and indexation, 89–95, 221nn. 26, 28, 30, 223nn. 33–41, 224nn. 42–45
and investments, 9, 85–89

Keynes's definition of, 25–26
measured, 4, 95–101, 212nn. 70–79, 225nn. 50–58, 276nn. 56–59
and measured GNP, 8–10, 95–101, 200n. 33
and monetary policy, 11, 101–9
and national debt and deficits, 19–21, 106–9
in Russia, 128–34, 232n. 51, 233n. 55
tax of, 12, 86–89, 220nn. 6, 12, 222n. 32
unanticipated (unexpected), 86
and unemployment, 220n. 4, 221nn. 22, 25
in the United States, 10, 24, 87, 97, 102–9, 201n. 41, 202n. 46, 207n. 30
volatility of, 85–89, 220n. 17
See also Central banks; Consumer Price Index (CPI); Deflation; Phillips curve; Price index; Price level; Reflation
Infrastructure
expenditures on, 18, 21, 23, 33, 57, 72
See also Public works; Government expenditures
Initiative, xi–xiv, xix, 32, 39, 40, 43–45, 154–65, 239nn. 33–34, 240nn. 35–44
See also Referendum
Innovations
commercialization of, 52–62, 80–83, 216n. 49, 218n. 73, 219n. 86
financial, 52–62, 87–89, 214n. 35, 219n. 84
and measurement of aggregates, 4–5, 15, 150, 178–94, 202n. 56, 218n. 76
and prosperity, growth, 52–62, 150, 159–61, 241n. 48
public policy toward, 19, 41–42
"social," 178, 181, 205n. 7
technological, 52, 59–61, 80–82, 141–43, 236n. 86